Marketing & Strategic Planning for Professional Service Firms

Marketing & Strategic Planning for Professional Service Firms

Stan G. Webb

amacom
A DIVISION OF AMERICAN MANAGEMENT ASSOCIATIONS

Library of Congress Cataloging in Publication Data

Webb, Stan G.
  Marketing & strategic planning for professional service firms.

  Includes index.
  1. Advertising—Professions. I. Title. II. Title:
Marketing and strategic planning for professional services firms.
HF6161.P89W4   659.1   81-66229
ISBN 0-8144-5687-1   AACR2

© 1982 AMACOM
A division of American Management Associations, New York.
All rights reserved. Printed in the United States of America.

This publication may not be reproduced, stored in a retrieval system, or transmitted in whole or in part, in any form or by any means, electronic, mechanical, photocopying, recording, or otherwise, without the prior written permission of AMACOM, 135 West 50th Street, New York, N.Y. 10020.

First Printing

Preface

In recent years, marketing among professionals has been a topic of concern for professional organizations. This is partly because of a worry that advertising practices would be demeaning to the profession and that solicitation of clientele would be unduly pragmatic or even unethical. Toward the end of controlling the activities of their various members, professional associations introduced strong codes of professional conduct and/or codes of ethics to restrict the practices of advertising and solicitation.

The codes of professional conduct and ethics have placed restrictions on advertising and solicitation throughout the history of the organization of the associations in North America. Recently, however, these restrictions on advertising have received severe criticism from several corners.

Government organizations have been one source of criticism. Legislatures and the judiciary have been increasingly interested in this matter in light of anti-combines legislation, restrictive trade practices, and price fixing. Even though these practices are frowned upon and legislated against in other sections of the economy, there is a resistance on the part of professional organizations to allow free competition to prevail. There is, of course, a very real concern by the professional bodies that if the advertising standards are not laid out for their members, this might bring about a proliferation of advertising and marketing techniques, which would bring discredit to the "ethical standards" of the profession. The committees and ruling boards of any professional organizations have visions of "sandwich boards," high-pressure TV commercialization, and high neon signs flashing out the name of a professional firm.

Their resistance to change has prevented large professional organizations from recognizing the significance of judicial and government action, such as the forced reinstatement through the courts of individual professionals who were discharged or reprimanded by their professional organizations for using advertising practices. Had the professional organizations been responsive to the needs of their legislators, the clients of the individual professional, and their own professional members, they might have allowed the use of advertising and recognized some marketing approach. Professional associations should limit themselves to providing solid guidelines, perhaps governed by their code of ethics, as to the manner, techniques, and applications of marketing tools.

Clients, too, have been critical of restrictions on advertising. The very real concern of the average client of any professional is that he is getting competent professional service. These concerns have been recognized by most professional associations and organizations in that they govern the conduct of their members through a code of professional ethics and, in recent years, through the adoption of continuing professional education (in some cases mandatory) for their members. The problem with voluntary continuing education is that there is no reporting on members' participation and/or application; the problem with mandatory continuing education programs is that from a social, psychological, and education point of view, you cannot force people to learn—they may very well attend an updating seminar, but they will not gain anything from the seminar if the only reason they are attending is because they have been forced to. Professional organizations are hesitant to try to change the attitudes of their own members. As with any human being, there is a built-in resistance to change, and many professionals much prefer the status quo. There are, however, an increasing number of professionals who enjoy the challenge and excitement of learning new techniques and procedures and accept continuing professional education as a professional obligation.

Clients, however, are often totally unaware of the differences in attitude among professionals—the common prejudice is that they are traditional, autocratic, and aloof. From a client's point of view, it is very difficult to obtain information about a particular professional who might be responsive to his needs.

The problem, then, is that the client is totally unaware of the services which may be available to him, and this has been largely brought about by the lack of advertising. The historical retort to criticisms of advertising restrictions is that "word of mouth" advertising is best. Referrals to professionals often come from neighbors, friends, or relatives, as well as business associates. These people, although well intentioned, seldom if ever have adequate technical knowledge of the profession to judge whether a particular professional would serve the client's best interests. More progressive professional organizations are helping to alleviate this problem by providing referral systems through their offices.

Unless some form of informational advertising is allowed, the client has no way of knowing the scale of fees, nor the services he can expect, when initially searching out a professional.

Finally, members of professional organizations increasingly recognize that public relations and good community image are a service to both the profession and the community which the professional serves. Progressive professionals are often frustrated by their professional organization or their firm's policies, which restrict free discussion and explanation of all fees and which make it difficult for them to help their clients understand that competent professional care is what they wish to provide.

There often is a total lack of sophistication in the application of a service-oriented approach to professional work and business planning, and this is mirrored by the lack of authoritive texts or guidelines in the area of marketing for professionsls.

The concept of marketing for professionals might at first appear abhorrent if one considered all the possible detrimental effects to the professional, his clients, and his professional organization. This fear appears to stem from an attitude that "selling" may ultimately lead to disservice to clients.

This book advocates taking the attitude that marketing means to serve. A professional must have goals in terms of servicing his clients well. Marketing is his professional undertaking to analyze his clients' needs and to plan, implement, and control methods to serve those clients well. Techniques in placing a marketing program for a professional vary widely from a commercial marketing application.

The purpose of this book is to highlight the marketing, planning, organizing, controlling, and communication (that is, management) functions that are most appropriate for a professional.

Stan G. Webb

Contents

Introduction 1

Part I: Marketing

1 The Nature and Scope of Marketing for Professionals 15
2 Practice Development for Professionals 24
3 The Client Is the Focus 31
4 Analyzing the Life Cycle of the Professional Firm 35
5 Environmental Analysis 49
6 Market Identification 62
7 Internal Analysis 72
8 Market Analysis and Segmentation 82
9 Client Analysis 91
10 Analysis of Professional Services 108
11 Service Distribution 120
12 Determining and Changing Fees 129
13 Market Orchestration 143
14 Professional Marketing Tools 153
15 Public Relations and Advertising 162

Part II: Strategic Planning

16	Establishing Market-Based Goals and Objectives	177
17	Designing a Market-Based Professional Firm	187
18	Defining Internal Resource Needs to Accomplish Objectives	201
19	Determining Organizational Structure	215
20	Strategic Planning for Management Information Systems	225
21	Market Planning, Information, and Control	238
22	Determining Policies to Attain Objectives	254
23	Summary	273
Index		281

Introduction

Professional managers know that planning is the key to stability and growth. They also know that a market and the revenue derived from it are the only reason for the business's existence. Planning is the attempt not only to predict the future but also to control it.

Markets must be considered when professional firms plan and set objectives. In planning for a professional firm, a model is made of a desired future, and work programs and methods are established to bring that future about. The planning effort must be directed at the realization of the professional firm's potential through a careful examination of markets and opportunities. The plan must also address ways to overcome complex problems.

Planning helps minimize a reactive and crisis atmosphere in a professional firm. The firm's markets and resources, including finance, facilities, and materials and supplies, must be analyzed. In this way, its personnel will be better distributed to accomplish the intended purpose and obtain good profits and results. This type of planning for a professional firm is expensive in terms of both time and money. But there is little doubt that, in the long term, no other function can provide a greater return on effort, investment, and time. There is no other function whose omission can prove as costly.

The Big Picture

No professional firm is a closed entity. It is not impervious to the influences of its environment. Unfortunately, external influences rarely are clearly understood, yet they can have the greatest impact upon the future of a professional firm. Major environmental considerations include economic considerations, technological advances, social influences, political inputs, competitive factors, and social responsibilities (see Figure I-1). Individual markets and competition are relatively easy to understand, but there are many other considerations which can have an immediate impact on the success or failure of a professional practice. Many architectural and engineering firms fail with the onslaught of a recession, which often begins with reduced housing and general construction activity. We are living in an age of rapidly advancing technology. Professionals must have a clear understanding, not only of the present state of technology affecting the profession, but also of potential future advances. Societal composition and thinking, values and demands, education and access to information, leisure activities, mobility, and buying and living habits are in a constant state of change and flux. Laws are passed, changed, or interpreted differently. Quasi-regulatory bodies, such as professional associations, change and place new interpretations on revised by-laws and codes of ethics. Competition may start up overnight. A professional employee may leave a firm to compete directly against it. Society is increasingly demanding a responsiveness from its professional members. Many of these changes occur slowly; but unfortunately, once they are apparent, it may be too late to do anything.

Figure I-1.   The "market"—demands and influences.

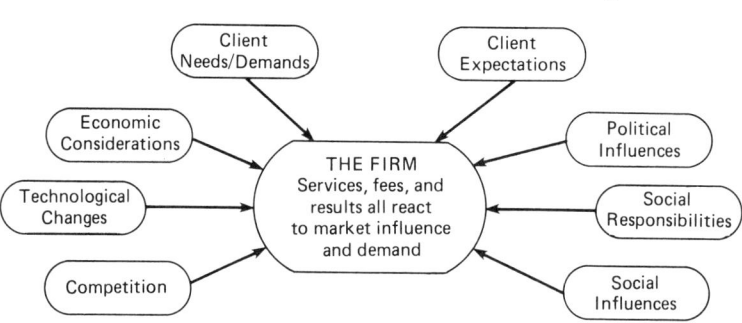

The market will determine the success of a professional firm. Many professionals and their organizations don't view understanding and analyzing market forces as an important function. They often react only when a crisis has developed—when a client is lost, the firm is unprofitable, or legislation is introduced, forcing a change. Through research and analysis, a planned management approach would recognize earlier that the professional needs to change, and would make the firm more responsive to the ever changing needs and expectations of the marketplace. An active, directed, and managed change by the professionals, rather than reactive, ill-considered response, is needed.

Forecasting external change is difficult, of course, and requires constant vigilance. One problem is that the number of external, or environmental, factors is so great that it is necessary to determine which are the most significant and to spend time and effort in analyzing those.

Monitoring activities must focus on those environmental areas or variables that are deemed critical to the professional firm. Active responses to these environmental issues require long-term and far-sighted planning, which must be thought of well in advance of critical periods.

Evaluating environmental developments takes a great deal of vision. It requires professionals to abandon the narrow technical aspects of their profession for the moment and concentrate on the shape of the forest, not on individual trees.

A Holistic Approach

If you accept that a professional firm must be fully cognizant of all major forces affecting the firm's success, then even the smallest professional firm must have a function that monitors and analyzes its environment. Environmental analysis is not a function which is performed only once; it is a continuous process of analyzing changes in the environment and evaluating their impact upon the firm so that the professional firm can be changed and adapted to the "new" environment (see Figure I-2). Environmental studies and analysis are usually performed by the senior professionals in a firm or by specialists specifically engaged to perform that function. The studies of the market, technological change, economic cycles and forecasts, resources, and so on are all an integral part of total planned management. The professional firm must also clearly understand the clients' perception of the environment.

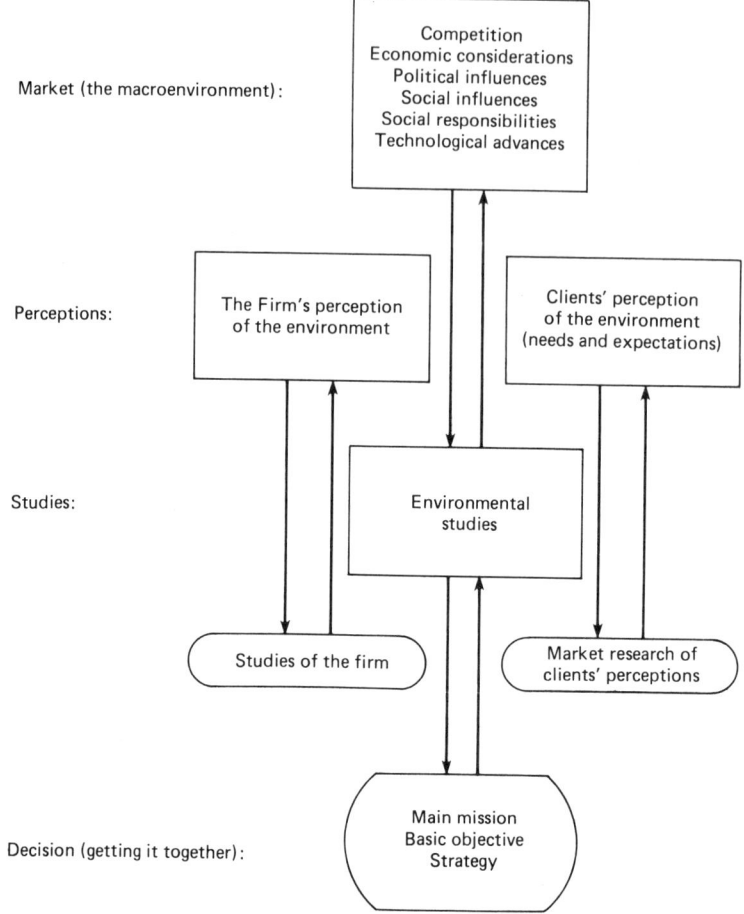

Figure I-2.   Being responsive to the market—a "holistic" view.

Environmental studies will assist professional managers to make decisions such as:

1. Designing the professional services to be offered to clients.
2. Defining the types of clients the professional firm wishes to serve.
3. Defining the market to be served, including geographic, social, and economic segments.
4. Defining the technology to be used to provide those services.

5. Deciding upon the types of professionals and employees to be hired, trained, and retained.
6. Deciding upon the types of equipment to be purchased, maintained, or abandoned.

In deciding on a basic objective, the professional determines what services will be offered and to whom, and how they will be delivered. He will respond to the stated client needs and expectations. It is difficult to be unsuccessful when you are providing the market (your clients) with exactly what it wants—if first you know what it wants. Setting basic objectives and strategic plans can be done only with an understanding of the market and the general environment.

Strategic Planning

Once environmental facors and market and client perceptions have been analyzed, the firm's basic purpose, main mission, objectives, and plans must be established. This is central to a modern "planned management" approach to operating a professional firm. Most professional firms take the following approach to planning:

1. State the results desired first. The central theme of planned management is that it works from results back to actions to achieve those results. It is different from crisis management in that it clearly states the end results to be achieved first; the task then becomes to look for means to accomplish those objectives. The first task, then, after analyzing the environment and client perceptions, is to list specific goals and objectives.

2. State the work methods necessary to achieve those objectives, including procedures, programs, and policies.

3. Determine the resource needs to accomplish the programs. This includes equipment, facilities, manpower, and financial resources.

4. Organize the operation so that there are clear-cut lines of authority and responsibility to respond to the goals of the professional firm. There should be clear decision-making capabilities at appropriate levels.

5. Control the operation by designing management information systems (MIS) to provide continuous feedback to management to allow it to correct operations or the plan as needed.

This approach is summarized in Figure I-3.

Figure I-3. Strategic planning for professional firms.

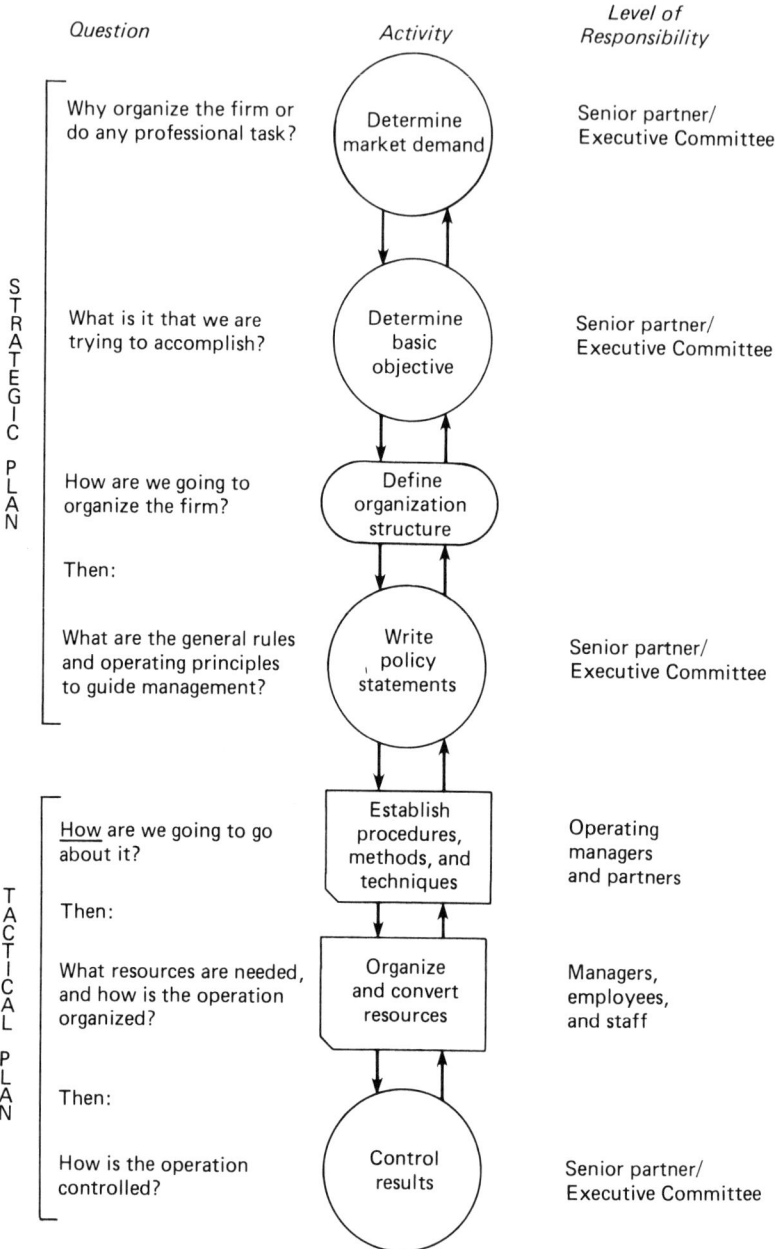

INTRODUCTION 7

Chapter Reference—Where to Look

Chapter 5 —Environmental Analysis
Chapter 6 —Market Identification
Chapter 7 —Internal Analysis
Chapter 8 —Market Analysis and Segmentation
Chapter 9 —Client Analysis
Chapter 10 —Professional-Service Analysis
Chapter 11 —Service Distribution
Chapter 12—Fee Determination and Changes

Chapter 16 —Establishing Market-Based Goals and Objectives

Chapter 17 —Designing a Market-Based Professional Firm
Chapter 19 —Determining Organizational Structure

Chapter 22 —Determining Policies to Attain Objectives

Chapter 13 —Market Orchestration
Chapter 14 —Professional Marketing Tools
Chapter 15 —Public Relations and Advertising

Chapter 18 —Defining Internal Resource Needs
              to Accomplish Objectives

Chapter 20 —Strategic Planning for Management Information
              Systems
Chapter 21 —Market Planning Information and Control

A professional firm cannot get good results by simply doing the technical or professional work; it must first know where it wants to go and how it expects to get there. The most common complaint of managers in a professional environment is that employees are not highly motivated. The most common complaint of those same employees is that senior professionals, or the firm, do not seem to know where the firm is going, or what the purpose of the operation is.

We are all familiar with the term strategic planning. It is long-term and results oriented. Strategic planning is different from tactical planning, which is very short-term. This distinction is important, because although both are integrated and related, there is a danger that tactical planning will replace broad long-term planning of the professional firm. Directing all effort toward improving next week's or next month's cash flow, revenue, or services, and totally ignoring long-term effects of such action, will not necessarily improve the professional firm's effectiveness in the long run.

Determining Strategic Policy

A policy is a general rule or operating principle established to achieve the objectives of the firm. Policies act as guides for consistent and continuing decision making. Whereas objectives are specific goals and procedures are methods of performing something, policies provide direction by tying actions to the basic purpose of the business. Unless there are clear and formal (that is, written) policies, it is difficult to control operations. It is recognized, however, that in certain confidential or extremely competitive areas policy will not be formalized.

Policy statements should be written holistically for the entire professional firm. This suggests that policy writing is the managing partner's job, since he alone can coordinate and integrate the policy-writing effort. Policies should blend with and reinforce one another and be in line with major objectives of the firm.

Major policy statements should be written for major areas of concern of the professional firm. The advertising and public relations functions and the firm's responsiveness to its clients' needs and expectations might be chosen as subjects for major policy statements. Policies might also govern relationships with debtors, government bodies, professional associations, competitors, and other major external elements. Policy often governs the financial structure of the firm, personnel relations, facilities, research and development, and the professional development of individual professionals within the firm.

The firm, as a whole, must work together toward a common purpose. Policies must be balanced and complement one another if the professional firm is to attain synergism in striving to attain its objectives.

Determining Operating Procedures, Techniques, and Plans for Improvement

A central objective of the professional management of a firm must be to optimize the use of its resources. Resources, including capital, facilities, materials and supplies, and personnel, must: be available (either through acquisition or by generating them within the firm) in the correct amount when they are needed, and they must be allocated to their greatest effectiveness.

Budgeting and financial resource planning are understood and used by most of us. Some of the major management problems center around the efficient use of assets. These problems can be at least partly solved with effective financial planning, initiated before a crisis occurs.

Planning for facilities, including equipment and premises, includes not only the purchase of new facilities, but planned replacement, optimum maintenance policies, and planned obsolescence. Geographic location of facilities is often critical for a professional firm. Facilities planning and choosing the right location are critical, because those facilities will project the image of the firm as professional and capable and responsive to client concerns.

Inherent in the planning process is the design of procedures to ensure that adequate materials and supplies will be on hand at all times to service clientele.

Personnel planning involves the allocation of people with the proper skills to implement the plans of the professional firm. It also presupposes that the total number of personnel will be kept to a minimum to enhance efficiency and total profitability of the firm.

Summary

To be well managed, a professional firm must be responsive to the needs of its environment, markets, and clientele.

The first thing to do is to get away from the detail of the technical aspects of the profession and to stand back and take a long, hard, objective look at the firm. Are you responsive to the environment and your markets? Do you have extremely well-satisfied clients? Do you, and other professionals working in your firm, find your work challenging and stimulating? Are you and your colleagues enthused and dedicated to providing professional services?

In marketing there is often no "right" or "wrong" way that something should be done—attitudes and personal interests and tastes are important. Perceptions, particularly how our clients feel toward us, are based upon emotion rather than reason. And sometimes it hurts us as professionals when we find that our clients are dissatisfied with our fee (the first indication of client dissatisfaction), the quality of our services, or the timeliness with which services are provided.

Clearly, a professional firm would be described as being successful when its clients are satisfied and appreciative. If a professional is meeting the needs, wants, and expectations of his clients, obtaining an adequate client base and profitability will be no problem.

But the "success" of a practice often has little to do with the technical competence of a professional and much more with his attitude of concern for his clients and his ability to deal with clients and others in a humanistic way. Except in the case of the specialty sections of a profession, approximately 80 per cent of a professional's new work comes from referrals from satisfied clients and from new work from those same satisfied clients. These referrals are usually from non-professional people, who are not really qualified to state an opinion on technical competence; instead they base the referral upon their perception of the professional's ability and his concern for their well-being.

The service that we are really providing to a client is to give him *peace of mind*, because he feels that his professional needs are being met.

There are two possible approaches to developing and running a professional firm. The superficial approach is basically technical or job-oriented: once the work is completed, the relationship with the client is finished. The "holistic" approach is centered on long-term concern with clients' welfare. The intent is not only to complete the current work required, but to continuously provide sufficient communication between the professional and his client so that anticipated problems and future work programs can be handled in a systematic manner. This suggests that the whole nature

INTRODUCTION

of the professional firm be client-oriented and not oriented toward the detailed technical aspects of the specific profession.

The superficial approach suggests that the professional views his practice merely as a means to an end, because work is not client-oriented and jobs are on a specific-assignment or short-term basis. Assistance provided by the professional is often temporary, unsatisfactory, or incomplete. The attitude of the professional may be to "get on with the job and on to the next client." This attitude may lead to suffocating self-interest, since the desired "end results" seem to be to create less annoyance and improve the comfort and income level—of the professional. Often the attitude is characterized by: "I am the professional—I know best."

That attitude, one of near-intimidation, is becoming very ineffective in an increasingly assertive and well-educated society. Today's clients are likely to respond with something like: "I know how I feel, and I want you to be responsive to my needs. After all, I pay the bill."

The second major approach, which is diametrically opposed to the superficial approach, is to build a client-responsive practice. This is the approach where a professional is really and genuinely concerned with improving the client's overall welfare and well-being in all matters which concern the client. This holistic approach requires more effort and work, and often calls for basic changes in the attitudes and thinking of a professional and his staff. The new attitude becomes almost a philosophy for the practice of the profession and will provide the very underpinnings of success —but first we must know what "the market" wants.

Part I

Marketing

1

The Nature and Scope of Marketing for Professionals

Professionals do not think of themselves as marketers. They do not think that they have to market their services. *Successful* professionals, however, have used marketing principles and techniques, whether or not they were aware of it.

The American Marketing Association says that marketing is "the performance of business activities that direct the flow of goods and services from producer to consumer or user." For a professional, a very broad definition of marketing is needed. This definition might be: marketing is the process of delivery of all services to all clientele and other "publics" we serve.

About the only thing that can be said about modern communications and marketing is that everyone feels that he is an expert. After all, we all speak clearly and precisely (don't we?), and our listener must have missed something we said. We are all bombarded daily with advertising and commercials trying to persuade us to buy. We observe the quality of the selling techniques used when we do such a simple thing as buying a new suit or an automobile. It is on this slim base that many professionals build their marketing techniques.

Comprehensive marketing requires an analysis of the whole process of value exchange. Where professionals are concerned, this value-for-value exchange means that the client is giving up something of value, most often his money, in exchange for professional service. A professional refining his techniques in the art of marketing is learning to plan, control, and execute that value exchange.

The client pays money in exchange for a needed (and expected) level of professional services. The level of the value of services might be measured by the amount of money that a client is willing to pay. If he complains about a high fee, it is because he perceives that he has not had professional services of a level of quality that would justify the price. His judgment will usually be subjective and emotional—not being a professional, he does not have the background to make an objective judgment of the quality of services. That is why an understanding of his perception and the continuous presentation of a "professional image" are so important.

Marketing relies heavily on the process of meeting the needs and services required by the professional's clients. It also requires that the professional establish an image that a client can relate to.

Professional marketing has to recognize the desires of the clients. The tools of the professional marketer are effective client communication, well-considered fee policies, and a desire to inform, educate, motivate, and service clients.

Marketing is the total systems package for the design, planning, promotion, and delivery of services needed by present or potential clients.

There are several important things about this definition. First, it is not a legal or economic definition, but a management definition. Second, marketing is not the process of selling. It is the process of careful planning that must take place before any effective selling can commence. It recognizes that the entire professional–client relationship should be built on the client's service needs. It is client- or market-oriented.

Third, marketing means that a professional should not attempt to be all things to all people. He should have carefully planned and selected the services that he wishes to provide, in a reasonable fee structure, to identifiable clients. Identifiable clients are known in marketing terms as the "target market." Professional marketers obtain elaborate programs of market research before even deciding which services to offer.

Fourth, marketing is a dynamic process using various programs and tools. It is not selling, which is only one aspect of the marketing process. Marketing is the interaction of many processes, referred to as "marketing mix." These include the design of the services to be provided to clients, setting fees, and the entire process of communicating with and informing clientele.

Fifth, marketing means that the entire program of services to be offered to clients will depend on what those clients' needs are. This is a very important point for a professional because of his unique position in offering advice to his clientele. Unfortunately, he may feel that he knows best what his client's needs are. Marketing does not end until the client's needs are fully met—it is a democratic, not autocratic, process.

Sixth, marketing is designed to enhance the value-for-value relationship between a professional and his client. The professional should offer services of significant benefit to the client so that the client is willing to pay a reasonable fee.

Seventh, the marketing process should be subjected to meaningful cost–benefit analysis. That is to say, marketing should derive a maximum return from a minimum investment in both time and money.

Eighth, successful marketing should enhance earnings over a long period of time, because clients should be satisfied enough to return and provide referrals to the professionals.

Finally, the image of the professional himself and the image of his profession as a whole should be enhanced by his marketing program.

Marketing involves the total integrated system. It is sometimes confused with merchandising, which means planning the services to be offered. Merchandising is also defined as getting the right product at the right price to the right market at the right time. Selling or solicitation is only one small tool in a total marketing scheme, and it is only one method of promotion.

Some Approaches to Marketing Management

There is a traditional attitude among some professionals that practice development and growth and the making of money are selfish motives and incompatible with the practice of a profession. A progressive professional, holding to the tenets of a marketing concept, would probably view the practice growth and increased income as a result of providing services needed by clients. In Chapter 12 we will deal with the important reasons why "success" is important for the professional, members of his staff, and even the clients he serves.

The traditional and the more progressive professional usually agree that service to clients is of paramount importance. Where they differ is in their attitude toward the application of modern marketing techniques. The traditional professional often is very passive in obtaining new clients, servicing existing clients, and expanding the scope of his services to his existing clients through adoption of continuing professional education programs. He often has the attitude of a dignified professional who will sit back to wait until clients come to his door. He sometimes will resist taking the time to explain even how he might further help a client, in the fear that this might appear to be solicitation of further business from the client.

A progressive practioner will take time to explain all of the ways that he might service a client, and he will actively pursue continuing professional education in order to learn ways to continually improve his service to the client.

To be of high service value to clients, a marketing concept or attitude toward client service must be translated into actual marketing management.

A professional and/or a professional firm must have clear goals and policies, established through a management planning process. The marketing efforts of a professional must be channeled to achieve those goals.

Marketing management must be recognized as an important management function if a professional's long-term personal and professional goals and the success of his practice are to be achieved. A professional or professional organization chooses a marketing management style which is consistent with his/its own goals and self-image.

The Traditional Approach—No Marketing Management

This is where most professionals are right now. If a professional firm does actively market, because of codes of ethics and rules of professional conduct, it is very careful to couch the naming of the marketing management function or the practice of marketing management in such phrases as "practice development" or "effective client communications." Most professionals downgrade the positive effects of marketing and prefer to stress quality of service. They do not actively perform marketing functions and presume that practice growth will come from a demand for their services.

In stressing service and avoiding the topic of marketing, these professionals often rationalize their position by explaining that quality service will lead to (1) retention of existing clients and (2) referrals through word-of-mouth as a result of good service to existing clients. Thus they are relying on one marketing tool—the offering of a professional service—to do the whole job. Although most professionals would admit that this is the only true and "ethical" procedure in practice development, it is based on three false premises:

1. Clients will have no market preference, as all professionals may very well decide to provide the highest quality of standards in service.
2. Clients are usually totally unaware of quality variations.
3. If other professionals adopted more progressive and appropriate marketing procedures, the traditional firm would be at a disadvantage.

A traditional firm manages the administrative and technical professional services, but fails to manage the marketing function. In fact, a typical organization chart such as Figure 1-1 totally omits marketing.

Figure 1-1.   Example of functional organization chart— marketing activities not managed.

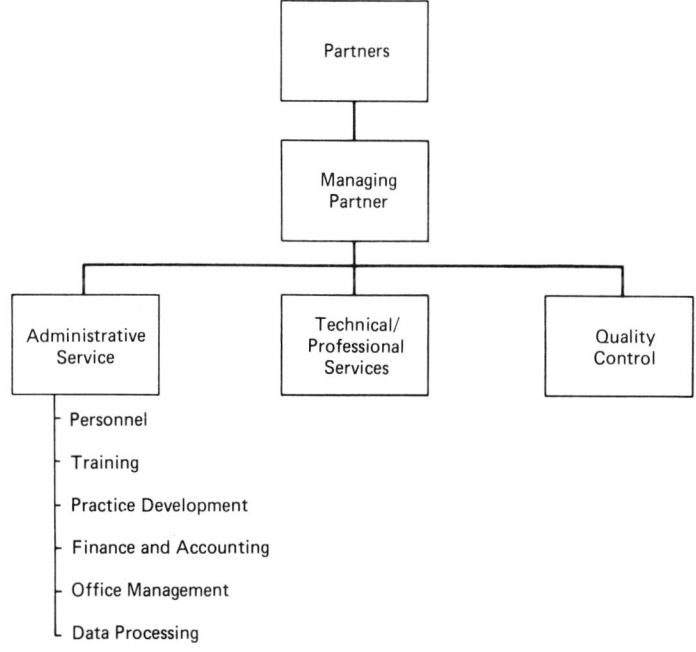

The Hard-Sell Approach

Aggressive marketing has the connotations of selling and solicitation. This is the marketing technique most prone to control by rules of professional ethics and codes of professional conduct. Aggressive selling tactics may be appropriate for soap manufacturers, cosmetics firms, and automobile dealers, but they would be deemed—and most every professional would agree—not in the interest of the professional image or in the long-term interest of the clients.

The most important reason, from a business point of view, for not using aggressive market techniques in a professional practice is that they do not work. The benefits of being aggressive as a professional are not self-evident.

Some major professional firms, although restricted by codes of ethics, do have aggressive sales techniques. These include lavish entertainment accounts, bonuses to partners obtaining new clientele, questionable pricing practices and discounts, and the occasional offhanded questioning of the standards of other professionals in their particular profession.

There are two very important reasons why aggressive selling does not work among professionals. First, the increasing sophistication of clients makes them highly resistant to hard-sell tactics. Second, the implementation of hard-sell procedures would actually detract from the practice of the profession, because clients, due to their increased sophistication and the greater sophistication of their professional advisors, are fully attuned to a false or aggrandizing statement. These statements often dwell on how professional the services are or contain claims that the quality of work is much greater than anyone else's. This does not ring true, because most business advisors, and most clients, recognize that quality professional help is in great demand and that when someone places himself in a position of solicitation, obviously his services are not in such great demand. In other words, if a professional has to solicit work, particularly by downgrading other professionals, something must be wrong. And the potential client knows it!

Balanced Marketing

Between the extreme of a total non-marketing approach with reliance on quality control and the opposite extreme of "hard-sell" techniques lies a balanced, management-directed, progressive marketing concept, which may be appropriate for a professional firm. This balanced approach would rely on a total marketing mix, that is, a blend of effective techniques, carried out in a professional and dignified manner, which might lead to the attainment of stated professional goals.

The problem with the non-marketing techniques used by most professional firms is that heavy reliance is placed on a single marketing element—quality service. The problem with the hard-sell marketing approach is the heavy reliance on promotion as the single marketing element.

A balanced marketing approach would seem appropriate in that it meets the various codes on professional ethics and the standards and image of integrity which most professionals attempt to establish and maintain. The approach should also meet requirements of a progressive professional in that there would be high-quality service willingly accepted by clientele, with a high degree of client satisfaction.

The marketing function is specifically identified in the organization chart of a progressive professional firm. Market research, communications, and relationships are managed functions (see Figure 1-2).

Why Professionals Should Market

At issue here is not whether a professional should market his services, but how effective he is in marketing those services. Whether we admit it or not, we all practice marketing to some degree.

By now it should be clear that technical competence is difficult to market. Technical skill is basic to developing a successful practice. If one thing is the determinant between a "successful" professional practice and all other professional practices, it is an honest concern and regard for the clientele. That concern can be addressed and techniques promulgated to assist the professional in achieving his objectives.

Balanced marketing, or *progressive professional marketing*, will identify and provide specific advantages to a professional:

1. *Improved efficiency in marketing technique.* A valid marketing program places heavy emphasis on a balanced, scientific management approach to identification of client service needs, pricing policies, effective communication techniques, and the development of new skills to service clients better.

In addition to these benefits, a progressive professional using

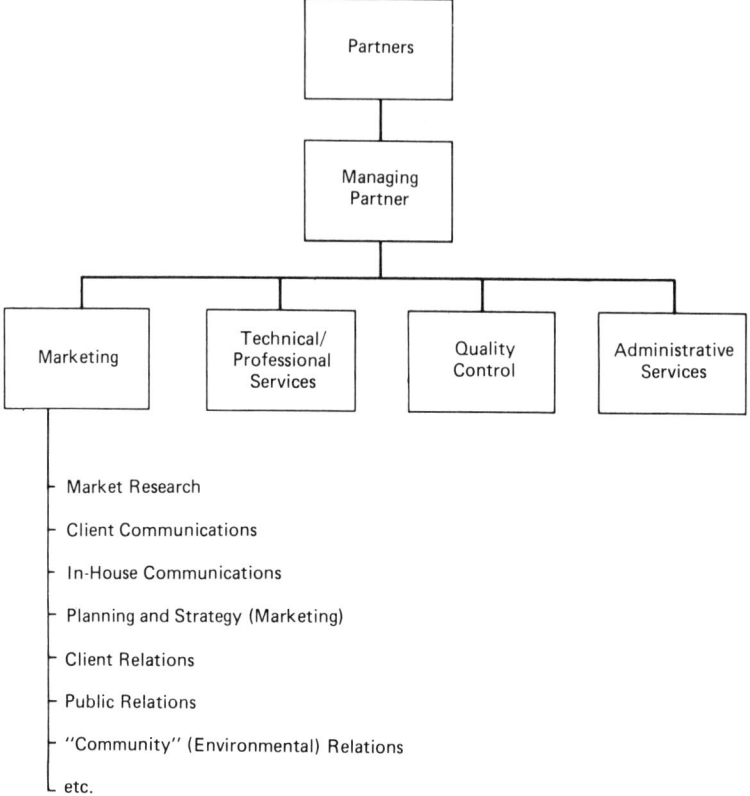

Figure 1-2. Organization chart for a professional firm in which marketing is a balanced function.

sound marketing techniques will obtain substantial cost savings over expensive and fruitless "selling" techniques, and will accelerate practice growth. That is, a professional marketing program has a positive cost–benefit relationship.

Needless to say, the first thing that must be addressed is the attitude of the individual professional or firm—there must be a willingness to learn what the client's needs are and learn techniques to satisfy those needs. The first benefit in changing this attitude within a firm is improved client satisfaction. Another major aspect of learning marketing technique is to learn the technical aspects of marketing mix.

2. *Client satisfaction.* Progressive professional marketing is designed to meet the service needs of clients. The whole idea is to

analyze and measure client needs in order to design programs that are responsive to those needs.

Where the professional firm has never used marketing techniques to study its clientele, there is every likelihood that the clients are being poorly served.

A very traditional practioner is often removed from his clients, resistant to learning new techniques and methodology, and unconcerned with client relationships.

In conclusion, very few professionals have switched to a marketing emphasis—an emphasis on determining and then meeting client service needs. There are many misnomers and misunderstandings and often total misinformation in professional marketing. Most professionals will not talk about this subject. Many marketing concepts are the same for commercial enterprises as for professionals; however, the techniques for placing a marketing program for a professional would differ widely from a commercial organization.

2

Practice Development for Professionals

The modern progressive commercial business manager is assertive, self-actualizing, and goal-directed, with a keen interest in human relations. There is no reason to believe that a professional should be anything less.

Historical Development

The professions really have no history of developments and techniques in the marketing concept. For the vast majority of professions, this is largely because of ethical considerations. Most professions actively reject the concept of a professional seeking business. This attitude among professionals, and particularly professional organizations, appears to be based on a total lack of understanding of the marketing concept when taken in its purest sense—as a desire to service client need—and on the confusion in definition between hard-sell "advertising" and true marketing. Unfortunately, the professions do not appear to be even willing to learn another point of view—a point of view currently being mooted by government and consumers everywhere—that everyone must meet consumers' needs and expectations. The professions' ostrich attitude is currently under attack throughout North America and Great Britain by legislative bodies as well as consumer action groups. In Great Britain, the Monopolies Commission issued a report suggesting that the professions' restrictions on advertising, together with price fixing or the use of minimum tariff schedules, are probably against the public's interest. In the United States and Canada, there have been major moves by legislators against professional bodies that censure their members, under the restrictions of the code of ethics, in relation to advertising. With a great deal of reluctance, the professional organizations are beginning to revise their advertising guidelines, and most professional organizations now allow "informational" advertising, meaning that members can advertise their names, addresses and telephone numbers, the hours of business, the services they will provide, and their fee schedule.

At a minimum, those would seem to be the areas in which consumers feel that they have a right to demand information. It is little wonder that the professions are being severely cirticized. Because the general public cannot gain any detailed information about the practices of particular professionals, there is an appearance of a closed shop. This is particularly true in the highly visible professions such as accountancy and law, where there is a high volume of work being done for many small clients and a great deal of public exposure. Further, there is a feeling among clients and consumers that these professions' codes of ethics and rules of conduct are designed mainly to protect the profession.

The failure of the professions to recognize the realities of the situation by insisting upon non-marketing has in fact led to a negative market image. The lay public, and even professionals of other professions, for instance, often accuse accountants and lawyers of providing minimum services for maximum fees. If the professional whose services have been rendered has an attitude of "take it or leave it" in regard to his fees, that certainly does not enhance the situation.

In most cases, of course, at least in the professional's own mind, the fee is justified, and there may very well have been a great deal of work done to justify the fees. Unfortunately, the client often does not know that. Their very unwillingness to accept a market concept has placed many professionals in disrepute because they do not have any apparent concern, in the eyes of their clients, for the client's well-being. The very fact that there is a bias by professionals against accepting feedback from clients and others is an indictment. Without an awareness of clients' problems and complaints, a professional cannot reshape his plans and may very well totally abhor the idea of changing his attitude.

One of the strange conundrums when addressing the question

of professional advertising is that professional organizations restrict the practice of marketing and promotion to their own members while at the same time using advanced marketing techniques in relation to the organization as a whole. In fairness, however, there are a few professional organizations that actually produce guidelines for their members and assist them in their marketing activities. The future will see an increasing demand by members of professional bodies to have those bodies assist in areas of progressive professional marketing. The marketing concept will eventually be adopted by professional organizations and integrated with the needs of individual members of those professional bodies. This would include such areas as market research, market analysis and forecasting, the processing and interpreting of data, the use of analytical methodology, and many other areas. At the most optimistic end, professional organizations will assist the professional in his marketing efforts.

This will come about as professional organizations recognize a need to be resposive to individual members' needs. In marketing terminology, professional organizations are known as "mutual benefit" organizations. The value-for-value relationship between the organization and its members is that the organization provides services to its members in exchange for their fees. This would seem at variance with a traditional doctrine, which suggests that a professional organization's purpose is to govern its members.

In early times there was no recognition of a marketing concept. Goods were produced and services provided to meet client and customer expectations and demands. From the period at the beginning of this century until the early 1960s there was a concept of "selling"—an aggressive marketing attempt to provide wide distribution of mass-produced goods—and this concept was widely abhorred by the leading professions. Under this concept, volume considerations were more important than quality control. It was built around the premise of volume distribution to maximize profits. The professions responded by introducing regulations to restrict the use of these tactics by professional members. Since the early 1960s the marketing concept has been increasingly in vogue. According to this concept, fulfilling consumer needs is in the best long-range interest of a company or organization. There is no reason to believe that this goal would be inconsistent with the practice of a profession.

The three stages in this historical development are summarized in Figure 2-1.

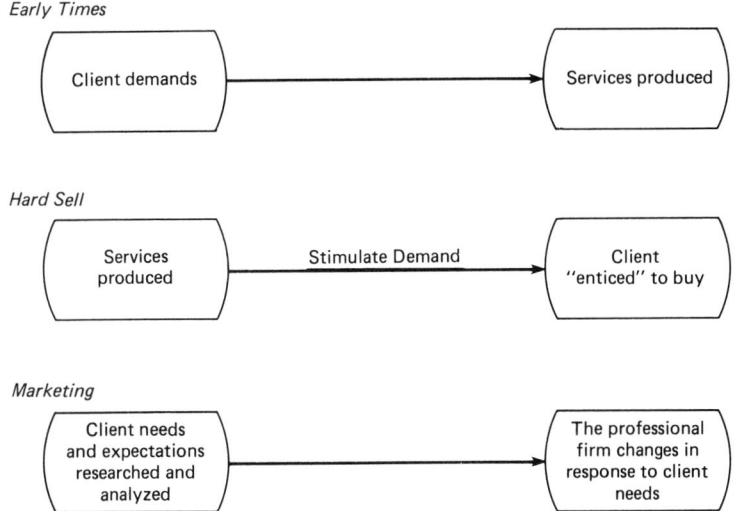

Figure 2-1. *History of marketing for professional firms: three approaches.*

Importance of Marketing

Many individuals who have not previously been exposed to professional care—and indeed many individuals who have been repeatedly exposed to professional care—are apprehensive, nervous, highly impressionable, and awed by the professional. Many clients and patients are intimidated by the use of professional jargon; to an unsophisticated client, the message of what you are telling him may very well be how little knowledge he has. The client may have anxiety about the fee he will be charged, and, most important, about the quality of the service he is receiving. He has no way of judging a professional in a discipline he is not familiar with. He is often literally placing his life in your hands. He is doing this in a physical sense with the medical and dental professions, an anesthetist, and similar professionals. He may be doing so with lawyers. Even with accountants, the possibility of tax evasion charges can be very real and threatening.

With all the fears and apprehensions of a client, it is important that a professional present a confident (marketing), self-assured (marketing), assertive (marketing) approach to his client's needs. Persuading a client to do something which would be in his best interest requires both empathy (marketing—feedback), and communication skills (marketing). Selling has sometimes been referred to as "the art of persuasion."

Most professionals would agree that it would be unethetical for a doctor not to try to persuade his patient to take his nitroglycerine pills if he has a heart ailment, or for a lawyer not to try to persuade his clients to stay within the tenets of the law, or for a tax accountant not to try to persuade his clients to follow the legislative requirements of the Internal Revenue Service. It is not a question of whether we do it, it is a question of how well we do it.

The Concept of Marketing

The marketing concept is based on two fundamental premises:

1. All of the professional's planning, organization, operating procedures, and policies should be oriented toward the client.

2. The professional's practice should be profit-oriented. The professional should be entrepreneurial in approach. The very important professional reasons for this are laid out in Chapter 12. The prime point of that discussion is that if a profession did not provide a decent living the professional might very well leave that field.

Fundamental to the philosophy of accepting a market concept are the recognition and acceptance of a client- or patient-oriented way of practicing a profession. Under the marketing concept, the client becomes the focus for the practice, and meeting his needs is the professional's main objective.

Furthermore, marketing is rooted in the profit concept and not in a volume concept. The corollary of this is that reasonable fees will be accepted where quality care of clients is considered paramount by the professional and where the client appreciates the professional's concern for his well-being.

Is Marketing Ethical for a Professional?

The three major arguments advanced against adopting a marketing concept are:

1. It is expensive and is paid for ultimately by the client.
2. It is manipulative.
3. It is intrusive in that it looks at the private wants, desires, and needs of clients.

We have previously discussed the view of many professionals that advertising or marketing is unethical and demeaning to the profession. This is particularly true in the area of client solicitation. The justification for these restrictions is often that clients would be offended by professionals offering more services than they needed. Also, many professions pride themselves in being remote from the "crass commercialization by the use of a marketing concept."

Many professionals are very traditional in their approach to practice management and development. They look at reducing expenses of any category as a way to increase their personal incomes. Why establish a whole new function? There is no doubt that marketing is expensive and time-consuming. Developing an attitude of client concern may require staff training programs, and there is the additional time factor in obtaining client feedback. Although concerns about the cost of the program are legitimate, it is important to relate those costs to the benefits derived. The benefits in this case are greater client satisfaction and quite probably improved income.

To the charge that marketing is manipulative, the answer may very well be yes. Many patients resent their doctor "telling them" to exercise regularly. The patient is nonresponsive to an authoritarian figure telling him how to run his life. But it is still in the patient's best interest for the doctor to try to persuade him to accept a regime of regular exercise.

Professionals should be very sensitive to the needs of the client and very careful not to impose their own standard of moral or ethical conduct on a client—the client has every right to be assertive and deserves the respect of the professional. This constraint poses a difficult moral question for the concerned professional. Is it better to tell the client what is best for him or to try to "persuade" him as a friend might?

The third major criticism leveled at using a marketing concept is that it is intrusive in that it pries into the clients' personal affairs. This is necessary if a professional is to truly understand the wants, needs, and desires of his clientele. A concerned professional must show consideration for the privacy of his clients and make them understand that the motivation for researching the needs of clients and their attitude toward the professional is to improve the service to clients.

Conclusion

Professionals and their professional organizations have been turning a blind eye toward marketing concepts and in fact try to ignore the fact that these concepts are being used in very successful firms and by individual professionals. The most respected and revered of the successful practitioners are often placed in the very hierarchies of the professional organizations which restrict acceptance of the marketing concept. Because marketing concepts are not taught in most professions, the younger and more inexperienced members of the profession are struggling against severe odds in establishing their own practices.

In this chapter we have seen the importance of establishing a marketing concept and learning about clients' needs, wishes, and expectations. We also began to discuss the techniques for meeting the client's requirements.

Marketing is primarily client-oriented—that is, it is designed to meet the needs of the professional's clients. Secondarily, there is a profit motive—the cost of marketing must ultimately pay off with higher profits.

In discussing whether marketing can be considered ethical, we examined the major complaints against the marketing concept. By now it should be understood that everybody markets himself and his profession, whether or not he recognizes it.

3

The Client Is the Focus

In every profession, clients have service needs, and both clients and other publics have every expectation that their needs will be fulfilled.

Publics may be defined as a distinct group of clients and outside parties that have a potential or actual interest in and influence on the professional. For purposes of developing a systematic marketing concept based on client service, the client becomes the center of research and activity for the professional.

A systems approach to marketing would require:

1. A thoroughly researched and realistic approach to determining the needs and expectations of the various publics served by a professional, but particularly the clientele.

2. A systematic approach to the management of a professional marketing program. Tools to assist this might include staff training programs and administrative coordination and integration. These will help ensure that the professional and his staff are consistent in their approach to the various publics served by the professional. The concept of marketing management is based on the premise that an integrated and coordinated professional practice is necessary to provide a profitable and efficient method of meeting the service needs and expectations of clients.

Synergy

A prime tenet of the theory behind a well-managed marketing concept is that planned management can bring about synergism within a professional practice. Synergism is defined in Webster's Dictionary as "cooperative action of discrete agencies such that the total effect is greater than the sum of the effects taken independently."

Basically, the effects of a concentrated marketing effort in one area depend largely on other related variables within the program. Thus a professional could not establish a promotional campaign without carefully considering the specific services he has to offer and the cost of those services to the client. For synergy to work, there must first of all be an awareness and concern for a client's well-being, with various tools and methods used to reinforce one another in the identification of client needs. As an extreme example, a client would not expect to pay very high fees where, for instance, the staff of a professional is sloppily dressed and the clients are required to sit on wooden benches in a waiting room. Synergism comes into play when a client walks into a well-appointed office designed to make him feel comfortable, and speaks to staff members who are responsive and concerned with his needs and exhibit a professional attitude and behavior. All this would make the client more responsive to reasonable professional fees.

The degree to which a professional establishes synergism within his practice depends to a great extent on his ability to manage. The ability to manage begins with a planning or goal-setting process. The professional must clearly define his personal objectives and express those objectives to his staff and other people he relates with. This will be dealt with further in Chapter 16. However, it is timely to mention these concepts here, as they are the initial considerations in the understanding of the marketing concept.

An Example of a Synergistic Approach to Marketing

The objective of this professional is to be concerned for his clients. To accomplish this, he has adopted a progressive professional marketing attitude, which he wants expressed to his clients consistently. Here are some of the things he might want to do:

1. Be well groomed.
2. Be warm and friendly toward his clients.
3. Be concerned for his clients' welfare.

4. Have an office that is comfortable and esthetically pleasing.
5. Train the staff working with him to be concerned for the clients' well-being.
6. Be concerned with learning new techniques and procedures in order to service his clients better.
7. Obtain feedback from clients he may have lost or who are disturbed with the professional attitude, in order that he might change his practice.
8. Willingly discuss fees and explain them to clients.
9. Assist clients in understanding his services and appreciating his concern for them.

If any one of those variable marketing tools is inconsistent with the professional's goals, a large amount of synergism will disappear. For example, if the professional is well-groomed and efficient and his office is esthetically pleasing, yet he is unwilling to discuss an unusually high fee with the client or leaves the client with a suggestion that he must "take it or leave it," the client might very well question the motives of the professional. For instance, he might consider the well-appointed office to be in the best interest of the professional. If the professional uses an autocratic method of bill determination, the client might very well question his warm attitude as a facade to promote the professional's own interests.

Obviously, ignoring or misusing one of many marketing tools might have the devastating effect of having clients questioning the integrity of the professional. It might appear as though the professional is acting primarily in his own interests.

Systems Approach to the Application of the Marketing Concept

A systems approach in marketing is a methodological orientation to the attainment of predetermined plans and goals. The approach is designed to make marketing efficient and economical by coordinating the appropriate marketing tools. The systems approach is implemented by:

1. Researching facts to approach the marketing problem.
2. Coordinating marketing methods and using synergy to implement the marketing program.

A system is defined as a group of interacting items or interdependent groups which, working together, form a unified whole. For a professional, the marketing system includes professional services, fees, distribution channels, and promotional activities.

The benefits from using a systems approach to marketing management are:

- It is a scientific approach to problem solving, encompassing all aspects of the problem.
- It coordinates appropriate professional marketing tools.
- It offers economy and efficiency in a marketing program.
- The professional manager can identify problems quickly through an understanding of the pertinent variables.
- The results can be objectively evaluated.

This approach will allow a professional to expand the scope of his professional practice to include other service areas which may be needed or desired by clients, as well as to deepen or reinforce services already being provided.

The difficulties in using the marketing systems approach are:

- The expense in time and money to implement the marketing concept.
- The lack of a standardized approach, as each professional would have to design and implement his own system.
- A lack of knowledge on the part of the professional of social and psychological factors that affect the behavior of people.
- A resistance on the part of the professional to abiding by research in which he may not have taken part, and failure to work toward predetermined written goals and other considerations including the necessity to conform as part of the system.
- An attitude prevalent among many professionals that they know what is "best" for their clients.

4

Analyzing the Life Cycle of the Professional Firm

Professional firms are originally started in response to clear-cut and obvious market demand. There is a clear and concise purpose for the firm's existence. Unfortunately, as the firm grows and becomes increasingly complex, a loss of direction and purpose may result, and bureaucracy sometimes replaces the original enthusiasm and spontaneity with which professional service had been provided.

The firm is increasingly trying to respond to more complex demands by new clients and demands for additional services by old clients. It builds an ever larger professional staff and employee support system. Internal communication may become increasingly difficult. Special demands are made by clientele and staff. An increasingly wider range of clientele, often with little common interest, makes demands on the firm. The original clear sense of external purpose fades, and professionals can become more concerned with the internal workings of the firm. Instead of responding to client demands, a professional might spend a disproportionate amount of time on his investment portfolio, tax shelters, oranization chart, job descriptions, staff relations, office and facilities planning—all of which detracts from the time available to be responsive to the clients' service needs. The job may be more important than the client.

That way of thinking is often deeply embedded in a professional's "psychological profile." He tends to be very task-oriented as opposed to people-oriented. This is learned partly through the very disciplined study required to even become a professional. Furthermore, the professions generally attract people who are very work-oriented. An educational feedback loop is formed.

Psychological theory suggests that if we work hard enough, for long enough, in a certain way, that is the way we become. An individual enters a professional course of study knowing it will take years of work to get a degree. He does the required work and study to obtain a degree, which demands further years of work and study to practice, reinforcing the work (job) orientation. Most professional courses take seven years of post-secondary study—during which time a student sets aside his friends and family to concentrate on studying for a degree. All effort is focused on that single goal—he is inured to the importance of passing exams and obtaining a degree, sometimes at the expense of the time needed to develop relationships with people, family, and friends.

He obtains his degree—the main purpose of his life to that point—and, after a few years of euphoria about that accomplishment, suddenly may realize that he can look forward only to more years of work and continuing study. At the same time he may be approaching a psychologically stressful age—"mid-life" crisis (32–42 years of age)—during which he will reassess all his values and life goals.

This book is not about psychology but about marketing and strategic planning; yet it is important to relate the two, because psychology will have a great deal of impact on the attitude and results expected from a professional, particularly a sole practitioner. The reasons for the changes which occur in many professionals in mid-career are still not clearly understood, although much research is presently being done in this area. It may be sufficient to say that a professional may feel trapped in an unhappy career choice, an unhappy marriage, few positive social relationships, and an unhealthy psyche.

He may be bored. That will usually change with time, and he will reemerge with a new, enthusiastic, and dynamic approach to his profession (or leave it!)—but it will be usually based upon a renewed interest in the clients' well-being and other positive social relationships. In other words, he will become *client-oriented* rather than *task-oriented* in his attitude toward the practice. The relationship is important in analyzing the life cycle particularly of smaller professional firms.

Organizations and professional firms in which professionals

ANALYZING THE LIFE CYCLE

work are "human" as well in that they are made up of individual people and the firm itself will be subject to change. Thus firms lend themselves to analysis based on somewhat human characteristics.

A Scenario

The following scenario was developed after close observation of more than 300 accountants, engineers, and lawyers and their firms. The scenario is not a specific vindication or vilification of any one but a generalized impression of them all. They were selected partly because they competed in a free, open, and unrestricted marketplace. There were no price-fixing practices or guidelines on the fees charged to clients—that is, there was no intervention by regulatory or quasi-regulatory professional bodies. Medical professions were specifically excluded because of price intervention; but except for fee charges, the scenario of the life cycle might apply here as well.

Such a broad generalization is dangerous, of course. Many individual firms would perform better or worse than the one in the scenario. Yet most professionals will relate, in retrospect, to most of the scenario in some way, particularly to the gyrations the firm went through to achieve maturity.

The time taken for maturation to take effect varies widely. Although seven years is not uncommon, we all know of professional firms that got stuck at the survival level for 20 years. They may have "20 years of experience," but it is more likely one year of experience repeated 20 times—they did not change and grow.

Stage 1: Planning and Survival

There is obvious demand for professional services. It is not usually understood, however, that the demand is for a high volume of professional services provided at low cost. For accountants, bookkeeping services are in high demand; for architects and engineers, drafting and similar services; for dentists and doctors, general practice and clinical and hospital work; and for lawyers, conveyancing. At this level, the market is usually saturated with professionals in preferred locations, and very competitive.

Clients often seek out beginning professionals and firms that are, in their vernacular, "hungry." They are often attracted by the modest fees usually charged. Competition, the level of professional work involved, and the excess time available to a new firm which does not have a wide client base (or, in the medical profession, "patient load") will also restrict the level of fees which can be charged.

The facilities are only functional, often not highly visible, and sometimes there is little consideration given to client convenience or comfort.

The professional tends to dress casually. He may be afraid of losing even one client because of the impact on his income and, hence, his ability to stay in practice. Whether it is a sole practitioner or an entire new firm, there is usually a great deal of self-doubt about the firm's capability to survive. Unfortunately, self-doubt usually leads to inadequate actions. The firm may be nonassertive and blindly follow a client's direction rather than professional dictates.

A marketing attitude or concept is usually lacking. The professional firm feels that clients *have to come in* to get some professional service done. Nothing is done to generate new clients through marketing management. A card may have been mailed announcing the opening; but often it was mailed to other, competitive professionals. Or a discreet advertisement may have been placed in the newspaper—often along with one hundred other "discreet" advertisements. Referrals are hoped for, but there is no structured program to attract new clients. The referrals are based on the firm's providing an "acceptable" level of professional service. But the firm has no external reference to judge the level of "acceptable" service—it has not analyzed the potential clients' or competitors' definition of "acceptable."

The firm grows, and at ever increasing speed, because it is young, aggressive, "hungry," and very intent upon increasing its market share—the *number* of clients it serves. Many of these clients were initially attracted and retained because of the major attraction that the professional services were moderately priced.

Then comes the first crisis: the professional firm does not earn enough net income. Yet the firm is afraid of losing clients if fees are suddenly, and greatly, increased. But a professional might earn as much or more, with less frustration and time commitments, if he worked for someone else.

This might be more appropriately called the "survival" state of a firm, because the professionals may sell out, merge, or abandon the practice. It also is a planning cycle in the sense that the professionals have learned through experience what their income needs are and have not planned a change.

The change is usually brought about by increasing the level of service through accepting only more advanced assignments at higher fees. The professional's reputation and firm are now becoming known.

Stage 2: Growth

Clients are now charged higher—and some would say "more professional"—fees. This is accomplished by having the senior professional do more senior work and delegating routine work to competent assistants.

The emphasis is still on increasing the market share, however. An increasing amount of the professional's time is devoted to systematizing, routinizing, and delegating the work so that professional services can be provided more efficiently, but at the same low cost, to a client. The purpose of this is to make the professional firm more profitable. Professionals have varying degrees of success in these efforts, since most are not trained as systems and methods analysts or managers. Rather, they are trained to provide competent professional services.

The fees charged provide an adequate and comfortable level of net professional income. There usually continues to be relatively intense competition at this level, but an adequate client base and relatively assured income result in a much more relaxed and easy pace and the development of a network of associates and professional relationships. Peer professionals—those in the same profession at a similar level—are not seen so much as adversaries and competitors but more as respected colleagues.

The office and professional service facilities not only are designed to be functional—to provide the service—but also are increasingly relationship-oriented. For instance, comfortable chairs in a "waiting room" would be provided, and clients might be greeted by a receptionist. It is still not totally designed for client convenience. The office may not be highly visible, and client parking and high office rents are of concern.

The professionals wear suits, and the firm is increasingly self-confident. There is not as much concern about losing a small client, but the firm is still very concerned about losing a large client. It is still a "reactive" concern, however, and there is a feeling that little can be done but to provide "good" service in order to attract new clients and retain old ones.

The firm continues to gain experience, and profitability increases as efficiency is improved.

The marketing aspect is usually summed up with a statement such as, "all new clients will come from satisfied clients who make referrals and from a discreet and professional advertising campaign." Both are wrong assumptions. Referrals come from clients who are *enthusiastic* about their professional advisors—but this is still not clearly understood by many firms. *Satisfied* clients are ones who get only what they pay for. Advertising in any form which appears solicitous does not work and may even be detrimental.

Still, nothing is done to gain new clients and stimulate demands from existing clients. A card may have been mailed to clients and peer professionals announcing the addition of a professional staff member or a change of location. Nothing else is done on a continuous basis, except, possibly, the continuance of the discreet advertisement placed in newspapers.

The firm still grows, and at a still greater pace, it would seem, in spite of itself. The firm is growing through its reputation of providing "good" (does that mean adequate, mediocre, or medium?) professional service. In other words, services that can be expected.

This is sometimes called the comfort stage of the cycle, because the professionals have a nice level of professional "salary."

The stage is set for another crisis, which will bring about another change. Remember that, while at university, the professional was conditioned to expect a great career—he was expected to be preeminent and successful. Even without this, he will somehow recognize that he is not only a professional but also a businessman. It seems reasonable to assume that the professional firm should provide not only an adequate salary but an additional profit level. Where there is risk, businessmen should allow for profit margins in addition to salary. The greater the risk, the greater that margin should be.

The professional recognizes some of the risk. He carries errors-and-omissions insurance; but what would happen to his revenues in a recession? He needs money to cover for that. What should be an adequate rate of return, in addition to his salary, on his investment in the facilities and equipment, staff, and buildings needed to operate his practice, let alone the tremendous investment of his time and money in getting the education in the first place?

An "entrepreneurial" profession is being born. The firm is about to change again, by raising the level of professional services, increasing efficiency, adding services, and expanding the client base. Increased net fees will be generated.

But the stage is also set for saturation, decline, and possible decay of the firm, because now there is increasing self-interest instead of client-interest.

Stage 3: Maturity

The professional firm has become relatively well known, and there are referrals. Revenues grow, though at a decreasing rate, and the firm is fully busy. More advanced levels of professional service and a degree of specialization are evident. Routines are delegated by the professional. Although he may be increasingly concerned that he is getting away from personal contact with his client, a great deal of his day is taken up with administration and staffing details. Budgets and more sophisticated management reports to control operations are called for.

Fees are maintained at a high professional level by offering more sophisticated, specialized, and senior levels of professional services. Routine client work is delegated to the lowest level possible (lowest cost) in the professional firm in order to enhance the net income.

The office and facilities are increasingly client-oriented. Clients are greeted in a reception area, not a "waiting room." Location of the facilities is now chosen for ease of client access, adequate parking, and high visibility.

The demeanor of the firm is increasingly assured and self-confident. The professionals dress and act professionally at all times. There is little fear of losing clients because of the broad client base. There is a temptation to become overconfident and begin to tell the clients what they should do. But there is plenty of professional work, and the professional is so busy that he has less and less time for client relations.

Marketing management is still not a function of the practice. The attitude is still that good professional and technical services bring clients through referral. Discreet advertisements still appear continuously. There is increasing social and professional involvement, especially through committee and continuing studies in the professional's association. This is sometimes done in the belief that it will enhance his professional reputation and, hence, bring more clients and higher fees. There is little doubt that it does, and the firm will continue to grow—but these activities may dominate the professional's life and detract from his ability to serve his clients.

Marketing management is still not a clear function. Although good service and advertising are still done, the professional feels that this might be better accomplished by increasing relationships, particularly with "feeders"—people who consistently provide referrals. There is also still the feeling that satisfied clients provide referrals, although there are some lingering doubts.

The professional is becoming dissatisfied with the practice. Routines have replaced spontaneity and enthusiasm. The professional may be doing the same old things for the same old clients for the past five years, and boredom may be setting in.

Stage 4: Saturation

Demand for professional services is steady and increasing, but the firm is overly busy and has difficulty responding to client demands consistently and on time. The professional finds it increasingly difficult to stay on top of current professional assignments and administrative detail. He may be increasingly bored with the detail and routine, which now make up a major portion of his everyday life.

The firm is so busy that fees may be charged at top levels—whatever the market will bear. Little reference is made to the costs to the firm of providing those services.

The firm is becoming overconfident. It makes demands on its clientele. It may be—or appear to be—unconcerned with the loss of a client.

Stage 5: Supersaturation and Decline

The focus of the firm has become even more internal. The professionals are sometimes impersonal with clientele and staff. Most things are systematized, routinized, and delegated. All this makes for an increasingly complex and rule-bound organization. Job descriptions, organizational functions, policy guidelines on just about everything, and established programs and techniques, including relations with clients, replace spontaneity and originality. Outside of specific authority limits detailed in the job description, problems and even opportunities are not addressed.

A great deal of time is spent monitoring and correcting errors of others. Few new ideas are forthcoming. Client services are defined by how they will be responded to—by what position in the organization. Perfection of detail becomes more important than a holistic concerned response to diverse client needs. Procedures for doing things become more important than end results. Old ways of doing things are continued—they're safest. Opportunities are missed.

Most important, *the professional firm becomes rigid and inflexible*—in a word, increasingly bureaucratic. The firm is rigid, but the world (and clients) is changing at an ever increasing pace. It is in danger of losing client market share and revenue, because it increasingly cannot respond to *changing* client demands, needs, and expectations.

It begins to lose clients, and clients increasingly dispute the amount of the fee as being unfair. They perceive that the professional firm is uninterested in them. They may begin to doubt and question the level of professional services they have been receiving.

The market "buzz"—what clients and others tell one another—is rife with negative remarks. "He's too autocratic," "He is too expensive," "I don't think he is keeping up to date," "He sure seems only interested in making more money" are comments which can kill a firm. That reputation can spread widely and quickly.

The firm loses clients (market share) at an ever increasing rate; clients fail to pay fees on time or don't pay at all; and the firm is unable to charge senior fees (market price), because its credibility has been eroded. The firm may fail.

With few exceptions, businesses and individual products follow a classic life-cycle curve. There is little reason to believe that this should exclude the professions; especially where clients are aware of a need for change and the services of a professional firm have remained static. This is compounded by the fact that professionals may become somewhat bored and complacent. Usually there are also enthusiastic and dynamic competitive professionals in the marketplace. There is no reason to believe that a firm will not decline—if there is no planned intervention (see Figure 4-1).

Planned intervention through market research and strategic planning will allow the classic life cycle to be modified. The firm will be changed to emphasize a client orientation, backed by an integrated and managed marketing program.

There are many things that a professional firm might have done to avoid the classic life cycle—to change and grow from the level of full maturity instead of allowing decline, or to start with full market-based programs and strategies in the first place.

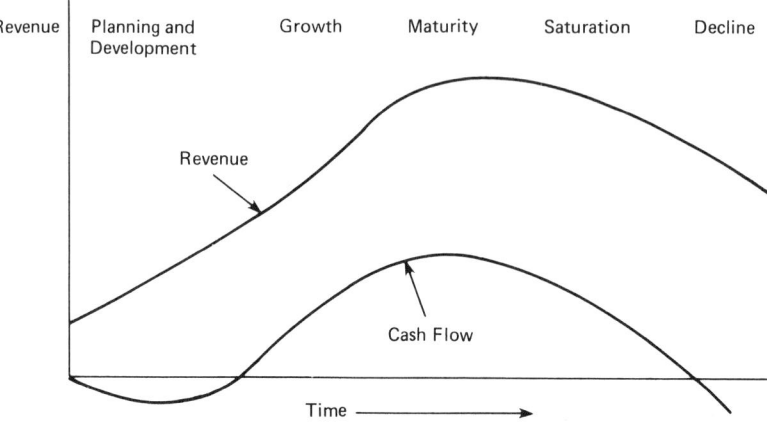

Figure 4-1.   Life cycle of a professional firm—unmodified curve.

The classic life-cycle curve can be modified by:

1. Developing a client-responsive practice.
2. Developing new services for old clients.
3. Developing new clients.
4. Redesigning the firm to improve appearance and efficiency.
5. Reducing the amount charged for professional services.
6. Providing motivation and enthusiasm to staff and professionals.
7. Managing a marketing program.

The effect on revenues and cash flows is illustrated in Figure 4-2.

The Client-Responsive Practice

The senior professionals are sought out for advanced consultation and continuing education of others in their profession. They provide senior consultation to their clientele. They devote a great deal (possible 70 per cent) of their time to management, marketing, client relations, and strategic (long-range) planning for their firm. The firm becomes recognized for the provision of advanced professional services.

Fees remain high, on the basis of more advanced levels of work. Low-fee areas may be avoided, or the clients may be willing to pay higher fees for the prestige attached to the firm. Quality profes-

ANALYZING THE LIFE CYCLE

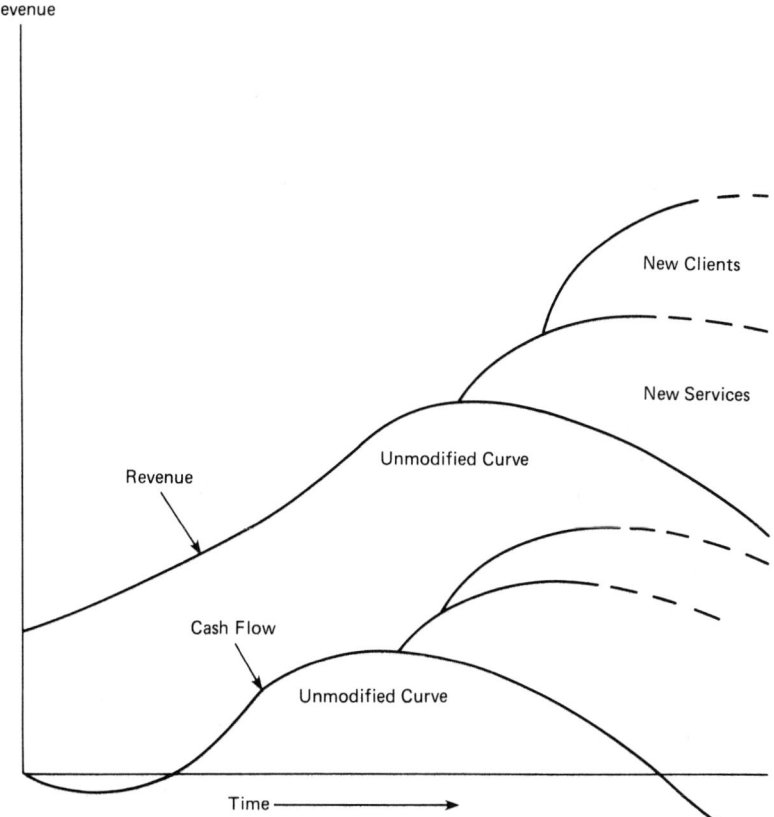

Figure 4-2. Life cycle of a professional firm—modified curve.

sional service, even in low-fee areas, is one of the hallmarks of the fully mature firm. This will be tempered by a concern about the client's ability to pay.

The office, facilities, staff, and professionals are all responsive to the client's well-being. Professional work areas are separated from reception and interview areas. Everything the client sees or perceives suggests that the firm is looking after his best interests. The professionals and staff are assertive and self-confident and always concerned about their client's welfare.

Marketing is now a fully managed function. The firm is cognizant of most things going on in the marketplace and the firm's environment. It monitors and adjusts to the changing perceptions of its clients, their aspirations, wants, needs, and expectations. It actively searches for ways to help clients more fully—not just by asking if there is any more to be done but by detailed research of potential client needs. It knows who makes referrals to it, and it provides positive reinforcement so that they will continue. It orchestrates the marketplace. It is not a passive and reactive firm but knows where it is going and is laying programs and taking action to get there.

It now knows that growth will not come from providing a "satisfactory" level of professional service or from referrals from satisfied clients. Dynamic growth will come only from enthusiastic clients. The firm knows, too, that possibly 80 percent of its referrals come from existing clients who should therefore become the principal concern and target in the firm's marketing efforts.

The problem for such a firm is not how to deal with decline but how to control the firm's continued growth and development.

Summary

The scenario discussed in this chapter suggests that there are two diametrically opposed viewpoints or attitudes toward the provision of professional services.

The first viewpoint holds that the way to develop and market a professional firm is to develop a cold and aloof professional demeanor—a nonresponsive (or negative marketing, or non-marketing) approach. This is a superficial and technical approach, in which the function of providing competent professional assistance is of paramount importance. Once the service is performed—the tax return done, the building plans completed, the divorce concluded, or the illness cured—the client or patient is sent away.

The second viewpoint is that a professional firm should become interested in the long-term welfare of its clients. The intent is not only to correct current problems, but to prevent recurrence in the future and to provide sufficient communication between the professional and his client so that anticipated problems can be avoided before they become major issues. Opportunities can be explored together, and often opportunities for the client are initiated by the professional. This suggests that the firm should be client-oriented rather than job-oriented.

The theory is further emphasized by the very nature in which firms respond to the two different value systems, even internally, within their own professional firms. A surprisingly large number of individuals—paid professionals, staff, employees, and clients—are still treated as children by many professional firms. Here is a brief comparison* of the two management styles—autocratic and democratic:

Autocratic	Democratic
1. People are best motivated by providing direction, authority, and control.	1. People are best motivated by discussion and acceptance, and by "internalization" of the firm's goals.
2. Be objective. Be rational. Never let human emotion interfere in professional life.	2. Consider all human needs. Emotional, psychological, interpersonal, and rational behavior can all be brought forward, openly discussed, and controlled.
3. Human relationships are important only to the extent that they help get the job done.	3. Human relationships are still important to meet objectives, but maintenance of the firm and response to the external environment are also important.

Clients have increased awareness and educational levels. They are increasingly assertive and demand that professional firms respond to their needs.

It is easy to recognize and diagnose an unsuccessful firm. The clients and the professional are both dissatisfied and unappreciative of the results. Clients leave to seek other professionals, fail to return, do not keep appointments, complain about the fee, and do not consistently follow the professional's advice. The professional is dissatisfied with his client base, does not earn enough income, faces expressions of client dissatisfaction with the quality of the practice, and is often "bored" with the practice and possibly the profession.

* Adapted from Chris Argyris, *Management and Organizational Development: The Path from XA to YB* (New York: McGraw-Hill, 1971).

Clearly, a professional firm can be considered successful only when it meets the needs of the individual clients and when clients are clearly satisfied, appreciative, and even enthusiastic about the professional services they have received. Beyond this, the individual professional and his staff must be personally satisfied with the firm and the profession.

5

Environmental Analysis

To this point we have attempted to address the validity of adopting the marketing concept for professionals. There are different marketing problems, strategies, and techniques for different professions. Even within the same profession, the size of the firm, its service capabilities, and other factors would indicate that different professional firms have different marketing problems and should implement different strategies to meet predetermined goals.

A professional organization can be looked at not only from a legal, moral, or ethical viewpoint, but also from socioeconomic viewpoints, political viewpoints, the professional staff's viewpoint, and the viewpoint of any other interested party.

The professional using marketing concepts will be interested in the interrelationships between his profession, his own practice, and the markets and publics with which he deals. He is interested in determining the value-for-value relationships and determining the exchange values—what a party is willing to give up in exchange for what he will be getting.

In order to understand the marketing problems of a professional, it is necessary to define markets, publics, and the concept of service on a value-for-value relationship basis. Only when we have classified a profession in a way which is relevant to the utilization of a marketing concept will we be able to proceed to adopt that concept.

Markets

In the traditional meaning, market is the total socioeconomic structure for the exchange of resources. In order to operate, even a professional firm must obtain at least: staff for a professional practice, necessary financial capital, supplies for the practice of the profession, office space, and proximity to the potential client market. In all cases, the professional must offer some of his resources in exchange for the market resources which he seeks.

The term market differs from the term publics in that publics are identified as individuals or groups with a direct or potential interest in or impact on a professional organization. Once a professional starts thinking in terms of value-for-value exchange with publics, he is thinking about the public in terms of markets.

Publics

Publics are defined as a distinct group of individuals or organizations that have an actual or potential interest in, or can have an impact on, a professional firm.

Every professional operates in an environment of publics. It is relatively easy to itemize the various publics with which any professional organization deals, categorize them between major publics and minor publics in the marketing sense, and/or classify them by function. The major publics might be diagrammed as in Figure 5-1 for a legal firm.

Functional Classification of Publics

In order to analyze the makeup of various publics, it is important to classify them by their functional relationships with a professional firm. This functional classification should be all-inclusive —that is, all the publics should be represented. In order to do this, a service-oriented professional practice might classify its functional relationships with its publics into four groups:

1. Internal publics—basically the professional organization itself, which converts the resources of various input publics.

2. Input publics—those publics which provide the resources and guidelines for the services. In the case of a law firm, this might include support publics (those who have provided capital, effort, and motivation to the development of the professional practice); supplier publics (those who provide the professional firm with the technical tools to practice the profession—these might include, in

ENVIRONMENTAL ANALYSIS

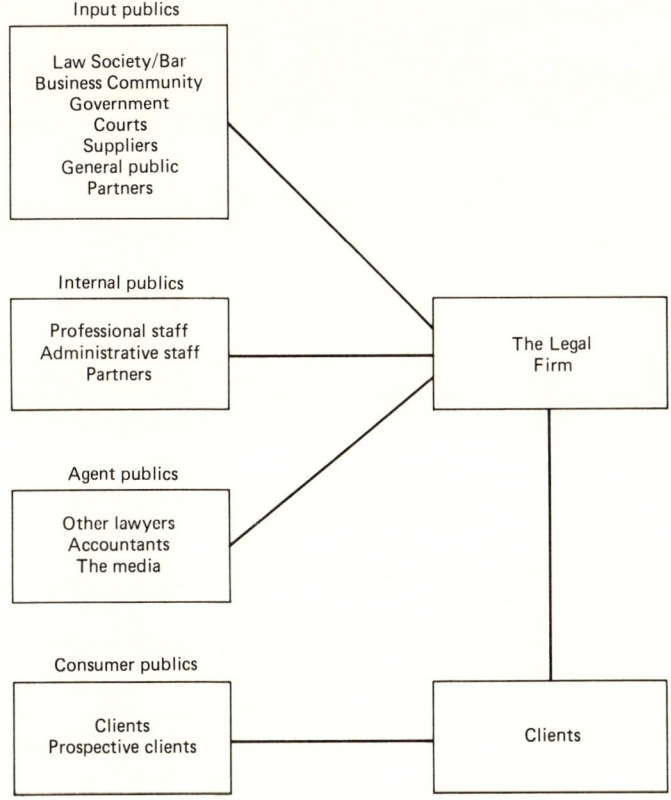

Figure 5-1.   The publics of a legal firm.

the case of lawyers, suppliers of preprinted forms, typewriters, and so on); and government and other regulating agencies that provide legal interpretations and a code of ethics and rules of professional conduct.

3. Agent publics—those who act as intermediaries between the internal publics (the professional firm) and the consuming publics. In the case of a lawyer, this might include a journal which has published his paper and in some cases might be the lawyer himself, who is acting in the dual capacity of an internal public as well as an agent public, passing the resources of his firm through to the client user.

4. The user or consuming publics are the clients of the professional as well as the general public. It is important to distinguish

between consuming publics (clients) and general publics. The major client publics of a professional are current clients and prospective clients. The general publics are indirect beneficiaries of the professional's services.

At all times, there is a possibility that a particular individual or organization may assume more than one functional aspect with a professional organization. For instance, a tax accountant is dealing with at least two functional aspects. First, the IRS in its relationship with the accountants acts as a regulatory public in that it provides guidelines for the preparation of tax returns. However, it also acts indirectly as a consuming public (that is, general public) in that it receives benefits from the professional tax accountant through more efficiently and professionally prepared tax returns.

Similarly, business clients of a professional might act as supporters, suppliers, and clients.

Classification of Publics by Importance to the Professional

Publics may be classified not only by their functional relationship to a professional organization but also by their importance to the organization, both quantitatively and qualitatively. Some publics, such as the clients, are very active in a professional's daily life and might be classified quantitatively. Other publics, such as regulatory agencies, may be passive in day-to-day business but very important in a qualitative sense. Obviously, such classifications would exclude a wide range of socioeconomic activities, organizations, and individuals who have no relationship to the professional firm and would not be deemed to be publics of that firm in any way.

This analysis of publics allows the following classification by importance:

1. Reciprocal publics are publics that have an interest in the organization and in which the professional's organization has an interest. Clients are a reciprocal public.

2. Sought publics are publics in which the professional has an interest, but which may not necessarily have an interest in the professional. Prospective clients are a sought public.

3. Unwelcome publics are the organizations or individuals who have an interest in the professional but in whom the professional is not interested. An individual who seeks free medical advice from a doctor at a party may very well be an unwelcome public.

A critical reason for classifying publics by their import is to allow the professional to understand the relationship between

ENVIRONMENTAL ANALYSIS

various publics and allow him to influence the development of those relationships in ways he desires.

Mutual Relationships Among Publics

Publics are related to the professional directly or indirectly, but they are also related to one another in many ways. Some publics can affect others' attitudes and behavior. For instance, a law firm that has established good relationships with clients will establish an enthusiasm among clients that affects potential clients and the general public. This would have a reinforcing effect on the pride of the staff members of the professional, and his pride in himself and his integrity. The enthusiasm would also increase the potential of obtaining new clients and reduce the danger of other professionals taking clients from the firm.

Alternatively, dissatisfaction expressed by any one of the publics with which a professional deals might have a synergistic effect on the attitudes of the other publics. Consider the example where a professional accountant, say, has a policy of not discussing any billings or fee structure with clients but suggests that the client "take it or leave it." The client might tell other clients that although the service was relatively good, the fee was exorbitant. In some cases, clients dealing with lawyers or accountants have even asked the regulatory agencies whether the fees were fair. Many times, regulatory or government agencies have little experience in professional fees and may even consider many professional fees to be excessive, reinforcing the doubt in the client's mind.

The following resources are left to a client who feels he has been treated unfairly in the fees charged by a professional:

1. He can try to discuss the fee with the professional and negotiate what he considers a more reasonable or realistic fee.
2. He might attempt to win the sympathy of other clients or the general public and thus bring pressure to bear against the professional.
3. He might go to the professional's governing body in an attempt to have the fees "mediated."
4. He might attempt to elicit the support of various activist groups, which have lobbied intensely in recent years against high professional fees.
5. He might seek redress through the courts.
6. He may very well stop being a client of the professional and seek professional services from a competitor.

The situation that specific professions such as law and tax accountancy are placed in is that the complexities of the law generally, and particularly of the income tax laws, require that a client obtain competent professional advice to make sure he conforms to the requirements of those laws. The client is often unaware of any value-for-value relationship if the only reason that he is seeking professional help is to meet statutory obligations. In the case of a tax accountant specifically, unless other services are given, the client is paying a fee just for the professional to compute obligatory taxes—a negative marketing influence if there ever was one.

A professional firm concerned with its clients' well-being must set up relationships with its clients that produce satisfaction for the clients. The professional's obligation is to determine which services to offer its important publics in order to obtain their support. Once a professional firm begins to consider the needs and expectations of its clients, it begins to think of those clients as publics and of a specific public as a market. That market is a group of valued clients and others with whom he wishes to exchange his services, usually for a fee, on a value-for-value basis.

There may be a great deal of communication going on about the firm of which the firm is not even aware. Clients, government bodies, competitors, professional bodies, staff, activist groups, and other publics may all be talking to one another. This is known as market "buzz." Often, the only direct communication link between client and professional is a client meeting or correspondence. It had best be very open and free from negative overtones, or the first time a professional may become aware of a problem will be when a third party—another lawyer or a professional association—brings it to his attention.

The Concept of Service—Value-for-Value Exchange Relationships

A professional has services to offer in exchange for value. Exchange requires self-evident conditions: (1) there must be at least two parties, and (2) what is being offered is of value to the second party.

Value is expressed in terms of human wants, needs, and expectations. Needs are, by definition, unsatisfied demands. If a client is not able to perform a job or technical or professional function himself, he will look to outside professionals to assist him. Those outside sources have value for the individual.

ENVIRONMENTAL ANALYSIS

In principle, clients can obtain professional services by three principal methods, only one of which is the exchange method:

1. Self-production—for instance, a lawyer might not look to others for legal advice.
2. Charity—to play on the charitable nature of people to provide something of value without anything in exchange.
3. Exchange—the process of exchanging goods and services on a value-for-value basis.

The marketing approach, of course, is based on only the last of these alternatives.

Exchange Flows

In marketing terminology, a transaction between a buyer and a seller, whether for goods or services, is known as a commercial transaction. The seller offers something of value—in the case of a professional, his services—in exchange for something of value to him, usually money but possibly also referrals.

The two parties to the transaction, the client and the professional, enter into the exchange because each sees something of value for himself—a way to satisfy his wants or needs. A client sees more value in obtaining the goods or services than in spending his resources elsewhere, and the professional obtains a desired profit through the exchange.

There are three recognized exchange transactions for professionals:

1. Commercial transactions—where goods or services are provided in return for something of value, usually money.
2. The employment transaction—where staff offer time and productive service to the professional firm in return for a salary.
3. Charity transactions—where a professional provides money or services and receives a feeling of well-being in return.

In addition, there are indirect relationships which come about as a result of exchange transactions. One example is shown in Figure 5-2.

The staff receives appreciation from clients for services performed. In this relationship, the intermediary is the professional, who obtains services from his staff and provides them to his clients in exchange for fees, which he in turn uses to pay wages to his staff.

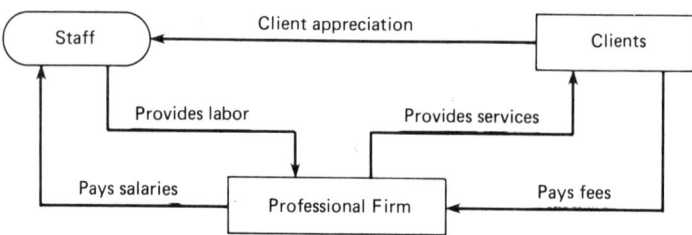

Figure 5-2.   Client-staff exchange relationship.

Professional Service Organizations

Professional firms differ from others in the exchange relationship in that services are exchanged for fees. It becomes obvious that if a professional is to service his client market, he must do the following:

1. Identify his target clients—the clients he wishes to serve.
2. Identify the needs of his target clients.
3. Design and implement services to meet clients' needs.
4. Provide those services in a timely manner for the client's benefit.
5. Communicate what services are available to the target client market.

Marketing problems arise where there is a fluctuating demand for the services of a professional. For example, a tax accountant is usually extremely overworked during and immediately prior to the tax filing deadline, and yet he may be underutilizing his capital and resources at other times during the year. No matter what the profession, there are periods of peak demand and periods of underdemand, and adequate market planning would take this into account and allow for a more timely and consistent level of service availability to the client.

Market Audit—Environmental Influences

To assess the total environment for the provision of professional services, a firm might develop a "market audit" to obtain information and analyze major considerations and perceptions in the marketplace—the macroenvironment.

The perception of a firm, and even an entire profession, will

ENVIRONMENTAL ANALYSIS

undoubtedly differ for various individuals or organizations surveyed, depending on their point of view.

For instance, the firm (and, indeed, the whole profession) may feel that it is providing excellent professional services and that fees are reasonable. The client may feel that services are adequate but fees are too high. Nonclients (the balance of the potential market) may feel that services are inadequate and fees are very high. The professional's staff may feel that clients are underserviced. Perception studies will allow a professional firm to set objectives and change in response to present (and potential) expectations. New firms may learn of shortfalls in the provision of professional services and structure themselves to be responsive to those market needs. Potential target markets may become self-evident in this market research. The professional organization might be very surprised by how it is viewed by others. Once it knows what those perceptions are, it can actively direct a marketing program to educate its publics and change those perceptions.

A market audit, or "macroenvironment analysis," may be built around a questionnaire such as that shown on the following pages.

MARKET AUDIT QUESTIONNAIRE
MACROENVIRONMENT ANALYSIS

Perception of:	The profession	☐
	The firm	☐
Perception by:	Total environment (holistically)	☐
(point of view)	Existing clients	☐
	Nonclients	☐
	Firm (principals) or partners	☐
	Senior professional staff (of the firm)	☐
	Support staff	☐
	Competing professional firms	☐

Survey of
Interviewee:

Name:_____ Title:_____

Firm's Name:_____

Address:_____

_____ Zip:_____

Telephone:_____

Prepared by:
(or interviewed by)

_____

_____

Date: _____ Time:_____

General Comments:_____

_____

_____

	Excellent	Good	Fair	Poor	Comments
ENVIRONMENTAL ANALYSIS					
1. How do you think the profession, as a whole, responds to wants, needs, and expectations of its clients/employers?	☐	☐	☐	☐	
2. What is your impression of how the firm responds to the wants, needs, and expectations of its clientele?	☐	☐	☐	☐	
3. What is your impression of how competitive forces work in this profession?	☐	☐	☐	☐	
COMPETITION:					
4. How good is the competition in providing service?	☐	☐	☐	☐	
5. Are there many sources of professional help?	☐	☐	☐	☐	
6. How competitive is the firm in terms of price (cost to clientele)?	☐	☐	☐	☐	
7. How do you rate the firm with respect to leadership in developing new methods, standards, and pricing?	☐	☐	☐	☐	
8. How good is the firm in:					
Research and development?	☐	☐	☐	☐	
Marketing?	☐	☐	☐	☐	
Promotion?	☐	☐	☐	☐	
9. How good is the firm in providing timely professional services?	☐	☐	☐	☐	
10. What is the firm's financial condition (that is, is it vulnerable because of lack of financial resources)?	☐	☐	☐	☐	

	Excellent	Good	Fair	Poor	Comments
ECONOMICS:					
11. How knowledgeable is the firm about how the economy affects the firm?	☐	☐	☐	☐	
12. How well are plans laid for major changes in economic conditions:					
A recession?	☐	☐	☐	☐	
Inflation?	☐	☐	☐	☐	
13. What is the response time (speed) with which the firm can respond to major economic changes?	☐	☐	☐	☐	
POLITICAL INFLUENCE:					
14. Does the firm have foreknowledge of (major) changes which may be imposed upon the profession:					
By government bodies?	☐	☐	☐	☐	
By the professional organization?	☐	☐	☐	☐	
(Note: Very few legislative changes in ethics or by-laws come as a complete surprise to involved professionals.)					
15. How do you rate the firm's knowledge of alternative policies of the government or professional organizations which may bring wholesale changes to a profession?	☐	☐	☐	☐	
SOCIAL INFLUENCE:					
16. How do you rate the firm's knowledge about society? (Note: Societal composition and thinking, values, demands, education/access to information, leisure, and mobility are always changing.)	☐	☐	☐	☐	

17. How prepared is the firm for shifts in population (size, location, and age makeup)?

18. How do you rate the response time (speed) with which the firm could respond to social changes?

SOCIAL RESPONSIBILITY:

19. How responsive is the firm to the needs of society and its environment—its professional organization, government involvement, charitable and social commitments, and so on?

TECHNOLOGICAL CHANGE:

20. How well does the firm keep up, in relation to other firms, with new developments in the profession through attendance at continuing professional education functions, journal reading, and so on?

21. How well are new methods, new materials, new techniques, new services, and new clientele studied and evaluated for their potential impact?

22. What is the firm's ability to respond to technological innovations? (That is, how fast could the firm adopt major new advances in professional technique?)

GENERAL:

23. How do you rate the firm in placing its clients' best interest first?

24. How do you rate the firm's technical proficiency?

6

Market Identification

The objective of this chapter is to define a "target" client.

It is impossible for any individual or professional firm to be all things to all people. Any attempt to do so results in the firm going in many directions (non-targeted) for many individual clients who demand many diverse services at the same time. Most important, it is difficult to develop a market research and marketing management program for a totally heterogeneous group. Mix the strong clients with the weak clients? The rich with the poor? The corporate with individuals? Bookkeeping with audit and consultative? House-drafting with chemical processing? Conveyancing with advanced litigation and lobbying? General practice with bone surgery? Only when a firm can identify a specific market can it structure its services, fees, and marketing program in response to those segmented needs.

The most important division is that between clients and all other "publics." A firm will survive or fail because of the client base. Yet, little differentiation is made by many professional firms. Who are the clients? What services do they need? What do they do? What do they use the services of the professional for? What will they be like in the future—will there be more or fewer of them, requiring more or fewer services? Assumptions may have to be made, but unless the clientele of a general practice is defined into very small segments (segments containing less than 10 percent of clientele revenue), it may be difficult to design services and marketing programs that are responsive to the needs of individual clients.

It is also important to define the competition in each market segment and to assess the firm's competitive strength for each individual type of client.

Along with a review of the professional's individual preference and goals, this sort of analysis will enable the firm to select a specific market position, objective, and strategy.

For instance, without market segmentation, many firms might set an annual growth rate of 15 percent over last year's volume. If the total market is growing at 15 percent and the firm has 60 percent of the *defined* market, its revenue volume has increased by 8 percent by just staying with the same market share. That is, it has not improved its position in relation to other firms; it has increased income only by obtaining 60 percent of the increased market for professional services, and it still retains only 60 percent of the defined market share. The balance of the increase—7 percent—could be accounted for by inflationary increases. In other words, the seemingly high growth rate of 15 percent is illusionary —there has been no increase in market share, and the revenue growth per client is just staying even with inflation. Segmentation will allow the firm to develop a strategic position and assess and measure its growth or decline by measurement against specific types of clients and specific types of services.

Segmentation by Individual and Corporate Clients

Many professionals serve not only individual people but also corporate bodies. In that case, the first distinction, or segregation, to be made is between individual people and corporate bodies. The characteristics and marketing strategies are often very different for the two segments. Certainly medical practitioners—dentists and doctors—usually deal only with individuals, particularly in a general practice. Yet, locum tenens organizations (other professionals filling in during absence) and hospital organizations would be considered a corporate body for identification purposes. Firms in other major professions, including accounting, engineering, and law, often specialize either in the corporate area (corporate accounting, industrial engineering, or corporate law) or in work for individual clients (individual tax preparation, home design, and criminal law, for example). General practitioners may work in many of these areas simultaneously. This is desired by many practitioners because of the variety of work and the challenge of a diverse client base. This may result in a less efficient practice, on a client-per-client basis, because without ever defining the type of client—corporate or individual—there may be little effort to design facilities and procedures that respond to the unique needs of the client.

Segmentation by Types of Client

Individual clients may be broken down, or segmented, by psychological profile, geographic location, and demographic characteristics—age, education levels, and so on.

Corporate bodies can be classified by similar means in order to ascertain characteristics of major (potential) clients. This will enable the firm to respond to the expectations of different groups of clients.

A psychographic profile of a corporate client might include an analysis of the "image" the corporation wishes to project—conservative and low-key or liberal and highly visible. It might be defined by benefits it seeks from a professional—low cost, dependability, timeliness of service, the professional's "image" (prestige value), and so on. Similarly, a client may have strong, medium, or no loyalty to its professional advisors.

The geographic location of a client can have a major impact on the selection and retention of professional advisors. Clients can be segregated by their physical location—country, region, state, and city—which can be further categorized by size and density.

Demographic profiles of corporate clients will be useful for further defining client preferences or establishing whether demand exists for more specialized types of services. The number of years a corporate client has been in existence may have a bearing on its management sophistication, or assist in locating its position on an industry "life-cycle chart." The type of industry it is in may also influence its choice of a professional firm. Many professional firms become recognized for services to a specific industry. The number of employees the corporation has is important in determining its size and identifying potential service areas. Similarly, gross-revenue information can help in further targeting a need for professional assistance. The blend of backgrounds and personalities of individuals within the corporate body—age, race, religion, nationality, and social class—will have a bearing on the choice of professional advisors. Education and knowledge—the degree of

MARKET IDENTIFICATION

management sophistication—will have an important bearing on the types of services sought.

A "scatter diagram" (see Figure 6-1) will help identify areas of concentration in the market structure and, if few other professionals are concentrating their efforts on specific areas, a competitive niche in which the firm can identify client service needs and target its services.

Concentration areas are often obvious from a visual examination of the scatter diagram. Some analysts remove from between 10 percent and 20 percent of the population at both ends of the array to determine the most common and representative areas of concentration. Quantitative analysis and other arithmetic and statistical techniques—often computer generated—can provide more specific results. However, since identification is often a very subjective process (how do you program a computer for client sophistication?), a simple examination of a scatter diagram is often sufficient for the purposes of a small professional firm. Of the averages—mean, median, and mode—we are looking for the mode—the most common areas.

Segmentation by Types of Services

The types of services and the degree of sophistication with which professional services are brought to the marketplace vary as widely as do the number of professions and individual clients.

Figure 6-1.   Client analysis using a scatter diagram.

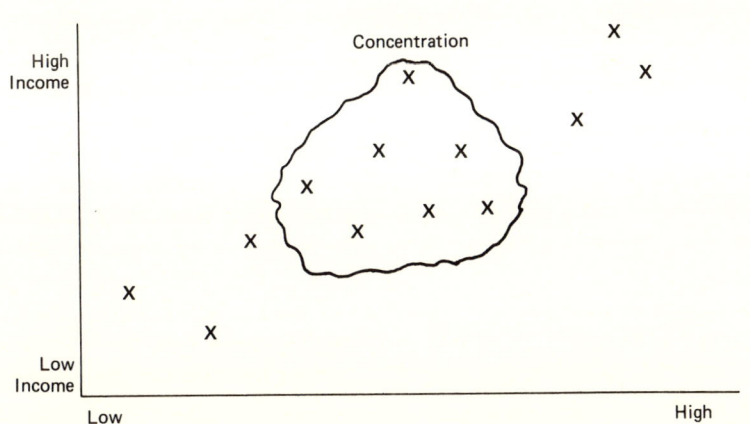

Most professional organizations attempt to define standards of professional services. But a standard is, by definition, a model of a desired result and is based on acceptable practices among average professionals. Yet, it rarely makes sense to talk about an average or "standard" client. The service needs of individuals and corporate clients are so diverse as to reach into almost every area of human endeavor. Some of the professions and various client needs might be:

Profession	*Client needs*
Accounting	Bookkeeping, accounting, audit, tax preparation, tax consulting, budgeting, forward planning, management consultation, cost reduction, profitability analysis . . .
Engineering	Civil, mechanical, electrical, chemical, nuclear, or structural; research and invention, design, project planning, production, construction, operations management . . .
Law	Civil, criminal, corporate, tax; conveyancing, litigation, judicial, maritime, international . . .
Medicine	Physical or mental; family practice, hospital, private practice; holistic, psychology, surgery, otolaryngology, osteopathic, research, urology

A scatter diagram (see Figure 6-2) will help segregate the types of services demanded by various clients (in this case, clients are

Figure 6-2.   Service segmentation—business clients of an accounting firm.

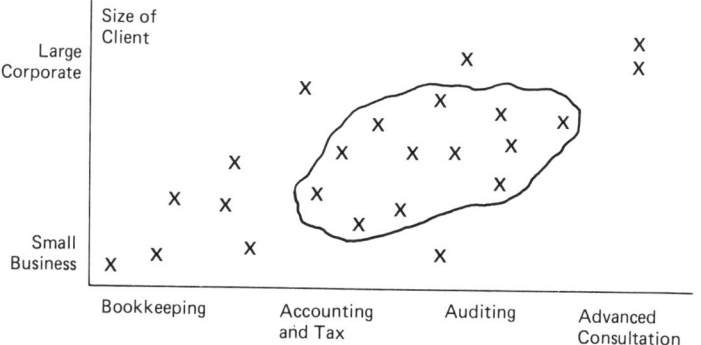

MARKET IDENTIFICATION

differentiated according to size). Again, where a segment of the market is not being concentrated on, or fully serviced, this may indicate a market position that the firm should take.

Segmentation of Other Publics

A professional must deal with many publics besides clients, including legislative and quasi-legislative bodies, suppliers, the business community at large, and professional staff. These might be segregated according to their importance and influence on the professional firm.

Influence	*Influencing Public*
Standards and direction:	Government and professional organizations
	Competitors
	Other professionals in the same profession
	Partners
Client response:	Clients
	Potential clients
	Ex-clients
Provision of service:	Professional and administrative staff
	Suppliers
Indirect influence:	General public
	Mass media
	Other professions

Publics might also be categorized by the function they fulfill in the overall provision of professional services. *Input publics* are those which provide resources for the practice of a profession. These supporters are universities and professional organizations, which provide education and professionals; government and professional organizations, which regulate the practice of the profession; and suppliers. *Conversion publics* are those which convert the input into client service—partners, professionals, and administrative and support staff. *Client publics* are the consumers.

Segmentation of Competitors

Competitors can be analyzed to determine whether they have a major or minor impact on the market. They can be analyzed for the number and types of clients they have, the services they offer, and, most important, whether they have chosen a specific market segment in which they hold a dominant position. If they have chosen a position, it will be very difficult to get clients to switch loyalties. These firms undoubtedly provide very efficient services because of in-depth knowledge, specialization, procedures, and techniques. For instance, a law firm might have 80 percent of the corporate litigation in a community, or an accounting firm might have specialized and be known to audit most of the banks in a state. They are known, reputed, and efficient in those market segments, and it would be difficult to compete for market share. An analysis of other professional firms will assist the professional in identifying an underserviced niche in the marketplace.

Market Positioning

We have shown in this chapter alternative methods of identifying the market for professional services. In order to be most successful, a professional firm should know the type of client it wants, the types of services those clients want, and the competitive forces in each of those market segments.

A Venn diagram (see Figure 6-3) will identify the client's needs

Figure 6-3.   Unstructured market positioning.

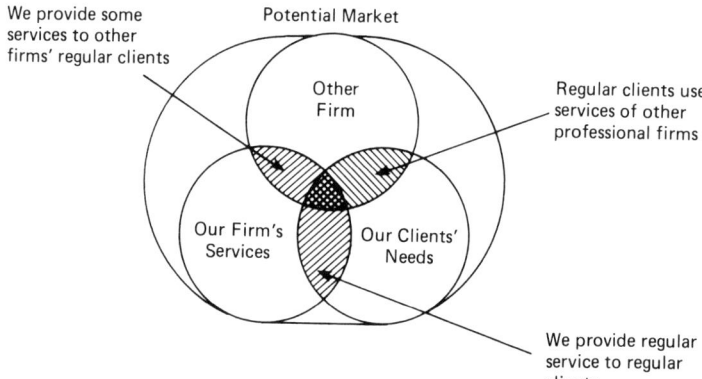

MARKET IDENTIFICATION

and areas where those needs are fulfilled by our firm or a competitive firm.

The purpose of market structure identification and analysis is to locate a market position or niche—a viable market segment, possibly with little competition and greater demand—from which to operate, rather than do the same things all other professional firms are doing and simply duplicate their client and service mix. This simply means to find out what other firms are doing—which type of clients they serve and which types of services they offer—and identify a number of client needs that are currently not served by competitors or at least not optimally served.

Additionally, needs of potential clients who do not use professional services should be identified.

Market positioning means that the firm will be able to meet most of the service for most of its clientele (see Figure 6-4). There is a high correlation between market demand and the supply of needed professional serivces by the firm. When clients are obtaining the professional level of services that they want, need, and expect, a high degree of synergism can be developed and the firm can increasingly respond and more efficiently service its target market. This will allow the professional firm to orchestrate its markets even better and build a marketing program to be increasingly responsive to client needs.

Identification of areas of current concentration and areas for potential development may begin with a questionnaire such as that shown on the following pages.

Figure 6-4.   Structured market positioning.

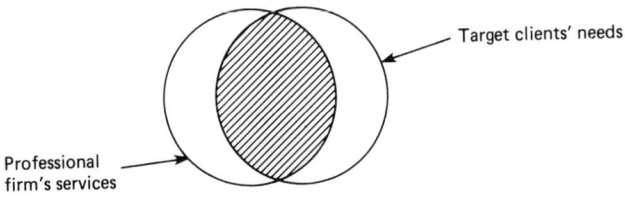

MARKET AUDIT: MARKET IDENTIFICATION REVIEW

Analysis of:　　　　The firm　　　　　　　　　　　　　☐
　　　　　　　　　Another professional firm　　　　　☐

Name of the other firm: _____

　　　　　　　　　Address: _____

　　　　　　　　　_____ Zip: _____

　　　　　　　　　Telephone: _____

Prepared by:　　　_____

　　　　　　　　　Date: _____ Time: _____

　　　　　　　　　General Comments: _____

　　　　　　　　　_____

　　　　　　　　　_____

CLIENTS:

1. Who are the (potential) major clients of the professional firm?

_____
_____
_____

2. What are the major market segments?

_____
_____
_____

SERVICES:

3. What are the major professional services?

_____
_____
_____

MARKET IDENTIFICATION

4. What are the characteristics and growth rates of each major segment?

5. What are the major considerations to meet present and future client needs and wants?

6. How do clients decide which professional firm to choose and which services to obtain?

COMPETITION:

7. How do clients and others see the professional firm and feel about it?

8. What firms might be classified as competitors (to the surveyed firm)?

9. Will competition change in the future?

7
Internal Analysis

A professional firm must know where it stands at the present time in relation to its internal environment—the microenvironment. An internal evaluation of the marketing system (if any) being used by the professional firm will assist in this.

The firm should establish and/or review its internal objectives. It should review its organizational structure to determine if it is appropriate for a market-based approach. Existing services should be clearly identified, and planning for new services or discontinuing inappropriate services should be considered. The existing client base should be clearly identified and categorized. Planning for additional clients or, in some cases, dropping old clients should also be considered.

The existing marketing program and strategies should be reviewed. The marketing program should include clear objectives and control procedures to ensure that results are obtained. Most important, are all marketing objectives, strategies, and plans client-oriented? Do they consider the needs, wants, and expectations of the firm's (potential) clientele?

The determination of a professional firm's market-based goals and objectives will be more fully discussed in Chapter 16. But many firms state goals and objectives that are very ethereal, not subject to measurement, and often totally internalized—that is, without consideration of market response. For instance, "to be the leading professional firm providing quality professional services

INTERNAL ANALYSIS

and earning a high level of professional income" sounds like a lofty professional objective. That may be so, but "the leading professional firm" compared to which other firm? The whole profession? "Leading" as to new client growth, net profitability, or quality of service? If so, by how much? What are the criteria for measurement? "Providing quality professional services" compared to what standards of quality? The average of other professional firms? The most expensive? "Quality" in whose eyes—the professional's or the client's? For instance, the professional may be giving the quality that he feels is appropriate, but the client may feel that that level of professional service (too high or too low) is inappropriate. "A high level of professional income" compared to which other professionals? How high is high? Measured against what investment? in education? office and support facilities? investment in the practice?

Obviously, lofty stated goals and objectives have little value other than for public relations. Even that value is doubtful, since such statements might sound very self-aggrandizing and pompous. A listener wants to know what you can do for him. For the objectives to be effective, we must be able to measure the results quantitatively against the objectives. Objectives must be concise and specific.

The professional firm should have an organizational structure that allows it to respond effectively and efficiently to stated client needs. For example, when a client telephones in for advice, is all the information he needs readily available from one professional, or must the client go from office to office, professional to professional, to obtain the information he needs? In an accounting firm, for instance, must a client talk to one professional about his year-end financial statements, another about his tax, and yet another about preparing a budget—and if one of those professionals is not available, how long must he wait to obtain the information? A functional (by type of professional job) organization chart can provide the firm with increasing efficiency through specialization, but if carried to the extreme, it will make client responsiveness exceedingly difficult (see Chapter 19 for organizational structure considerations).

Existing professional services should be carefully identified and categorized. Does each person in the firm perform all professional services needed by each client, or can administrative and backup routines be delegated to assistants? Can some of the professional-level services be delegated to a highly trained subordinate who is subject to the control of the professional? Often, through this analysis, opportunities will be found to add other advanced professional services or to refer a unique type of professional service to another specialized professional, rather than trying to keep current in those areas where the time and effort required are greater than the potential benefits.

Similarly, clients can be analyzed and categorized into groups with various characteristics. It may be appropriate to confine professional services to the group that would benefit the most from the firm's efforts and refer to other specialists those clients who would obtain more appropriate professional services elsewhere.

The market audit questionnaire that follows may be helpful in conducting an internal review of the current marketing system.

MARKET AUDIT: INTERNAL REVIEW OF EXISTING MARKETING SYSTEM

Perception of: The firm

Perception by: Principals or partners ☐
Senior professional staff ☐
Support staff ☐

Perception of: Name: _____ Title: _____

Branch or Department: _____

Telephone: _____ Local: _____

Prepared by: _____

Date: _____ Time: _____

General Comments: _____

INTERNAL ANALYSIS

OBJECTIVES:

1. Does the firm have long-term objectives?   Yes ☐   No ☐
   What are they?

   _____

   _____

2. Does the firm have short-term objectives?   Yes ☐   No ☐
   What are they:

   _____

   _____

3. Does the firm know which clients it wants and   Yes ☐   No ☐
   what services to offer?
   What type of clients are wanted?

   _____

   _____

   What kinds of professional services does the firm want to provide? (Be specific as to the *kinds* of services, *not* quality.)

   _____

   _____

   _____

4. Who is responsible for setting objectives?
   Name: _____

5. How actively does he/she work to ensure that objectives and plans are met?

1	2	3	4	5
Hardly Active		Moderately Active		Very Active

6. Do you help in the planning process?   Yes ☐   No ☐

7. Would you like to become more involved? Yes ☐ No ☐

8. Do the objectives seem reasonable for the firm? Yes ☐ No ☐
   (Consider competition from other professional firms, the size of the firm, and opportunities for development.)

9. What do you consider to be the firm's major strengths?

   _____
   _____
   _____

10. What do you consider to be the firm's major weaknesses?

    _____
    _____
    _____

ORGANIZATIONAL STRUCTURE:

11. Do you understand and practice the marketing concept?

    Yes ☐ No ☐

    How often do you respond efficiently and fast to client service needs and expectations?

1	2	3	4	5
Seldom		Usually		All the Time

    How often do others in your firm respond efficiently and fast to client service need?

1	2	3	4	5
Seldom		Usually		All the Time

12. Is the firm organized to respond to client requests? (Consider staff, facilities, services offered, location, and so on.) Yes ☐ No ☐
    How could this be improved?

    _____
    _____
    _____
    _____

INTERNAL ANALYSIS   77

13. Are all staff members adequately trained, supervised, and evaluated on
    the basis of their ability to be responsive to client needs?

                                              Yes ☐   No ☐
    How can this be improved?

    _____

    _____

    _____

14. Are there any incentives for attracting and retaining desired clientele?

                                              Yes ☐   No ☐
    What are they?

    _____

    _____

    _____

15. Is a senior principal or partner responsible for the firm's marketing
    activity?   Yes ☐   No ☐

    Name: _____

SERVICES:

16. List the kinds of services provided by the firm by level of importance
    to the firm's clientele and who is responsible for them:

                                         Kind of   Who Is
                                         Service   Responsible

    Major professional services   _____   _____

                                         _____   _____

                                         _____   _____

                                         _____   _____

    Minor professional services   _____   _____

                                         _____   _____

                                         _____   _____

                                         _____   _____

                                         _____   _____

Administrative and support services   _____ _____
　　　　　　　　　　　　　　　　　　　　　　　_____ _____
　　　　　　　　　　　　　　　　　　　　　　　_____ _____
　　　　　　　　　　　　　　　　　　　　　　　_____ _____

17. Can some of the senior professionals' work load be delegated?

　　　　　　　　　　　　　　　　　　　　　　　　　　　　Yes ☐　No ☐

　　How?

　　_____
　　_____
　　_____

18. What kinds of professional services should be increased?

　　_____
　　_____
　　_____

19. What kinds of professional services should be decreased?

　　_____
　　_____
　　_____

20. Are there other kinds of related professional services which should be performed for clientele?　　　　　　　　　　　　　　Yes ☐　No ☐

　　What kinds?

　　_____
　　_____
　　_____

　　Why?

　　_____
　　_____
　　_____

INTERNAL ANALYSIS

21. Are there certain kinds of professional services which should be discontinued? Yes ☐ No ☐
    What kinds?

    _____
    _____
    _____

    Why?

    _____
    _____
    _____

CLIENTS:

22. List the kinds of clients of the firm by level of importance to the firm and who is responsible for them:

	Kind of Client	Who Is Responsible
Most important	_____	_____
	_____	_____
	_____	_____
	_____	_____
Least important	_____	_____
	_____	_____
	_____	_____
	_____	_____

23. Which types of clients benefit most from the firm's professional services?

    _____
    _____
    _____

24. Which types of clients benefit least from the firm's professional services?

_____
_____
_____

MARKETING PROGRAM AND STRATEGY:

25. What is being done to achieve growth objectives?

_____
_____
_____

26. How successful do you think the program will be?

1	2	3	4	5
Totally Unsuccessful				Very Successful

27. How do you think it can be improved?

_____
_____
_____

28. Is the marketing effort aimed at the right place at the right time? (Consider quality of service, client contact, timeliness of service, and so on.)   Yes ☐   No ☐
How can this be improved?

_____
_____
_____

29. How often are resources (principally staff) adequate for a full—and quick—response to client needs?

1	2	3	4	5
Never		Usually		All the Time

INTERNAL ANALYSIS

30. Are enough time, effort, and resources directed to marketing and client relations? Yes ☐ No ☐
    How can this be improved?

    _____

    _____

    _____

MARKETING EFFECTIVENESS (Implementation and Control):

31. Is there a marketing plan, at a minimum prepared annually?
    Yes ☐ No ☐

32. Are there specific objectives as to how many clients should be added or dropped? Yes ☐ No ☐
    How many clients, or what percentage?
    Increase No. _____(%)   Decrease No. _____(%)
    When?
    Next month _____ Next year _____ Don't know _____

33. Is the targeted objective for growth or decline realistic?
    In terms of clientele?   Yes ☐ No ☐
    In terms of service?   Yes ☐ No ☐

34. Do management reports contain information on marketing activity?
    Yes ☐ No ☐

35. Are studies done to determine the effectiveness of the marketing (including advertising) effort? Yes ☐ No ☐

36. Are controls in place to ensure that marketing objectives are being met? Yes ☐ No ☐

37. Other comments you would like to make:

    _____

    _____

    _____

    _____

    _____

    _____

8

Market Analysis and Segmentation

A market has been defined as the potential environment in which a resource exchange can take place. The professional firm receives resource input principally from the professional market, supplier market, and labor market. Its job is to convert those input resources into viable professional services that can be used by the client market. There must be exchange value to all of them.

A market, then, is a *distinct group of individuals who have resources that they wish to exchange, or would consider exchanging, to their advantage.*

Marketing considers the exchange (or trading) value when dealing with publics—those people who could have an impact on the professional firm.

Once the professional firm starts thinking in terms of value to the client or public, it is, in effect, beginning to use a marketing approach. It is beginning to estimate the value of its services from the clients' or publics' viewpoint. At the same time, it realizes that almost every public involved potentially has a unique viewpoint. There are thus many variables to be considered.

Major variables can include the psychological, geographic, and demographic characteristics of individual clients.

Psychological characteristics of clients. The personality and lifestyle of clients will have a bearing on the choice of a professional. Awareness, assertiveness, and compulsiveness may have an effect. Prestige associated with a professional can have a major influence—not only on the choice of a professional by a client, but also on his willingness to pay professional fees. The loyalty of clientele and the esteem in which others hold the professional—all can be broken down and analyzed.

Geographic factors. Along with competitive considerations, the country, state, county, or city location of clientele will certainly affect the choice of a firm by clients. Those locations can be analyzed for population density, number of clients per professional (firm), types of clients or service per professional, commercial versus residential type of industry, and types of individual engagements—such as residential property sales per conveyancing lawyer.

Demographic characteristics. Age, education level, family size and structure, income level, nationality, occupation, race, religion, sex, and social class may all have an effect on which professional a client chooses and what level of professional services he seeks. These can be sensitive areas given equal opportunity legislation, yet they may have a major impact on the success or failure of a practice. Other than provisions in some government contracts, there is no legislation forcing a client to choose a professional on the basis of equal opportunity legislation.

Major variables can assist in defining "target" clientele. Much of the information needed for an analysis of these variables is publicly available. The analysis of these variables is known as *market structure analysis,* which differs from client analysis (Chapter 9) in that it analyzes the whole marketplace—defines the (potential) clientele, segments that clientele into cohesive units, determines the strategic market position to best serve the chosen (target) clientele, and defines programs to orchestrate the marketing strategy.

Client analysis is the process of determining and maintaining current knowledge of clients' perceptions, needs, wants, and expectations once the firm has positioned itself within the market structure.

Segmentation

Most professional firms treat the entire marketplace as a homogeneous unit. Little effort is made to differentiate the clientele, let alone their unique and distinct needs for professional services. The professional firm is suggesting, in effect, that it has an equal appeal and responsiveness to everyone. Mass marketing and broad "public relations" types of advertising attempt to convey this notion. The single "image" that a firm projects seldom attempts to respond to the needs and expectations of individual clients but only attempts to bend the publics' point of view to that of the professional. A professional firm that tries to convey the impression to everybody that its services are best, for everybody, is using this strategy. This undifferentiated approach, with little emphasis on market (client or service) differences, is not as effective as segmentation, because little attention can be given to exchange value—the "pay value" to individual clients.

When a firm has divided its markets into segments, it can concentrate on the service needs of individual segments. This will result in a much greater impact on each of those segments. If only one target market group is identified, a concentrated marketing effort can be directed at that one segment. The objective is to structure the services and the firm to be extremely responsive to that market segment's needs. The firm designs its promotional activities and professional work programs and services directly for those clients so that they will receive the greatest benefit by employing that firm. By defining that segment carefully and concentrating on market strength with existing and potential clients in that segment, a firm can expect to become reputed for its area of expertise. No doubt the firm will, initially at least, have clients in market segments on which it has not concentrated. Those clients might get the same type of professional services, at the same cost, as they would get from another, undifferentiated professional firm. Over time, however, they might drop the firm or, more appropriately, be referred to another firm that is better equipped to meet their needs. As an example of concentration, a lawyer might specialize in corporate law, further concentrate on corporate taxation, further concentrate on the forest industry, and ultimately concentrate on a single company—"corporate income tax law as it affects forest company X."

However, most professional firms would prefer not to concentrate totally on an individual company—they might better be hired directly by that company as an employee. Also, there is the risk that this company will run into financial difficulty or decide to change its professional advisors. For those reasons, many "targeted" professional firms prefer to concentrate on an industry or a function, but not a single company. For a tax lawyer, this might be "taxation as it affects resource-based industries"; for an engineer, "energy conservation as it affects manufacturing companies."

Often, however, professional firms do not concentrate on a single market but decide to provide two or more kinds of professional services to two or more types of clientele. Market segmentation has still occurred, and differentiated marketing techniques—providing for analysis, professional identification, a responsiveness to client needs, and promotional activities—can still be directed to *each* of those specific segments.

Differentiation by patient (client) has occurred where a general medical practice or clinic offers its services to "families," "underprivileged," or "senior citizens." Differentiation has also occurred, by the *kind* of professional service, where there is "specialization" of function. Otolaryngology (ear, nose, and throat), radiology (X-rays), and urology (urinary or urogenital) are examples from the medical profession of differentiation by function. Where this occurs, there is often little differentiation by type of patient.

Client Mix

A homogeneous market is defined by a common need binding together many types of individual clients. Most people need accounting and tax, engineering, legal, and medical assistance at some time in their life. They will seek it out when they *realize* that they need competent professional assistance. Clients will usually seek professional assistance only when there is positive exchange value to them—when the value of services received is greater than the costs of obtaining those services.

Yet, when only need is considered, many of the other variables —the unique characteristics, traits, and expectations of a variety of clients—are often ignored. There is no effort to structure unique services in response to unique client needs. The professional firm will likely offer the same services to all clients. Opportunities may be missed because of the failure to differentiate.

Another professional firm might segment its clients in the extreme, obtaining a "profile" on each individual client. This is certainly necessary in the medical profession, but not for marketing purposes, unless one or a few clients can be segregated and grouped by the resources they have available and the services they are likely to seek. For instance, various types of professional services can often be correlated (see Figure 8-1) to the size of the client organization. As the client organization grows, it develops the capacity to do its own work internally.

Many professional firms do try to determine the needs of each individual client and attempt to provide specific services in response to each individual client's needs. The problem with this approach is that every client has unique needs and the firm may not have the resources or professional capability (or "specialty," if you prefer) to respond to every demand of every single client. The firm would have to spend an inordinate amount of time doing "research" to try to fulfill the client request. This could be expensive for the client and, especially if the work is being done in an area in which the firm does not have previous experience, ineffective as well.

Service Mix

A homogeneous market also exists where many needs are expressed and many professional services provided, but to few types of clientele. For instance, some people will do little if anything without first obtaining the advice of a professional advisor. General medical practitioners, lawyers, and business advisors are particularly aware of this phenomenon. An otherwise steady and reliable client will not take a step without first discussing and obtaining "clearance" on just about everything in his daily or business life. Yet, he is probably the only true "expert" on many of the things he is seeking advice about. To be consulted and used as a sounding board is one thing, but when a client shifts responsibility for his life or business away from himself, there are inherent dangers. Few professionals, with the possible exception of psy-

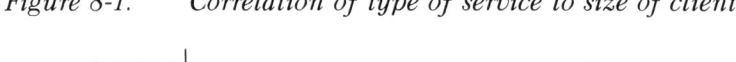

Figure 8-1. *Correlation of type of service to size of client.*

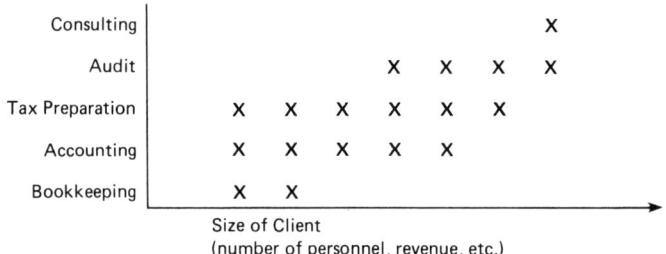

chologists, are trained to accept that continued level of responsibility.

This admittedly extreme example of a failure to identify the service mix indicates that, on occasion, extreme demands can be placed on a professional by certain types of clients. Client knowledge, self-confidence, and the ability and desire to learn new techniques and develop new awareness may result in a reduced need for professional services as the client learns about these himself.

At the opposite extreme there are many clients who are so independent (and overconfident?) that they seldom seek professional advice until a problem is almost overwhelming or major opportunities have been missed. They fail to use the appropriate mix of professional services at the appropriate times.

Service segmentation (service mix) occurs where there is an identification of a specific need for a specific group of clients. This might include a breakdown of services requiring specialization, advanced professional technical skills, routine professional services, or administrative support. The service needs could be further broken down by very specific types of professional service.

Market Positioning

Once a professional firm has analyzed the *market structure* and reviewed its internal operations and capabilities for responsiveness—including deciding what it wants for itself—it can begin to locate a place, or position, in the market that will be most beneficial to both the (potential) clientele and the firm. It can begin to define a target clientele and target services. A niche in the marketplace may be revealed which provides great opportunity.

Figure 8-2 shows an example. Firm A supplies the broadest range of legal services, with emphasis on high-demand low-cost services. It may specialize, and even set up departments for conveyancing and estate work to increase efficiency and provide low-cost services. Firm B is positioned to provide more individualized services, but because it tends to compete directly in areas serviced by cost-efficient firm A, its fees may remain relatively low. Firm C offers more specialized services and may remain smaller than firm A or firm B. Because of its ability to provide efficient, unique service, albeit in low-demand areas, it may be more profitable. Since it does not compete in the same markets as firm A or firm B, it might receive referrals from both those firms.

Market research should be completed to ensure that there is

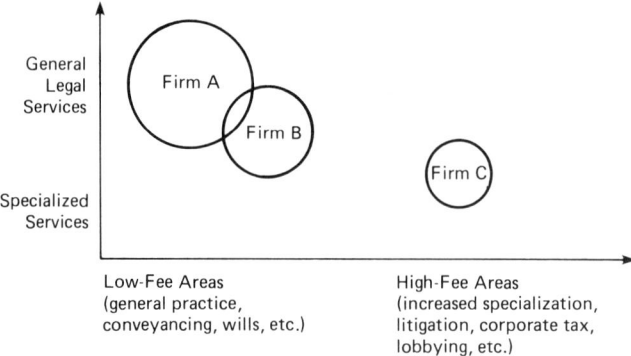

Figure 8-2. Market positioning for law firms.

sufficient demand for the services in the market niche in which a firm is considering placing itself. For a professional this might consist simply of general discussions with other professionals to obtain information on services that they perceive are needed to "back them up"—ones which in future they would hopefully refer to your firm. Client-based research can be done on (potential) client perceptions and expressed needs and demands for professional services. Unfortunately, however, professionals often "structure" their firm on how they *feel* about the demands of the marketplace. Their unresearched perception could be wrong.

In the previous example, firm A is responding to the areas of greatest demand, but if it chose to remain small, there would appear to be an opportunity for a viable new firm in that market position. Firm B could expand its services to meet the demand, but it may also choose to remain small, and that would increase the viability of a new firm. If, however, firms A and B remain fairly large and competitive in the same area of high demand, they may be fulfilling the demand of that market segment well. It would be difficult for a third firm to be effective and profitable in that segment.

Firm C will probably remain small, since it is in an area of low general demand. Its specializations are unique and sought out, so fees for the specialization may be fairly high. The marketing strategy for this type of professional firm would be very different from that for a "generalist" professional firm, which responds to a wide range of client service needs. Yet, despite marketing

MARKET ANALYSIS AND SEGMENTATION   89

efforts, firm C may have trouble getting known for the unique services it provides and may have problems maintaining sufficient revenues. There may not be enough demand from clients for the "specialized" professional services, and the firm may not be reputed as being a leader in the profession. Although firm C offers a degree of specialization, this area may be sought by many other (potentially competitive) professionals.

A firm thinking of entering this market can consider many alternatives. It can compete in the service areas of firms A and B because of the broad and strong demand for a wide range of legal services. It can compete against firm C by offering similar specialized services, because there obviously is demand—firm C is doing some work. Or it can consider some new and untapped market segments whose demands are not met by any of the firms.

A professional firm considering a position in the market should consider long-term viability and profitability. Future changes in demand for the services (the client base may change location, or technological advances may replace unique specialities, and so on) should be considered. Competitive firms may position themselves in the same market niche. However, in our example there may be an area where a firm that offers more specialized services can obtain higher fees than firm A or firm B, or there may be a whole area of specialization where needs are not being responded to (see Figure 8-3).

Firm D might position itself in a median position between a wide range of general legal services and extreme specialization. Its medium fee range might appeal to middle-income clientele. Firm

Figure 8-3. *Potential market segments available for positioning law firms D and E.*

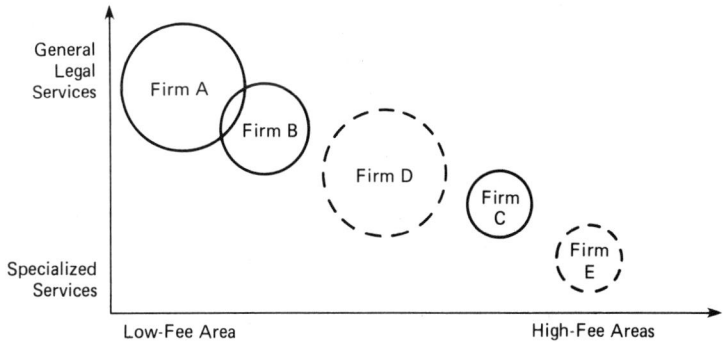

E might position itself where there is high demand for a very specialized service; its unique service capability, and even the high fees, will help it in its marketing efforts.

In this example, firm A might be a "storefront"-type law office and firm B might be a general practice in a relatively low-income area. Middle-income people might feel uncomfortable in both environments. Firm D might respond to this unmet demand by locating in a middle- to upper-income neighborhood and structuring its services to meet major needs of that type of clientele. It might, for instance, avoid criminal law but concentrate on marriage breakdown—separation or divorce, conveyancing, and wills and estates.

Firm E might respond to an area of unmet demand by offering unique services. It might locate in a prestigious neighborhood and assist in estate probate, death duties, and state taxes, for instance. It might locate in the professional district of the town or city and specialize in tax law, accepting engagements only on referral from other lawyers and professional accountants.

Summary

Market positioning usually involves structuring services so as to respond to one type of client. Other types of clients and publics are not a major consideration. A firm first attempts to establish its relationship and position to the major markets of (potential) clients and services. Then it considers its relationships with other publics—legislative bodies, professional organization, and so on—as well as staff requirements, facilities, location, and so forth.

Every time we look at markets and segments from a different point of view, we will obtain a different perception. If we design a marketing program around that perception, we can expect to get different results. Markets and perceptions change. Certainly clients and their perceptions change. Professional firms change their perceptions of those clients and the entire market structure. New and different segmentations, whether by age, occupation, location, or psychological breakdown, will offer new methods to identify exchange value to clients, and new opportunities for professional service. Obviously, marketing, and particularly correct segmentation, is much more an art than a scientific activity.

9

Client Analysis

Once the firm has identified a particular market segment to which it would like to respond, it can begin to gather resources, including education and experience, to provide services to that target clientele. Before even doing that, however, the firm must understand and appreciate the perceptions, wants, needs, and expectations of those clients. One of the reasons it was important to segment the market was to allow the firm to offer consistent levels of professional services, to a consistent type of clients who can be expected to respond to a specific and consistent "image" and marketing program of the professional firm.

Assessing Needs

Most clients have extreme difficulty identifying the needs they wish fulfilled. However, client-oriented professional firms must know what those needs are if they are to fulfill them and provide any degree of client satisfaction. A firm must know the different needs of different types of clients, the levels of those needs (is there great demand or very little?), and the changes that may affect the needs of those clients in the future.

Needs, which by definition are unsatisfied demands, are not the same as dreams, wishes, or desires. In a marketing sense, a market exists only where a client is willing to exchange something of value (money) in order to satisfy needs. For instance, if an individual wishes he had an engineer to assist in designing a home and deal with contractors but is not willing to pay for the services, there is no real need, only a wish—and no market would exist. The nonclient has placed no exchange value on the wish.

The client survey questionnaire for a CPA firm at the end of this chapter is designed to obtain *direct information* from clients about their feelings, wants, needs (demands), and expectations. One of the most apparent obstacles to the provision of professional services, aside from the clients' difficulty in identifying need, is that many professional firms do not even tell clients what the existing range of professional services is.

In our example, many individuals use CPAs to prepare tax returns, but clients can only guess that a CPA might also be available for business planning, family money management counseling, or business/financial consultation.

You may share the opinion that many professions, in not allowing any form of advertising, have failed clients and the general public by not keeping them informed of many invaluable professional services available to them. However, client surveys and interviews work well only when clients can identify their needs and are willing to divulge their feelings and perceptions to the firm. Unfortunately, dissatisfied clients usually do not complain to a professional directly, but complain about him to other (potential) clients, other professionals, or the professional's governing organization. Obviously, a firm cannot change in response to those indirect demands until it knows what they are.

Fortunately, there are two other methods that may be used to ascertain client needs.

The first of these is the *simulation method.* This involves providing the client with a model or visualization of how a professional service could be of benefit to him. It allows the client to "experience" the results of obtaining the service and allows the professional to gauge the clients' reaction.

For instance, an engineering firm might do a "mock-up" of a completed project for presentation in a bid to obtain the engineering portion of a contract. A lawyer specializing in estate planning might prepare a client "information package" containing examples of typical planning techniques, comments, and forms for the purview of prospective clients. In addition to providing minimal management information on the client-requested tax return, an accountant might analyze a client's profitability by department, before he was asked to do so, to show how the information would be useful to the client. A dentist might profile the costs of corrective dentistry over a patient's life and compare them to the costs of preventive dentistry through regular checkups. The possibilities of simulation are endless, but the intent usually is to make clients aware of latent (unstated) demand.

A second alternative is the very indirect *projective method,* including principally role play, sentence completion, visual association or completion, and word association. Human motivation and psychology are very complex, but indirect methods can be very effective in uncovering basic needs.

If a CPA were to role-play with his client before the client's presentation to his bank for funding assistance, the perception of areas where the presentation was weak is an indication of need for further professional work (and possibly client training) in the request for funding assistance.

If a client, in a neutral atmosphere, completes the sentence "I feel that all professional fees are far too high," this could in reality express his feelings about a particular firm.

A rough sketch by an engineer can prompt a client to fill in many details (stated needs) in a conceptualization of a building project.

Word-association and active listening skills are important to all professionals. Clients sometimes rationalize the late payment of a fee by stating that the work was not satisfactory or completed late, when in reality they are not able to pay as promptly as they might otherwise. Blame is sometimes shifted to the professional, but by carefully listening to the feelings and meanings behind the words and generating key phrases and words, the professional may be able to infer a client's true needs.

Image Assessment

We are admonished by our professional associations, peers, and others to project a "professional image." Yet no one seems to be able to define exactly what that means. Many professionals mistakenly construe it as a visual image—the way we dress, the decor of our offices, and the like.

Other professionals relate image to the way we conduct our practice (for example, like a "top professional") and the way we deal with our clients (for instance, objectively). Again, this is incorrect.

A professional's image is the sum total of the attitudes, beliefs, and concepts conveyed by a professional to his publics, including clients.

Images may be simple or complex, and they may be clear and concise or quite indistinct and fuzzy.

The perception of the image varies from individual to individual, depending on the person's point of view, perception, needs, experience, and beliefs.

Image may be based on visual impressions—the type of facilities, decor, and equipment in a professional's office and the clothes that he and his staff wear. Image can also be based on a human perspective—the attitude of a professional and his staff, the promptness and efficiency of the work, and courtesy toward the clients themselves.

Question 23 of the client survey questionnaire at the end of the chapter is designed to provide systematic information on the client's visual perceptions of a CPA firm. Office appearance, telephone manners, correspondence, financial statements, and the dress of the staff are all important visual perceptions on which a client will base his judgment of the overall quality, standards, and image of a CPA firm. Most of the balance of the client survey questionnaire deals with human factors: the professional's competence (question 6), his responsiveness (questions 7–10), his willingness to serve (questions 11 and 12), and his concern for the client's welfare (questions 13–22).

Images can be measured in many ways. Image attributes may be assigned externally by the general publics. Market buzz may take the form of "everybody knows that lawyers are very expensive and often do not get results (or questionable results)."

Image-making firms and consultants use public response surveys and judgment to analyze the image perceptions of the marketplace.

Many professional organizations spend millions of dollars per year on "image enhancement" public relations programs to build public confidence in and esteem for the profession. Unfortunately, this does not always work unless the professionals themselves are willing to change. Even when professionals are very reponsive to public needs, it takes a long time to change the former prevalent image.

The general public may not even be familiar with the services of a particular profession, and some may hold all professionals, as a class, in disrepute. Some professions are well known for the types

CLIENT ANALYSIS

and quality of services they provide, and some are regarded with higher public esteem than others.

Image and Client Attraction/Retention

Certain types of clients will seek out a professional on the basis of a complex interplay of their perceptions of the professional's attributes, both visual and human. If a potential client is unimpressed by the visual characteristics, he seldom will engage the professional. If he is already a client, he could seek professional assistance elsewhere. The rationalization for doing so is to receive more appropriate services; but in fact, the client perceives, and rightfully so, that his own image will be related to the professionals he associates with. If the professional is held in high (or low) regard, so will the client.

A professional may be perceived by clients as being authoritative, aloof, cool, and objective. At the opposite extreme, clients might perceive another professional as spontaneous, warm, and down to earth. Some clients prefer one type of professional over another. Different clients might assign those very different attributes to the *same* professional individual. Different professional profiles are appropriate at different times, depending on the services required by the client. If you assigned your lawyer to collect an overdue accounts receivable, you would hope that he would be firm and autocratic in demanding payment; but if you were going through a divorce, you would hope that he would be "sensitive" to your cause. In an operating room, you would hope the surgeon would be cool, objective, and concentrating on his *task;* during a general examination, you might hope he would be pleasant and human and have "warm" hands.

Therefore, image can also be very situational. It may be appropriate for a professional to change his image depending on the task at hand or to find some middle ground upon which to base a consistent image, yet be flexible without going to extreme (high task or high relationship) orientations.

Image, however, is like a mirror in the sense that if a professional is highly task-oriented, he will usually attract the type of work that demands productivity. If he is very relationship- or people-oriented, he will usually attract clients who respond well to a warm and friendly atmosphere.

Role Models

Most of us are familiar with the technique of role modeling—looking to leaders in our field, determining which of their characteristics we would like to emulate, and then copying them.

Another technique is constructive synthetic visualization. Basically, we build a model of the ideal image for ourselves or our firm. We visualize our surroundings, the atmosphere of the practice, the image, the types of clients, and the services we would like to provide. Once the visualization is complete, it can be expressed by a clear and concise written objective. The task is then to change attitudes, professional services, and possibly clientele to match those idealized attributes.

Modeling allows testing for various attributes and responses before major changes are made. Specific clients can be "tested" for their response to new attitudes, or provided simulated models of new professional services. For example, before moving facilities to a new location, the firm can test clients' responses to identify the best choice. The result might look like this:

Client Response	Low Rent (Practical)	Medium Rent (Comfortable and Modern)	High Rent (Ostentatious)
Favorable	50%	80%	30%
Unfavorable	50%	20%	70%

Or attributes and characteristics of a professional can be assigned values by clients' priority or expectation:

Knowledge and intellect	3
Honesty	1
Concern for clients' well-being	2

Analyzing existing clients' perspectives can be painful for many professionals. The first time a firm does this analysis, it may find, for instance, that clients think of the firm as slow and expensive, and even question the quality of the professional work. The market-based approach is designed to allow the firm to know what those perceptions are and, if they are negative, to change before clients are lost. An inherent danger in analyzing client perceptions and then *not* changing the firm if the perceptions are negative is that clients will now become familiar with previously unknown or unstated needs—and may look to other professionals to fulfill those newly discovered needs. For instance, on the basis of his limited personal experience with one firm, a client may have thought that all professional accountants are slow and unresponsive. But the very survey may suggest that some firms are not.

Client Expectations

One interesting phenomenon which occurs in client analysis is that the professional's perception of why clients go to his firm is almost always different from the client's actual reason. Professionals usually stress quality standards. Clients usually identify an attitude of client concern as their priority in choosing a professional firm. It is not unusual, for instance, to find that 80 percent of a firm's growth from referrals is a result of the professional's expressing a responsive attitude to clients' concerns, whereas only 20 percent of the growth might be attributed to professional knowledge and expertise.

As an exercise, you may wish to list the priorities you use in selecting the services of an unrelated professional firm. Question 5 of the client survey questionnaire at the end of the chapter lists some of the criteria useful in all professions. Later, without reference to those results, list the attributes that you think your clients would look for in choosing your professional firm. A comparison of the two lists might be revealing. A client's criteria for selecting a professional firm are almost invariably different from what the professional expects. You probably chose the other professional for his human attributes; yet you probably decided that clients sought out your firm largely because of your technical skills and competence.

A sample questionnaire designed to aid in analyzing the clients of a CPA firm follows.

CLIENT SURVEY QUESTIONNAIRE FOR A CPA FIRM.

Note: The purpose of this review is to allow our firm feedback on how you perceive us, and to assist us in developing our firm to better meet your needs.

We hope that you are honest in your evaluation of our firm and that you will feel confident in discussing areas which may be of concern to you, both now and in the future. It is only through your dialog with us that we can improve the quality and timing of the services which we now provide to you—and develop the firm into new areas in which you may wish assistance.

Client Name: _____

Address: _____

_____ Zip: _____

Telephone: _____

Interviewee: _____ Title: _____

Interviewed by: _____ Title: _____

General Comments: _____

_____

_____

_____

1. What is your broad business classification (e.g., construction, contractor, manufacturer, wholesale distributor, retail store, etc.)? _____

_____

2. Approximately what are your total gross (sales) revenues? (Check one.)

   Under $100,000 _____
   $100,000–$250,000 _____
   $250,001–$500,000 _____
   $500,001–$750,000 _____
   $750,001–$1,000,000 _____
   $1,000,001–$5,000,000 _____
   $5,000,0001–$25,000,000 _____
   $25,000,001–$50,000,000 _____
   Over $50,000,000 _____

3. What was your overall revenues growth rate for the past five years?
   _____% per year

3a. What do you expect your overall revenues growth rate will be in the next five years? _____% per year

4. What services do you expect from your CPA firm?
   Bookkeeping—writeup, payrolls, etc. _____%
   Non-audit financial statement preparation _____%

CLIENT ANALYSIS

Audited statement preparation   ____%
Providing financial advice   ____%
Government reporting   ____%
Systems (accounting) design   ____%
Taxation—preparation   ____%
    —consulting   ____%
Other consulting (management advisory
  service) areas   ____%
Other (please specify)

  _____ ____%

  _____ ____%

  _____ ____%

                                                                                                                                         100 %

5. What are the most important criteria you have for selecting a professional accountant? (Please number in order of importance)
    A professional image   ____
    Timely advice and work   ____
    Low fees   ____
    Quality work   ____
    Concern for client well-being   ____
    Tax knowledge   ____
    Audit experience and knowledge   ____
    Ability to provide information helpful in improving profitability____
    Other (please specify):

    _____ ____

    _____ ____

    _____ ____

    _____ ____

CLIENT CONCERN

6. How do you perceive the attitude and knowledge of the staff and professionals of the firm in the following areas:

	Excellent	Good	Fair	Poor
Professional accounting and auditing knowledge	☐	☐	☐	☐
Tax knowledge	☐	☐	☐	☐
Knowledge of your business	☐	☐	☐	☐

Ability to assist you in improving
your profitability ☐ ☐ ☐ ☐
Provision of timely work in
accordance with your needs ☐ ☐ ☐ ☐
Quick response to your
telephone queries ☐ ☐ ☐ ☐
Informativeness (on new tax
legislation, other services
the firm offers, etc.) ☐ ☐ ☐ ☐
Knowledge of work schedule and when
you can expect work to be completed ☐ ☐ ☐ ☐
Other (please specify):

_____ ☐ ☐ ☐ ☐
_____ ☐ ☐ ☐ ☐
_____ ☐ ☐ ☐ ☐

General Comments:

_____
_____

7. How often do the firm's professionals or staff telephone you (other than in the performance of regular annual work)?

Every _____ weeks

8. How often would you prefer a member of the firm to telephone you?

Every _____ weeks

9. How often do members of the firm visit you (other than in the performance of regular annual work)?

Every _____ weeks

10. How often would you prefer a member of the firm to visit you?

Every _____ weeks

11. Some CPA firms offer management advisory services to clients. Which of the following areas might you wish to discuss?

Corporate development areas:
  1. Corporate planning ☐
  2. Executive search—personnel evaluation and selection ☐
  3. Government assistance programs ☐
  4. Long-range goal setting ☐

CLIENT ANALYSIS

    5. International operations ☐
    6. Management performance audits ☐
    7. Costs of marketing and distributing services ☐
    8. Interpreting statistical results for management ☐
    9. Merger and acquisition considerations ☐
  10. Model construction and simulation (econometric, PERT, CPM, etc.) ☐
  11. Scientific decision making (programmed decision trees, etc.) ☐

Capital acquisition and general management:
    1. Business valuations ☐
    2. Capital budgeting ☐
    3. Business cycles analysis and forecasting ☐
    4. Human relations problems ☐
    5. Optimum use of funds ☐
    6. Organizational structure ☐
    7. Management and utilization of "other" assets ☐
    8. Wage and salary administration ☐
    9. Work simplification, both for staff and line ☐

Cost reduction programs and other operating advice:
    1. Budgets—forecasting (pro formas) and profit planning ☐
    2. Corporate strategy ☐
    3. Cash flow predictions ☐
    4. Cost reduction programs ☐
    5. Cost studies ☐
    6. Credit and collection—policy and procedures ☐
    7. Data processing—own, computer service, liaison, consulting ☐
    8. Installation—project accounting ☐
    9. Inventory management ☐
  10. Decisions on produce mix ☐
  11. Production planning and control ☐
  12. Profit analysis—price/volume and cost relationships ☐
  13. Ratio analysis ☐
  14. Systems design ☐

Accounting and Systems:
    1. Inflation accounting ☐

2. Management information systems (MIS) ☐
  3. Performance reporting—variance analysis, management by exception, control reports ☐
  4. Research and development evaluation ☐

12. What effect would it have on your use of the services offered by the CPA firm if you were called on:

  (a) Twice as often?   Change + _____
      Why?   −

  _____

  _____

  (b) Half as often?   Change + _____
      Why?   −

  _____

  _____

SCHEDULING

13. Do you experience difficulties in your relation with the firm in regard to work scheduling (getting your work on time)?

     Yes ☐   No ☐

  (a) If yes, what are these difficulties (late response to telephone queries, late tax filing, late information for bank, late information for management information, etc.)? (Record below)

  (b) Are the difficulties serious? (Record below)

  (c) How frequently do they occur? (e.g., 10%, 30%, 90% of time)

Difficulty	*Serious*	*% of Time*
_____	_____	_____
_____	_____	_____
_____	_____	_____

  (d) What do you think you could do (provide basic information earlier, for instance) to assist the CPA firm in getting earlier, more timely information to you?

  _____

  _____

CLIENT ANALYSIS

14. When you wish to obtain additional service or advice, how soon is information available?

    Immediately ☐
    In satisfactory time ☐
    Too late ☐

15. How frequently are your instructions followed in regard to deadlines for work completion?

	% of Time				
For:	30	50	70	90	100
Tax deadlines	☐	☐	☐	☐	☐
Deadlines for bankers	☐	☐	☐	☐	☐
Deadlines for management information	☐	☐	☐	☐	☐
Others (please specify)					
_____	☐	☐	☐	☐	☐
_____	☐	☐	☐	☐	☐

16. For information on the status of work being done:

    (a) Who is your main contact at the firm? _____

    (b) Whom do you contact when he/she is not available? _____
    _____

    (c) How long does it take to get information? _____ hours

    (d) What difficulties, if any, do you experience in getting this information?
    _____
    _____
    _____

    (e) If there are difficulties, what problems does this cause you?
    _____
    _____
    _____

    (f) How frequently do you have difficulty in obtaining needed information? _____ % of time

(g) How many calls, on the average, are required to get needed information? _____ calls

17. When work is delayed by the firm:

   (a) Does someone call you to advise you of the problems encountered? Yes ☐ No ☐

   (b) Does the firm ask you if there is a special reason for placing a "rush" on your work? Yes ☐ No ☐

   (c) How often is work delayed in getting back to you after promised deadlines or after you would have hoped to have your files back? _____ % of time

   (d) After your year-end date, how long does it take to get your financial statement and tax returns completed? _____ months

   (e) How long do you think it *should* take to complete these year-end statements and returns? _____ months

   (f) How soon would you *like* these statements and returns completed? Within _____ months

   (g) What difficulties have you had as a result of the year-end statements not being available sooner?

   _____
   _____
   _____

18. For queries about financial statements, your record keeping, tax advice, and other problems you encounter:

   (a) Do you ask the firm to advise you on the problems encountered? Yes ☐ No ☐

   (b) If you do not call the firm, what other sources of information are available?

   _____
   _____
   _____

   (c) When you encounter difficulties in accounting and record keeping, how often do you telephone your firm?

   _____ % of time

CLIENT ANALYSIS

(d) How often would you prefer to call the firm?

_____% of time

(e) If there is a discrepancy between how often you call and how often you would prefer to call, what are your major reasons for not calling?

_____

_____

_____

_____

19. For information on fees:

(a) Who is your contact in the firm? _____

(b) How often are the fees within the range you would have expected?

_____% of time

(c) When the fees are different from what you expected, are they higher or lower, and by how much?

Lower ☐   Higher ☐   by _____%

(d) Do you experience difficulty in understanding how professional fees are determined?   Yes ☐   No ☐

(e) Do you get timely invoices and explanations of work done?

Yes ☐   No ☐

How could this be improved?

_____

_____

(f) Are you satisfied with the credit policies of the firm?

Yes ☐   No ☐

Would you recommend any changes?

_____

_____

20. Are there important areas where you need to get more information from the firm?

_____

_____

21. Do you feel that your financial statements could contain more information which would assist you in managing your business?

   Yes ☐   No ☐

   What other types of information would you like?

   Gross margin % ☐
   Breakeven sales ☐
   Expense analysis ☐
   Breakdown of revenue and gross margin by product, department, etc. ☐
   Other: ☐

   _____

   _____

22. Do you feel that the overall appearance of your financial statement could be improved?   Yes ☐   No ☐
    How?

    _____

    _____

23. How do you perceive the professional image of the firm?

	Poor	Not Bad	Always Top Professional
The appearance of the reception area in the office	☐	☐	☐
The appearance of the individual offices	☐	☐	☐
The way in which the telephone is answered	☐	☐	☐
The appearance of the firm's correspondence with you	☐	☐	☐
The appearance of the financial statements	☐	☐	☐
The dress code of the staff	☐	☐	☐
Other: _____	☐	☐	☐
_____	☐	☐	☐

CLIENT ANALYSIS 107

24. Do you refer potential clients to your accounting firm?

 Yes ☐   No ☐

 How often? _____ % of time

25. What general comments do you wish to make about the firm?

_____

_____

_____

_____

10

Analysis of Professional Services

In a way this book is about specialization, but not in the traditional sense of specialized functions. It is much broader than that. It is about the professional's choice of a *market*. Markets are chosen and their needs analyzed. Output exchange values—what clients are willing to pay for the services—can then be considered. Input and conversion markets are analyzed to determine the appropriate costs (exchange value) to provide those professional services.

Once target markets are selected, marketing instruments can be chosen to enhance the value of the professional firm to its clientele. The mix of instruments is known as a marketing mix. Instruments within the "mix" are normally categorized in four ways:

1. Location of the professional firm.
2. Level of professional fees.
3. Types of services provided.
4. Type of promotion used by the firm.

Traditionally, the term professional "specialization" has referred only to the type of professional services provided—for instance, chemical engineering, income tax law, auditing in accounting firms, or radiology in medicine. Increasingly, there are professional "specialists" by other instruments within the marketing mix. Professional firms are increasingly established in residential areas, especially regional shopping centers, as opposed to downtown and

ANALYSIS OF PROFESSIONAL SERVICES

professional districts. This is to allow more client convenience. Some firms "specialize" by offering low-cost services—consider low-fee "storefront" law offices, incorporation and divorce "kits" offered by lawyers, and the like. Promotion instruments are becoming increasingly sophisticated, targeted, and "specialized."

Professionals who are marketers define the pattern of the market and its professional suppliers. In terms of the market:

1. Who are the (potential) clients?
2. What do they do?
3. Why do they buy the professional services?
4. How are they going to use the professional services?
5. Will they become repeat clients?
6. Are needs for the professional services—across the market—increasing or decreasing in the future?
7. Will individual clients use the offered professional services increasingly or decreasingly in the future?

Markets are then segmented into homogeneous groups—types of clients who obtain the professional services largely for the same reasons. A professional marketer realizes that (1) there are distinct characteristics that vary from one segment to the next, and (2) each segment requires different strategies and promotion techniques. The objective is to find a unique pattern of professional services which would respond to a specific *niche* in the marketplace. For instance, if two professional firms were supplying the general professional service needs of 60 percent of the marketplace and six firms were supplying 80 percent of the market, it would be very difficult to establish a new general professional service firm in the same market. Either new markets must be found for the same services or very unique services must be found for the same market.

Once a market need is established—by location, level of fees, types of service, type of clientele, or any other criteria—a firm can "specialize" by becoming the major factor in that segment.

Service Concept

Normally, professional service is thought of simply as the provision of services which are needed by (potential) clients. Yet, professional services can be considered to have many different characteristics when considered from the clients' viewpoint.

A *core service* is one which is the central benefit to a client. The real "service" that a professional offers in this category is *peace of mind*—the client is assured that his needs are being met. An accountant's client seeking tax advice is not paying just for that; he also wants to assure himself that he will remain within the bounds of income tax law and not go to jail for tax violation. An engineer's advice is sought not for the detailed technical drawings but to provide some assurance that the building will not collapse. A lawyer's advice is sought not to learn all about a section of some obscure piece of legislation but to receive assurance that what one is doing is legal or will not be discovered. A doctor's advice is sought not to provide a detailed diagnosis but to help the patient live longer. The visible and tangible service is the package under which those benefits are sought.

A *tangible service* is the actual (and traditional) definition of the professional service being offered to the marketplace. It is the description of the *physical and functional services* being offered —for instance, tax preparation, design, litigation, and eye surgery.

In their totality, the benefits and costs of professional services to a client are known as *augmented services.* A client must not only get the service and pay the bill, but locate a professional firm, telephone for an appointment, wait, travel to the firm, wait for service, discuss the file with a professional, travel back from the appointment, wait for results from the professional, telephone for an appointment, travel back to the firm, wait for service, review results with the professional, pay the bill, and travel back from the appointment. The benefits of professional services will be weighed by the client against the total of all these costs. Augmented-service improvement might include location convenient to client, no need for an appointment, no waiting, and immediate results.

We speak of a professional *service line* when a professional firm offers more than one type of professional service to its clientele. Many professionals are extremely specialized and offer only one type of service, often on the basis of referrals only. Most firms, however, offer a range of services to a variety of clientele, or one type of clientele. Thus an accounting firm might not only prepare individual tax returns but consult on family financial management, and a corporate lawyer might not only appear in court as counsel but prepare agreements for his clients.

The diversity of a practice is determined by the number of clients and the number of services provided to those clients. Depth of service refers to the range of services offered within a class of services—for instance, the number of (corporate) services

ANALYSIS OF PROFESSIONAL SERVICES

of a corporate law office. The width of service is the total number of services offered by a professional firm

There are a number of alternative ways in which a firm can expand. It can:

1. Offer new professional services to new markets.
2. Offer new (or improved) services to existing markets.
3. Offer the same services to new markets.
4. Increase its share of the market by taking away work from other professionals (market penetration).

A professional firm would determine alternative strategies to expand its market, on the basis of its analysis of current market conditions.

Potential Expansion Area

1. New professional services to new markets.

2. New services to existing markets.

3. Same service to new markets.

4. Increase market share.

Example of Strategy

1. Accounting firm to open office in shopping mall for high-volume processing of 1040s.

2. Consulting firm in mechanical engineering expands to plant design and project supervision to existing clients.

3. Law firm working in corporate law seeks new clients.

4. Medical clinic seeks increased work by expanding client base (new clients come from other medical professionals).

Adding Service Lines

New service lines are essential in a rapidly changing professional environment. Technological, social, and legislative changes all occur at an increasing rate. Computerization has made the traditional bookkeeping function redundant in many accounting and professional firms. The introduction of fluorides has made the practice of corrective dentistry almost obsolete in many localities —many young people simply do not get cavities.

Most professional organizations recognize the rate of change by providing their members with continuing professional education, often on a mandatory basis. New concepts and techniques are offered to update traditional methodology. However, unless demand continues for its type of professional service, a professional firm must add new service lines if it is to remain viable. Many firms, however, do not rely solely on updating in the traditional fields in which they work but analyze the need for related services by the existing client base, and structure the firm and learn new skills to respond to that demand. This can be one of the greatest opportunities for growth, since the client base already exists. The question of "solicitation" is academic, since the firm would upgrade its qualifications to better serve existing clients.

Ideas for new service lines can come from clients, staff, or the professional himself. They are often the topics of public debate and coverage by mass media, or derived from indications of the future directions of a profession as a whole.

It is interesting in this respect that most of the following were not even considered major opportunities, or problems, in 1960.

Profession	*Direction*
Accounting	Computerization and consultation—*planning* with historical reporting.
Engineering	Computerized drafting, technological change, functional design changes.
Law	"Storefront," legal liability, television advertising.
Medicine	Medical plans, legal liability, joint practices, clinics for the "disadvantaged."

New service possibilities can be generated through client discussions and brainstorming sessions conducted by the professional and his staff. Once candidate services are identified which have potential exchange value to the clients, a firm can test the demand for those services by questioning a range of clients. If there is an indication of heavy demand, a firm would subject the new service to economic analysis to determine the potential benefits and fees to the firm over the costs of providing that service. If the benefits are sufficiently greater than the costs, the firm would proceed to develop the new services. Education, experience, and knowledge would be considered along with the other resource needs—equipment, facilities, capital, and staffing. At this stage, testing of the (proposed) service can be done on a select number of clients to ensure that professional standards, techniques, and timing are appropriate, and to ensure that there is, in fact, adequate demand for the service. Only after all these stages are passed should a new service line be added to the firm and promoted widely to large segments of clients.

Reducing Service Lines

Once a professional firm begins to think in terms of objectives, it begins to analyze its existing service lines to ensure that the services it is performing are in line with its objectives. And the services will change as the professional firm matures and becomes more sophisticated and targeted. Old service lines may be inappropriate, redundant, or uneconomic. The objectives of the firm may have changed. Consider a doctor who decides to specialize in mid-career: he would, most appropriately, sell his general practice.

An accounting firm may drop the preparation of individual 1040 tax returns because of increasing demand from corporate clients for tax, audit, and consultation. A lawyer may become known for his divorce experience and spend an increasing proportion of his (and his firm's) time in that field—at the expense of conveyancing and general services for individual clients. But all these examples suggest that a professional is reacting to service demand instead of managing that demand. The 1040 tax clients might receive less timely and concentrated services as the accountant was meeting increasing client demands in the corporate area. The lawyer might be increasingly unresponsive to general client needs as he spends more time in the divorce court.

Professional firms tend to avoid the elimination of service lines. New firms, particularly, struggled very hard to get any work in the first place. The psychology of the entire firm may be to continue increasing services and clientele at all costs. If services are eliminated, some clients and services may suffer, and many professionals are concerned about this. Often, however, old lines are retained on the basis of some rationalization. For instance, the accountant may keep a wide base of general small clients on the rationalization that exposure through preparation of individual tax returns will eventually bring more corporate work through referrals or when clients go into business for themselves. The lawyer may think that keeping a large number of general-service clients will lead to referrals for what he hopes to concentrate on—divorce—and he knows that nearly one out of four people gets a divorce, at some time.

Yet, tying up time, effort, and money and providing increasingly poor service in lines that are weak is very costly. Clients are poorly served, the professional and his staff are going in many directions at once, the service may be unprofitable or subprofitable, and the retention of that service line has the effect of stopping or retarding the development of new services to preferred clients. Existing services to preferred clients may also suffer—be untimely, expensive, and so on—because of the firm's inability to concentrate on improving its performance for that clientele.

A number of criteria would seem appropriate for the regular review of professional services to determine if it is appropriate for the firm to continue those service lines. Each and every type of service should be reviewed at least once a year to determine if:

- The firm still wishes to provide that service.
- The firm is able to respond to that market segment with high-quality, timely, convenient services at competitive prices.
- There is sufficient revenue for the firm from that type of professional service.
- There is sufficient profit from that professional service.
- The service adds to the firm's ability to provide a range of services to a "target" clientele.
- The service is congruent with the major objectives of the firm—that is, it should reinforce other services, not detract from them.

If a firm decides to reduce the number of service lines it has available, there are two courses of action it can follow:

1. It can immediately stop providing the service or sell the service line to someone else. It is not unusual, for instance, for an accounting firm to sell its 1040 clients, as a block or individually, to another accounting firm or tax preparer. A sale or transfer is usually preferable to dropping the service, since it will be less disruptive to clients unless they are redirected or referred. It is advantageous to the professional, since he will be able to transfer files and avoid heavy client complaints.

2. It can gradually eliminate the service line to allow the firm time to reorganize itself and give the clients time to obtain those professional services elsewhere.

Modifying Services

Many techniques are available to modify services—provide new features or provide the services to previously untapped markets. Services can be upgraded, systematized, and delegated for greater efficiency. Standards of professional presentation, and quality, can be improved. The image of the service or firm can be changed, which may have an impact on the usefulness of a professional service to clientele. Clients might get reports and correspondence that they can better understand, and use to better manage their affairs.

For instance, many clients of accounting firms do not understand what a balance sheet (position statement) is, let alone what it does. Lawyers and medical practitioners often use professional jargon in their communications with clients. Engineers sometimes prepare such elaborate and detailed plans and specifications that a client has difficulty in understanding the basic concept behind the plans.

Services will be modified, too, by many seemingly irrelevant changes—a change in location, office decor, and the attitude and personalities of professionals and their staff.

The core service or objective can be changed from "providing professional services for profitability (high income) to the professional" to "providing professional services for which there is an expressed client need," which is much more client-oriented.

Choosing Appropriate Service Lines

Clients could consider many aspects when seeking professional assistance. They may consider the resources available to the professional firm and its ability to continue to serve them over a long period of time. They might consider the firm's flexibility to learn and change as the clients' needs change and grow. They may consider the intellect of the professionals in the firm and the image of the firm.

An individual client might also consider his service needs, both short-term and long-term, from a profession as a whole. He would classify the types of services and then search out the firm that seems ablest to meet most of those service needs.

Once client markets are mapped out and the types of clients the firm wishes to serve are identified, the firm is in a stronger position to attract clientele, because it will be able to offer the range of professional services those clients are demanding.

The questionnaire that follows is provided to aid in analyzing professional services.

QUESTIONNAIRE FOR PROFESSIONAL-SERVICE ANALYSIS

1. What are the major professional services of the firm?

   _____
   _____
   _____
   _____
   _____
   _____

2. What are the functional services (for example, accounting, administration, reception, quality control, marketing)?

   _____
   _____
   _____
   _____
   _____
   _____

NEW SERVICE LINES

3. What new services could be added? List:

   _____
   _____
   _____
   _____
   _____
   _____

ANALYSIS OF PROFESSIONAL SERVICES

4. Will these services meet needs of specific clients?

5. Are there enough (potential) clients?

6. Will the clients understand the services and their benefits?

7. What effect will these services have on the firm's other services and on clients?

8. Will these services be preferred over the same or comparable services offered by competing professional firms?

9. What effect will adding these services have on the cost of operation? (Consider facilities, manpower, education, and so on.)

10. Will the clients be willing to pay additional professional fees to obtain additional services?

SERVICE LINES TO BE DISCONTINUED

11. What service lines could be discontinued?

12. Why do they not meet specific client needs?

13. Will the clients understand the discontinuance of a service?

14. What effect will this have on the firm's other services and on clients?

15. What effect will this have on the firm's cost of operation?

ANALYSIS OF PROFESSIONAL SERVICES

16. Which clients will be lost? Is that beneficial to the firm?

___

SERVICE MODIFICATION

17. What would be the effect of moving to a new location?

___

18. What would be the effect of changing the level (up or down) of professional fees?

___

19. What would be the effect of changing the quality of professional services and the time spent on providing professional service?

___

20. What would be the effect of changing marketing and promotion techniques?

___

11

Service Distribution

Marketing takes into account not only the types of professional services, their price, and their promotion, but the whole delivery system. This includes the level of service, quality, and location(s). The objective is to be in the right place, at the right time, with those professional services which are in demand.

Distribution channels may be chosen for professional services just as for other types of goods and services. Traditionally, however, most professional firms use a direct marketing model. They establish themselves in one location, with one level and quality of professional service, and hope that clients will come to them. In that case there is no recognized marketing channel.

Level of Client Service

Many professional firms are managed for the convenience of busy professionals. For instance, clients may have to wait to get their tax returns completed, or a patient may have to wait for a physician in a clinic setting. A professional firm could provide a higher level of service and reduce the clients' waiting time by hiring additional professionals. It could reduce the clients' inconvenience by locating the professional office(s) nearer to the client to reduce client travel time. Alternatively, the professionals may travel to the clients.

All these alternatives may increase the costs of operating a professional firm. Those costs would normally be passed on to the client, so the question of his ability or willingness to pay for convenience must be addressed. Many professional firms develop a balance between client convenience and cost of operation by offering less than optimum client convenience in order to maintain lower costs of operation—and, ultimately, lower fees.

Quality of Professional Services

Many professional firms continually admonish their staff to maintain a consistently high standard of professional service. Many professional organizations, similarly, govern their membership with by-laws and codes of ethics which demand the ultimate in quality. Unfortunately, this is often done with little consideration to resulting costs to clients. The firms and organizations often provide little support or direction on how the staff or professional members can maintain reasonable quality but at lower costs through efficiency improvements.

Many clients and consumers rebel at the often extraordinarily high fees brought about by a total dedication to ultimate and perfect professional service at all times. Consider that a quality control department which reviews all professional work and correspondence in an accounting office can result in a 10 percent increase in client fees.

In a global sense, major advances in medicine, paid for largely by taxation, have resulted in very expensive methods to prolong life. The costs to society are increasing at a much faster rate than inflation or the taxpayer's ability to pay. At some point society may have to make a decision to stop some medical treatments before their costs exceed the total gross national product of the nation.

There is a certain degree of risk in discussing the sensitive issue of quality control at a time when most professional organizations are really pressing for perfection. Practice licensing, research and development, quality control inspectors appointed by the professional's organization to review every firm on a periodic basis, "peer reviews"—reviews of other firms by practicing professionals —higher education and entry standards, quality control guidelines, inclusion of lay people on the boards of professional organizations, and reinforced codes of ethics are all being used by most professional organizations to some degree to enhance the quality of service provided by professionals. Those procedures are all very expensive to implement and administer and must eventually be passed on to clientele in the form of higher professional fees. At the same time, a major complaint of the general public is the high cost and inaccessibility of direct professional services.

Most firms eventually balance the degree of quality control between the costs and risks associated with a reasonable quality standard.

Decisions on Geographic Location

Most professional firms do not recognize structured marketing channels in their location decisions. Certainly, location is considered for professional convenience, but beyond that there are many ways to look at location, organization, and administration techniques in managing the distribution of professional services.

A regional firm might provide one level of a marketing channel by providing direction and administrative support from a main or head office. A second level might be the provision of direction and support by those regional offices to smaller community or neighborhood offices. Regional and national professional firms, however, seldom go to that second level of marketing channels.

A major consideration which must be addressed is location accessibility by the type of clients the firm wants. The facilities must also be accessible to professionals and staff. Parking facilities should be adequate for clients and staff. Collateral professional services should also be considered. Ideally, a surgeon should have his office close to a hospital; an accountant's office should be conveniently located with regard to lawyers, offices, and banks.

Location decisions are critical to the business-related success of most general professional practices. Highly specialized practices often are not as concerned about location, since the type of services they provide is unique and often is provided on the client's premises. Before a professional considers opening a general practice, however, he should establish that:

- There is sufficient demand for client services at the proposed location.
- There are sufficient resources, including (potential) staff to operate the office.
- There is accessibility—the office is convenient to clients and staff.
- There are collateral support resources from other professionals.

Centralized versus Decentralized Offices

Most professional firms are centralized and provide professional services directly to clients. Usually it is most economical to have only one office and centralize the professional research libraries, reception, professional staff, administrative support, equipment, and facilities. As a professional firm grows, this has the added advantage to clients of offering all types of services centralized in one location.

Both clients and professionals may be inconvenienced, however, and higher costs may be evidenced by increased travel time, higher rent in centrally located major centers, and growing complexity and costs of administering and managing a large central office. Functional internal and administrative positions are often created to meet the needs of a large central organization. Office managers and personnel managers, for instance, do not supply direct client service. Large centrally located firms may be quite remote from major (potential) clientele.

Decentralization and the opening of branch offices may alleviate some of these problems by providing needed services more convenient to client locations.

A number of new issues must be considered if a decision is made to decentralize a professional firm:

- Where should branches be located?
- How large should each office be?
- How will the activities of each branch be administered and controlled?
- Should quality control be decentralized and made the responsibility of each branch manager? If it is, will quality be consistent within the firm on a regional or nationwide basis?
- How many branches should be opened?
- What are the service needs of clients at each branch? Are they the same or unique from branch to branch?
- If unique services are required, how will the branch obtain the resources and specialists necessary to complete the engagement?
- How will branches be staffed, particularly in remote locations?

Many larger professional firms have found that a branch organization, with support from professional specialists at the main office where needed, is appropriate for handling the widest variety of potential clients. This is a blend of centralization and decentralization, with only specialists and administrative support services being centralized.

Figure 11-1 shows an example of a regional law firm with branch offices. The conveyancing, litigation, and administrative "specializations" of the main office support branch activities. Client contact, work assignments, and promotion take place mainly at the branch level.

Franchises

One of the concepts carried forward from the 1960s and 1970s is franchising. Interestingly enough, professional and "near-professional" firms are increasingly considering this form of business organization to provide regional and community service in the 1980s. Franchising may be appropriate to high-volume, relatively simple forms of professional services. Many ethical restrictions are placed upon this type of venture, particularly where full-time attendance of a qualified professional is required. Neighborhood law clinics, tax preparation offices for individuals, and "pain and stress" clinics may be run as franchised offices of large professional firms. This form of business organization, however, may be dangerous without detailed client market analysis, because demand may be based not on end user (client) demands but on the franchisee's demands—location and ability to pay for the franchise.

Franchising may result in services and locations being opened

Figure 11-1. Organization chart for a regional law firm with branch offices.

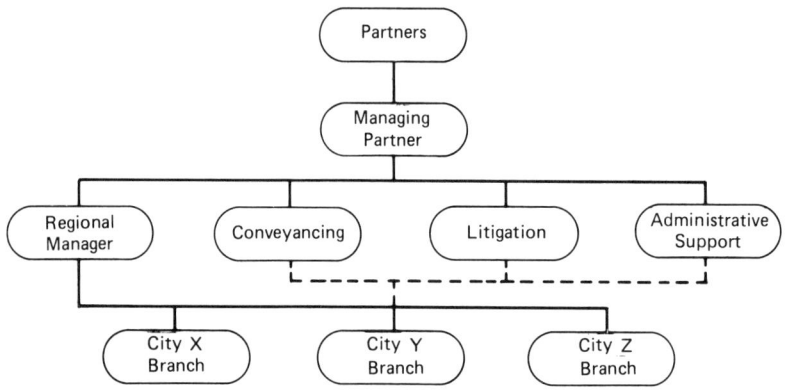

without consideration of the entire market structure. It has the major advantage, however, of allowing rapid expansion even when a professional firm is short of major resources—principally money and professional expertise.

Client Considerations

Some clients continually look for quality professional services, competence, and image when seeking professional firms. Most professional organizations strive to impress upon the public that all members within the profession have the same high standards and dedication. Many codes of ethics and unwritten or written rules of conduct reemphasize the commonality of high standards within any professional group. If that were true, then most clients would seek out professional assistance largely on the basis of the convenience of the firm, particularly its location.

Many clients do just that. Certainly, most family medical practices are located where there are families, and most engineering firms specializing in residential construction locate where there is considerable house construction activity. If a professional firm is convenient and appears professional, it may be initially selected by many potential clients on the basis of those characteristics alone. If professional services are timely and in line with the client's expectations, a long-term client–professional relationship may be established. The image of both the location and the decor of the office can, however, have a major impact on the selection or retention of a professional by his clientele. For instance, for middle-income clientele, a balance must be struck between a bright, clean, and comfortable location and decor and one which appears ostentatious. Consideration should also be given to possibly incompatible images projected by nearby businesses.

Professional Service Considerations

A professional firm should have a clear indication not only of the level and quality of the services it is willing to provide but also of the types of services it wishes to provide. All of these will determine which type of location is appropriate for the firm. If the firm offers highly specialized professional services, it might locate in a professional "core" area of a major city. A general practice offering services to a wide variety of clients might consider locating in a regional shopping center or a smaller community setting.

Most important, the types of clients that a professional firm wishes to attract will have a major bearing on a firm's location. High-income or low-income districts, population density, and the direction of population movement (change, growth, or decline) would be considered.

An Example of Failure to Do Long-Term Planning in a Small Law Firm

A small, single-practitioner law firm was located in a major city and was aware of a smaller community located 40 miles away that did not have a full-time practicing lawyer.

The lawyer decided to open a part-time (one day per week) office to better serve the clients in that second community. He felt that the office would provide $2,000 per month in higher fees and cost $700 per month to operate, including automobile and office rent expenses. The accompanying table shows the figures.

	Main Office	Part-Time Office	Total Firm
Revenue	$6,000	$2,000	$8,000
Less expenses:			
Office	3,000	500	3,500
Travel	—	200	200
Total	3,000	700	3,700
Net income	$3,000	$1,300	$4,300

The second office was very successful and soon demanded more time from the lawyer. This increased his travel time, and the amount of time and expenses of being away from the main office. Yet the main practice was growing as well. The lawyer was unwilling to relocate or hire another professional and eventually closed the second office. There were several reasons for that decision:

1. Clients at both offices were inconvenienced and upset while the lawyer was at the other location.

2. Travel expenses had grown and the lawyer realized that the amount of time he spent traveling (two hours per day while at the second office) was time that would otherwise be productive and billable.

3. There was not enough work in the main office to keep him busy full-time, resulting in higher gross fees. His net income would be much higher if he closed the second office, because he would not have the high travel costs and the office expenses at the second location.

4. Maintaining the second office and expenses attached thereto resulted in higher charge-out rates to all his clients in both locations.

Choosing Appropriate Locations

The specific choice of a professional office or building would be contingent upon a number of factors:

Amenities (banks, restaurants, and so on).
Drainage and soil conditions.
Land and development costs.
Utilities (electrical and telephone).
Waste disposal.
Water supply.
Zoning by-laws and regulations (especially with an eye to future growth).
Maintenance.
Lighting.
Heating and air-conditioning.
Security.
Decor—carpets, furniture, fixtures, and the like.

Location, equipment, furnishings, and decor influence the professional's staff and clientele. Clean, comfortable, and attractive surroundings can promote a sense of well-being, accomplishment, and pride among staff. Most clients respond favorably to well-appointed premises.

When new professional facilities are being planned, it is important to consider the lead time needed from conception to completion. Projects are often not completed on schedule because of the unavailability of supplies or subcontractors.

Trends within the area in which a firm is considering locating should be analyzed. Population shifts, orientation of development toward industrial or residential, traffic flow, property maintenance, the impression the neighborhood gives, and registered permits for rezoning may all provide an indication of changes in the level or types of professional services which will be in demand in the future.

Most important, a professional firm must establish that there is unfilled demand in the area for the professional services it is proposing, and it must have the resources to become a recognized professional leader in supplying that market.

12

Determining and Changing Fees

A professional firm is a business organization with revenues as the core of its continued growth, development, and existence. Professional fees should provide for an adequate professional standard of living, the costs of staff training and continued professional education, and adequate time for reflection and relaxation to allow a professional to "recharge," as well as office administration and downtime (coffee breaks, luncheons, unbillable explanation time, vacations, and so on). In addition to considering and analyzing nonbillable time, a professional might analyze billable time to determine strengths in fees and sources of revenue.

There is a growing realization by professionals that they are also businessmen and subject to risk. There is an increasing requirement for working capital in the firm as the practice grows. There is exposure to bad debts. Professional liability is an increasing concern. There is the risk of practice failure. The rewards of practicing a profession should be sufficient to attract young people to the profession and provide them with sufficient income for succession (that is, the ability to pay out an existing practitioner from future income).

As businessmen, professionals feel, more than ever, that they should earn a profit comparable to the industry and commerce sectors of the economy. When one takes into account the extensive educational and practical experience requirements (approximately seven years beyond high school for the average professional), this is understandable.

At the same time there is increasing pressure from society to minimize professional fees. Many people feel that they have a basic right to obtain certain professional services at minimum or even no cost. The services of the medical profession and of lawyers are often provided at nominal or no cost to the disadvantaged. Many people feel that tax preparation fees should be the responsibility of the collection agency, because of increasingly complex tax laws and filing procedures. Home design, construction and design standards, and government inspection of building plans are increasingly subject to regulation.

There is little doubt that there will be increasing government intervention in all professional–client relationships and activities. One of the rationalizations for that intervention is that government, through subsidizing professional education at the university level, has an obligation to ensure availability of professional services to society at large. However, many professionals still have the right to determine an appropriate fee level.

Profit Maximization

Some professionals feel that the idea of profit maximization is foreign to the concept of professionalism. Some even feel that it is somehow unethical to charge "what the market will bear."

Profit maximization means that an organization must set its price, above cost, and understand what effect price will have on the demand for professional services. There is a concern among many professionals that there is absolute demand for many types of professional services. For instance, if a doctor were needed in a lifesaving situation, or a lawyer to obtain an injunction, clients might have little concern, at the time, about the costs of the needed professional services. There is opportunity for the professional to charge unreasonable fees. The alternative is for a professional to charge a "fair" fee. In a totally free market environment, however, there is little price elasticity—demand will fall as prices are increased. Services which were "needed" may be redefined as "optional," and clients may seek other professionals, attempt to do some types of professional services for themselves, or simply not seek a professional firm's assistance when they feel that fees are unreasonably high.

The key to profit maximization is to set a professional fee high enough above costs of operations to earn the maximum revenue per service offered, yet low enough so that there will continue to be adequate demand.

As price is increased, profitability will improve to the point where there is market resistance (see Figure 12-1). Further increases in prices will result in lower demand for professional services as clients seek alternatives. The resultant drop in client services, with the high fixed costs of operating a professional firm, may result in dramatically lower profit levels. Maximum profitability will be attained when there is sustained demand for services, probably at medium rates.

A professional would think that if he underestimates the value of his services to his clients, the client may consequently underrate the professional's abilities. Fee setting should be considered from many angles, not the least of which is the clients' psychological response to the fee.

Professionals are not all equal in ability or performance and should not expect the same return. Professional services are not all the same, nor should they bring the same return. More senior professional services and specialization, for instance, will usually produce a higher fee, but a higher total profitability only if there is adequate demand.

Figure 12-1.   Relationship between price and profit level.

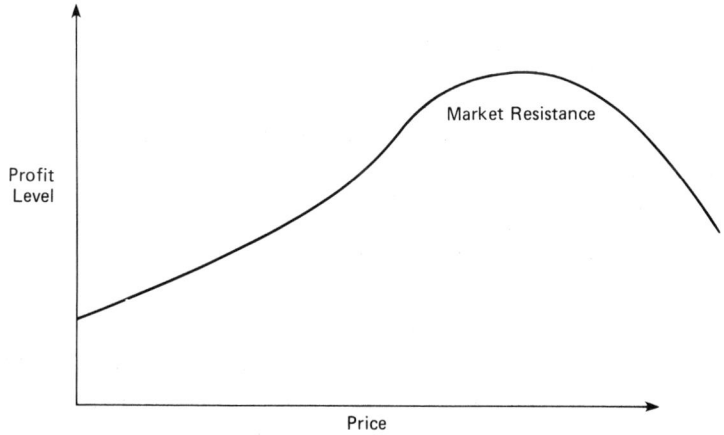

Objective versus Subjective Fee Setting

Objective fee setting means establishing a fixed fee for a service, or an hourly charge-out rate, and simply multiplying that rate by the number of services or hours worked. Only accurately measurable items such as the number of services or hours, plus disbursements, are used. Sometimes these fees are discounted before clients are billed if inefficiency or need for staff training is evident. Seldom are fees adjusted upward.

The advantages of the objective approach are that it is largely mechanical and consistent, which means that fees are easy to determine and easy to defend. The disadvantage is that it rarely takes into account that an individual client's perception of the value of the services to *him* may be different from the value placed on those same services by a different client. It does not take into account the vagaries in individual clients' wants, needs, and expectations. It is also somewhat subjective in that the fixed fees are rarely negotiated but are set by the professional firm. The fees may be high or low compared to those of other firms.

Subjective fee setting involves adjusting the basic, objectively determined billing for value and acceptability to the client. Some professionals, however, do not maintain time or service records, so the entire billing may be a subjective guestimate. A number of subjective elements enter into the determination of professional fees, including the professional's estimate of his efficiency, the comparative value of professional skill and experience, the professional's reputation, the type of work and degree of difficulty, inconvenience to the client, unusual expenses, the level of professional fees in the community, and overtime if required, as well as value and acceptability to the client.

Even within the same profession there are widely divergent points of view on the appropriateness of either method. Many professional services may be somewhat mechanistic, and some professionals would argue that an objective billing method is appropriate in most cases. Those professionals who argue that practicing a profession is an "art" would argue that the subjective billing approach more truly expresses their professionalism and the value of services in the clients' eyes.

Many discussions are held on the subject of professional ability and efficiency. Inexperience, false starts, lack of adequate supervision, the use of overqualified senior personnel, and doing unnecessary professional work may all result in a client having a legitimate complaint against a high fee.

Cost, Demand, and Competitive Considerations

Most professional firms base their fees on the costs of providing professional services. The major advantage of cost-oriented fee setting is that it is relatively simpler than demand-oriented fee setting. Prices do not change as a result of fluctuations in demand. Cost-oriented fees also appear fairer to both the professional and his clientele. The professional will retain an adequate level of profitability, and the client will not be subject to unusually high fees when demand is high. Since most professional firms use cost orientation in fee setting, there are often very similar fees charged by competing firms, because the underlying costs and profit margins of most professional firms are similar.

Example of Cost-Oriented Fee Setting

In an analysis of the commercial and industrial sectors, it is not unusual to find a price-earnings (or investment-to-profit) ratio in the 3 to 10 range. Generally, the smaller the organization, the lower the P/E ratio. For smaller publicly traded firms the P/E ratio is often in the 3 to 5 range. This reflects the higher risks of being a smaller organization. These risks include those of competition, failure, higher leverage (debt/equity), and limited service capabilities for broad markets. (These P/E ratios are stated on an after-tax basis.) There is a growing awareness among the professional community of these risks and the commensurate requirement for adequate margins to cover these risks, in addition to the payment of a fair salary to a professional. The amount of the principal's salaries should be considered in light of the fact that the average professional has ten or more years of post-graduate experience behind him.

An example of the revenue required for running a professional accounting firm (see Table 12-1) should include the principals' salaries and should provide for a reasonable return on invested capital.

Traditionally, in proprietorship and partnership accounting there has been only one earnings account—profit or net income—against which "drawings" were made. In reality, however, there are three major components of that earnings account:

Table 12-1. Cost-oriented pricing—small accounting firm.

Cost Component	Amount	Percent Cost
Principals' salaries	$ 32,000	32.0
Staff salaries:		
Reception	9,600	
Bookkeeper	9,600	
Intermediate accountant	18,000	
Total staff salaries	$ 37,200	37.2
Other overhead items Promotion, travel, stationery, equipment, depreciation, office rent, etc.	$ 26,800	26.8
Return on capital invested in the firm (10% on $40,000)	$ 4,000	4.0
Total "cost factor"	$100,000	100.0
Margin (P/E ratio: 4)	$ 33,000	33.0
Total revenue required	$133,000	

1. Salary for the proprietor or partners.
2. Interest on investment in the capital needs of the firm.
3. Net income or profit after adjusting for principals' salaries and cost of invested capital.

This includes no adjustment of profit to account for tax considerations.

The model in Table 12-1 equates the "value" (price for the firm) with one year's gross fees ($133,000) for P/E ratio calculation. The "margin" and "cost factor" might be equated to the value of the firm traded in the open market, where valuation is based on pure return on investment calculation. (This is an oversimplification, because there may be many other factors affecting the market price of a "going concern" professional firm.) On analysis, however, Table 12-1 brings home one important fact. If a professional expects to be able to purchase a firm, he is looking at a seven- to nine-year pay-out after tax. This would be calculated on the basis of other income, but the very fact that a salary is drawn (to

$32,000) implies a tax rate of more than 40 percent on the margin. Shrinking the margin to less than 14 percent and increasing the P/E ratio to greater than 7 would not be out of line with other successful small businesses in a competitive risk environment.

Once a professional firm has ascertained its costs, and the fees it requires to maintain an adequate level of profit, it can work backward, using the weighted value of each professional and staff member, to determine the appropriate hourly fee for each individual in the office. Many professional firms establish 1,200 billable hours per year as a reasonable base for establishing a charge-out rate (see Table 12-2). A receptionist position would have fewer billable hours because the work is largely interrupted and administrative.

Different people in the firm have different value to the clients. By valuing the relative worth of each person, it is possible to calculate (Table 12-3) the hourly charge-out rates necessary to achieve the revenue required.

Fee determination among professionals is becoming a highly subjective process that takes into account the value of the service to a client.

Table 12-2. Billable hours per year.

	Number of Days	Number of Hours @ 7 hours/day
Total Year	365	2,555
Less: Weekends (52 × 2)	104	728
Statutory holidays	10	70
Vacation	15	105
Funerals, weddings, illness	10	70
Administration and routine	24	168
Waiting for clients	5	35
Long lunch	10	70
Long coffee breaks	5	35
Education	10	70
Total "downtime"	193	1,351
Total billable time	172	1,204

Table 12-3. Fee determination: cost-oriented pricing.

Position	Relative weight of "value" of service to client (subjective)	Chargeable hours	Weighted hours (A×B)	Weighted fee*	Charge rate (A×D)	Employee fees generated (B×E)
	(A)	(B)	(C)	(D)	(E)	(F)
Principal	8	1,200	9,600	6.52	52.76	$ 62,588
Reception	3	800	2,400	6.52	19.56	15,647
Level I student	3	1,200	3,600	6.52	19.56	23,471
Level IV student	4	1,200	4,800	6.52	26.08	31,294
Totals			20,400			$133,000

*Gross fees required ÷ total "weighted hours" (133,000 ÷ 20,400) = weighted hour fee ($6.52)

Many professional firms use demand-oriented pricing, basically charging "what the market will bear" without heavy regard to the costs of providing professional services. This does not mean that the fee will necessarily be high. This will only happen if there is high demand for professional services. There is also an increasing probability, in some firms and professions at least, that rising competition and faltering demand may result in lower charge-out fees.

There may be price discrimination. Client discrimination exists where fees vary with the clients' ability to pay. Service discrimination exists where the fees for services vary with the type of service. Time discrimination occurs where different rates are charged on the basis of demand, discounts for early work, overtime rates, and the like. Location discrimination occurs where different rates are charged in different geographic locations. All these require some degree of market segmentation to determine costs, demand, and profitability of each segment.

A third type of pricing, dominant in most professions, is competition-oriented pricing. Under this method, professional fees are set at a level equal to, or higher or lower than, the fees charged by other professional firms providing services in the same or similar markets. The major advantage of using this method of determining an appropriate fee is its simplicity. Simply ask other professionals what their fee levels are, or refer to a "tariff" of average fees published by many professional organizations. The major disadvantage is that it provides only average fees, in average markets, with average operating costs, *which result in average profitability.* Little use can be made of those averages, other than as a reference, in pricing many types of unique or specialized services, to unique clientele or where unique costs must be considered. There is usually little segmented information available from competitive professional firms or professional organizations.

Positive Pricing Models

Many clients equate quality with price. In commercial marketplaces, many new products or unique services are introduced with initially high price structures, and this appeals to certain segments of the market. Some types of individuals and companies like to be the first in obtaining unique, rare products and are willing to pay the costs for the status or prestige value associated with the purchase. We are all familiar with individuals who are constantly in the forefront—the first in clothing style changes, new cars, video recorders, and a multitude of consumer goods and services.

Products and services are often repackaged and reintroduced as "new," "unique," or "first offering" because of customer appeal in the much wider general market. This may encourage customers to make a purchase decision, and there is reason to believe that the majority of clients will respond to professional marketing in a similar manner.

Clients may be proud of the fact that their professional firm is the most expensive firm to deal with. In effect, they equate quality of professional services with the higher fees. They also prefer the personal prestige of being associated with a leading professional firm. We are all familiar with clients who state, "My doctor is renowned for . . ." or "My lawyer defended. . . ." There is a certain amount of clients pride in associating with leading professionals, and clients are often willing to pay higher fees for that association.

Higher fees can also allow those professional firms to provide forever increasing client service and support through reinvestment in continuing education, office facilities improvement, image enhancement, and so on.

The high fees can reinforce the notion, synergistically, that the professional firm is the acknowledged leader in a field. We have all had clients who have acknowledged that a professional is "very good, but very expensive." Yet, if he was not expensive, certain types of clients would question the quality of professional services given. The important point, in the clients' mind at least, is that advanced professional quality demands a high price because it is rare and could not be maintained without the high price.

Setting higher prices could actually stimulate demand. The amount of the fee could lead to referrals, since many people would associate it with high-quality service.

The major disadvantage of setting high prices is that the professional services could be beyond some lower- and medium-income clients' ability to pay. This may lead to client dissatisfaction, bad debts, or delayed payments and complaints. Clients may be lost, possibly to moderately priced professionals. Unless the professional firm is preeminent in its field and totally irreproachable, many clients might switch to another firm. Few people or corporations are willing to admit that they are changing to another firm because they cannot afford the fees. Common market buzz and rationalizations from clients take the form of "The firm was so large that I didn't know who to talk to, or who was handling my account," "They were so slow," or "They are not structured to meet the needs of the small client."

Obviously, the fees must be structured to be acceptable to major client segments. Not all clients have the same psychological profile—for example, the need to associate with preeminent professionals—and most (potential) clients are not in the most prestigious income brackets and thus cannot afford the highest professional fees.

The professional firm should know not only the psychological profile of its clientele but also how fees are set in its markets—on a competition, demand, or cost basis. The firm might also promote itself by considering some special fee arrangements on a temporary or full-time basis. Most important, the firm should understand the impact of higher or lower fees on demand for its services.

Recommendations for Fee Setting

Professional fees are areas of continuing vital concern for the professional, particularly in an era of high inflation and increasing competition. Fee setting is a basic area in which proper data are essential. Professionals are sometimes lax, and often feel helpless, in determining the level of professional fees in a competitive market. Often, fees are determined by levels considering only competitors' fees.

Here are some of the major considerations and attitudes in determining a fee structure *for profit:*

1. Prices should be based on the costs to the professional firm. There should not be slavish adherence to market fees or competitors' fees.

2. Selective fee increases should be used where competition precludes general fee increases.

3. Prices should cover direct costs, fixed expenses, and a reasonable margin for profit.

4. Fees should be under continuous review. Procedures should be in effect to review fee levels and policies of each item, service, and/or department at least annually. During periods of high inflation, fee policies should be reviewed more often—on a quarterly, monthly, or weekly basis—particularly for highly volatile cost items.

5. Many professionals, particularly small professional firms, resist implementing fee increases because they fear client dissatisfaction.

Breakeven charts can assist the professional in visually demonstrating the effects of cost changes, changes in expense levels together with changing volume, and their effects on profit.

It should also be recognized that many professionals are underpriced, because increases in fees rarely keep pace with the inflationary increases in costs and expenses. Declines in gross margins (revenue minus salaries), as evidenced by comparative financial statements, usually are evidence of underpricing.

Once fees are determined, reference should be made to competitive fees as well as other market fees, but only as a comparative check on the fees. If fees are widely divergent from market fees, this may indicate a much different cost to competitors or different expenses or profit expectations of other professionals. The important point, however, is that the firm must use its *own costs and expenses* as the decisive guide in determining fee structure if it is to remain profitable and viable.

We will restrict discussion in this section to breakeven fee setting. This requires gathering data to determine minimum revenue to cover overhead, minimum support prices (the minimum prices that allow enough gross margin to cover fixed expenses), and a reasonable profit.

Determining a breakeven point requires clear segregation of direct (variable) costs from fixed expenses. This varies with each firm, depending on the nature of the profession, the size of the account, whether the expense could be reduced in direct relation to revenue volume, and whether the expense is shared, proportionately or disproportionately, by other departments or services.

Major items considered as variable costs include supplies, direct labor, and direct payroll taxes and fringe benefits (which are usually expensive—fringe benefits often total from 15 percent to over 35 percent of direct labor costs). Professionals increasingly tend to allow 2 percent to 10 percent of direct costs as a safety margin—a margin for error, price increases in an inflationary economy, interest costs of short-term holding of inventory, delays, and unforeseen contingencies.

Major items usually considered fixed—unchanging in relation to the level of professional activity and revenues—normally include office rent, utilities, insurance costs, and professional dues.

The breakeven point is the point at which revenue equals direct (variable) costs plus (fixed) expenses. This can be expressed algebraically as

$$S = V + F$$

where S = level of revenue at which the firm will have zero net income
V = variable expenses
F = fixed expenses

The following example is very basic, but it will lay the foundation for further discussion. In this example, variable costs for a given firm are $130,000 and fixed expenses $50,000. The total revenue (R) of the firm is $200,000.

$$\begin{aligned} S &= \frac{V}{R} S + F \\ &= \frac{130{,}000}{200{,}000} S + 50{,}000 \\ &= .65S + 50{,}000 \\ .35S &= 50{,}000 \\ S &= 142{,}857 \end{aligned}$$

Therefore: V (at 65% of $142,857) + F ($50,000) = $142,857.

This would be charted as in Figure 12-2. Profit will increase at an increasing rate once fixed costs and variable costs are recovered. The point of cost recovery is the breakeven point. The following points should be emphasized:

1. Where fixed expenses increase, revenues must increase at a ratio of variable costs to revenues (in the example, 200M/130M)

DETERMINING AND CHANGING FEES 141

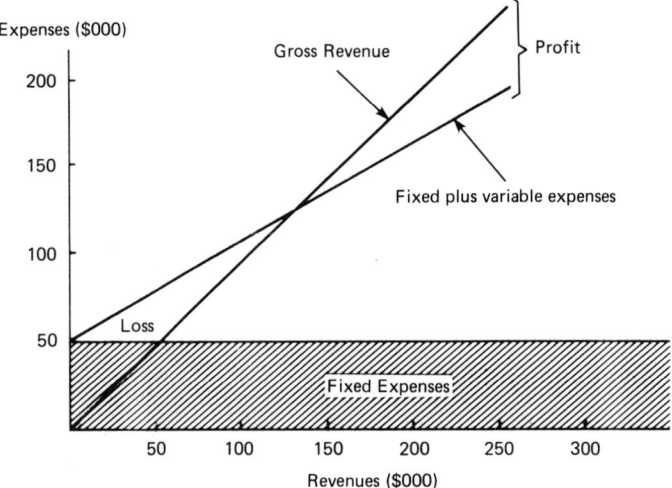

Figure 12-2.   Breakeven chart.

to cover increased fixed expenses. That is, the *gross margin* (not revenue) must increase in direct relation to increases in fixed expenses.

2. Ratios of revenue, variable costs, and fixed expenses are in constant flux and must be reviewed to ensure current validity.

3. Breakeven charts can clearly show the interrelated effects of revenue volume, direct (variable) costs, and fixed expenses.

Decisions to review fees must concentrate on adequate knowledge of cost/revenue relationships and their effect on profitability. Once a decision to change fees toward more profitable levels has been made, careful consideration should be given to planning and introducing fee increases. If you are not an accountant, you may wish to obtain professional advice from one.

Initiating Fee Increases

Fee increases should be made on a timely basis to allow maximum benefit to the professional and the least concern to his clientele. Most professions have seasonal fluctuations in demand, and it is usually most profitable to increase fees just prior to increased demand for services. If some clients are lost, the firm can better afford it at that time. Similarly, widespread publication of major general consumer price increases might prove a psychologically better time to notify clients of fee increases.

Most professionals do not announce their fee increases but quietly change them when dealing directly with clients. Those professions which provide service to government, industry, or through a professional purchaser should notify those clients in advance of billing. Reasons for increases in fees should be given, and notification might be made in the form of a proposal of fee adjustments in order to allow maximum flexibility and further negotiations with clients.

In order to minimize losing clients from fee increases, professionals should stress the benefits of the services they provide. Some professionals also notify their clients directly of the labor and operating cost increases and attempt to relate these increases to other increases of which the client is aware. Notably, in recent years, price increases are related to increases in all forms of taxation.

Where there are several fee changes—some heavy increases, some minimum increases, and some fee declines—professionals usually stress areas of minimum fee increases and place heavy emphasis on fee decreases. Clients may accept selective fee changes more easily than general fee changes.

Some professionals use fee increases to stimulate services by providing prior notification of proposed increases. This also is a tactful approach to introducing a new fee level, since the client has the option of obtaining scheduled professional services currently at "old" prices.

The professional will consider the psychological and marketing impact of introducing fee changes. Increases should be announced only sporadically, not on a continuing basis (thus it is better to announce a 6 percent increase at six-month intervals than 1 percent increases every month). Fee changes should be made on a selective basis, rather than across the board, to allow flexibility. The professional should also be willing to provide reasonable explanations to all clients about fee increases, and should try to ease the impact of those increases through increases in the quality of professional services. Finally, he should clearly express his concern to meet the clients' needs.

13

Market Orchestration

We had described synergism as the cumulative effect of independent actions, events, or attitudes which together provide a result greater than the sum that could be expected of the independent parts. In synergy, the independent parts reinforce each other. This concept is critical to a well-managed marketing effort and the orchestration of key variables. Once a firm has chosen, through market analysis, its strategic position in the market—whether defined by client group, professional type or level of service, fee level, geographic location, or whatever—it can establish objectives, policies, and programs that will help it become the dominant force in that segment. It will not try to dominate the whole range of services, prices, clientele, locations, and promotional activities of the whole profession. However, if the firm cannot devise unique strategies for any unique professional service it has to offer, it should consider withdrawing from that service and/or rewriting its objectives until some unique variable becomes apparent. The objective of this exercise is to develop a firm that is unique and *preferred* for a specific service by a client group. Once that position is chosen, and only then, can a professional firm organize its marketing activities so that they are mutually reinforcing and synergistic.

If more than one segment is chosen—that is, if the firm picks a target market range—it is important that those segments be compatible with one another and a decision be made as to how important each is to the firm's total operation. Take the case of an accounting firm. It could do work ranging from payrolls and basic bookkeeping up through auditing and advanced financial consulting, and this work could be done for small businesses, medium-size businesses, government agencies, banks, specific industries, or hundreds of other types of clients. Without segmentation, revenue sources might appear as in Table 13-1. This sort of array is typical of most accounting firms, but atypical of most professional firms today, in which services and clientele are often amorphous.

Most professional firms, particularly small firms, provide services across the board. They seen to accept every possible type of engagement available to them. This is possibly a result of early conditioning when revenue increases were necessary for the survival of the firm. Yet, even when the firm is relatively secure, the push to grow—in quantity, as opposed to quality—continues. For instance, the professionals in this firm might justify individual income tax preparation as being done to get exposure, in the hope that there will be referrals or that this group will eventually go into business and form companies. The problem, however, is that without a clear indication of the eventual client/service segment there can be no carefully targeted and orchestrated marketing program. The firm is also using tremendous resources to maintain an acceptable level of service to all individual client groups. In Table 13-1, for instance, 14 percent of the firm's total revenue comes from individuals, 77 percent from companies, and 9 percent from others, yet the research, study, knowledge, administration, and scheduling for the 14 percent would typically be as expensive as for the companies, which represent 77 percent of the income. There would be a larger number of individual clients, at lower rates—say, 500 clients for 1040 individual income tax preparations—and perhaps only 130 corporate and business clients in a small six-person professional accounting firm. A full 59 percent of the services of the firm, as shown in the blocks on Table 13-1, are for only four services—bookkeeping, accounting, non-audit financial statements, and corporate tax preparation, for companies and other than individual clients.

The heterogeneous client/service mix makes it difficult to develop new services for existing clients for which there is unmet demand. For instance, the firm may be so busy preparing individual income tax returns during the income tax season that it has little time to explore and respond to the needs of its corporate clients—typically, by offering financial advice, tax consultation, and ad-

Table 13-1. Percentage income breakdown by service/client group for an accounting firm.

	Individuals		Companies			
	Middle Income	High Income	Small	Medium	Others	Total
Individual tax preparation	5	2	—	—	—	7
Bookkeeping, payrolls, etc.	2		12	5	3	22
Client accounting			10	3	2	15
Non-audit financial statement			8	4	2	14
Audit				8	2	10
Financial advice		1	3			4
Government reporting			2	3		5
Systems (accounting) design			2	1		3
Corporate tax preparation			5	3		8
Corporate tax consultation			2	3		5
Estate planning	1	3				4
Corporate consulting			1	2		3
Total %	8	6	45	32	9	100
	14		77		9	100

vanced consulting to assist corporations in improving their profitability. In addition, the firm may not develop the skills and resources to respond to those needs. By not clearly stating its objective, it has almost by default defined itself as a tax preparation firm for individuals, at least from February through April in each year.

The orchestration problem that this professional firm faces is that its clients and service demands will conflict with each other. Individuals could be unhappy if tax returns were filed late, and corporate clients would be unhappy if they had to wait a long time for financial advice they need now. The high costs (through increased staffing) of preparing individual tax returns over a short period would result in the firm getting lower than acceptable results, unless it were specifically organized to immediately reduce costs or increase other services when the tax season was over.

Orchestration is addressed when the professional firm begins to develop compatible clients and services and a marketing program that is aimed at bringing about the desired mix. It means deciding upon the mix of segments that can be most efficiently and effectively served by the firm. Once that is done, the firm can be organized to be responsive and to target its advertising, promotion, and marketing efforts to a specific market range. It can decide upon the most effective promotion or publicity campaign. It can decide on an appropriate advertising medium, budget appropriately for market research and promotion, and design effective themes, procedures, and copy. Most important, it will provide a consistent image of what it is, what it does, how well it does it, and where it is going.

For instance, in the example of the accounting firm, if the firm decided that the target range was all services listed for corporate clientele, it would typically reorganize everything in the firm, from the reception area to service results.

Synergism—from Office Reception to Service Result

You are attempting to show staff, clients, and all others that you clearly know the type of firm you are building. Your activities must be in harmony. Only in this way will you obtain the type of clientele requiring the types of services that you desire to provide.

The most important area is the attitude of the firm and its staff. There must be constant awareness and effort to become client-responsive. Clients know when the firm is concerned with their best interests. A dynamic professional firm will search for ways to help every client on an individual basis. Staff will be trained to review professional work and files, not just to ensure that adequate quality control over professional services has been exercised, but to be aware of areas where there is a potential need for service. Clients, without professional training, often do not know or cannot perceive a need for professional service, and often do not even know the other types of services which may be available to them from a professional firm. Therefore, the professionals themselves often must initiate that search. Clients seldom request a unique, new, or different service unless they can clearly perceive the benefit to them. Professionals often must also point out the benefit to the client which may be perceived only by them. They must be able to communicate those benefits in terms that the client can understand. Professionals alone have the knowledge and experience to help clients avoid repetitive problems and to provide a broad perspective of opportunities.

For instance, an accountant can point out how a tax shelter can save a specific client $1,000, or an engineer can point out a rough concept to a client that may lead to a $5,000/year reduction in energy costs. The point is that the client, by himself, will not ask for professional advice, because he does not know that $1,000, or $5,000, or whatever, is available to him as a benefit. Once the professional has pointed out the costs and benefits of a proposal, the client is free to decide whether he wishes the professional firm to go ahead.

The point is that clients *do not realize what they do not know,* and unless the professional takes the initiative, he may have recurring problems or continuously miss opportunities. Yet, many professional firms think that this is a "selling" stance and will provide only services that are specifically requested of them.

Initial Impressions

The first impression somebody gains is usually a lasting one. Someone walking into a professional firm will "look at the walls" and develop a feel of how he will be treated and the type of firm he is dealing with. That impression will take two or three minutes to form—but for the next two-hour consultation and over months and even years, he will justify that initial impression and expect always to be treated in accordance with it. If he is initially treated curtly, and then a staff member is warm, friendly, and courteous, he will mistrust the intent of that stance. If, however, he is initially treated with courtesy, and then someone in the firm is short with him, he will generally pass this off as being the exception and find an excuse to justify the action—bad weather, illness, or whatever. That does not justify any discourteous attitude to clients—ever; but it does reinforce the notion that first impressions stick. First impressions are critically important. They had better be well orchestrated, and be the ones that the firm wishes to create. This implies that the entire office reception function must be well managed.

Often the first contact with a professional firm is by telephone. All staff and professionals should be coached and trained in telephone manners and etiquette. A cheery "good afternoon," followed by the name of the firm, gives a warmer impression than "Tim Connor, Attorney-at-Law. Who is calling, please?" If a staff member is temporarily busy, a caller could be asked whether he would like to hold, if the call could be returned, or if someone else can help. The caller can be asked about the nature of the call, or if there is anything the professional will need, so the professional can be prepared and immediately responsive when he calls back. If a professional is going on holidays, he can call his clients to ensure that they will not need him while he is away, or just to advise them of arrangements he has made to cover the practice. When a professional calls a client, he should be well prepared and know what he is going to say and the results he expects from the call. A goodwill call, enquiring about generalities and the weather, wastes both the professional's and the client's time. Professional firms should make a habit of promptly returning calls—every day. There is nothing more frustrating than for a client to telephone (expressing a need) and not be called back for days or weeks, with no reasons given. His impression is that the firm probably doesn't really care about him—and he is probably right. Above all, keep appointments and commitments—if you say you will call, do it.

The waiting room is one of the most underused promotion vehicles imaginable—yet it is freely available to most every professional. It can be made warm and relaxing, demonstrating obvious concern for client comfort. Which would you prefer: a carpeted, color-coordinated, upholstered, spacious room or a cold, tiled one with hard plastic furniture?

There may be no reading material to put clients at ease—they may be forced to stare at walls. If there is reading material, it is often placed without thought of content—there may be general-interest magazines and material instead of material that relates to the reason for the client's visit or that leads directly to how this firm can better serve him. Here are some examples:

Accounting:	"How a budget improves profits."
Engineering:	"How to save energy costs through building modification."
Law:	"How to avoid family disputes through planning your will."
Medicine:	"How to improve your disposition."

If they are written by the firm, so much the better—the firm's interest in serving its clients becomes immediately more obvious.

Hardly anyone can walk past a library without checking what interests the professional. If the books are carefully selected, the library would *not* contain the same books in every firm. Books about the profession or how to run a firm are of professional interest, but not of client interest. Books with titles such as "Helping Law Clients Administer Their Practice," "Saving Space in Building Design," "Tax Savings for Corporations," or "Losing Weight" will show the client that the law, engineering, or accounting firm or medical practice is interested in him. These titles were made up, but the firm can choose titles which make the client directly aware of how the firm can help him with specific services. Some firms lend these client-oriented books to their clientele.

Personal appearance is also critical. A business client, for instance, will have difficulty reconciling the overly casual appearance of professionals and staff members with a quality professional product.

Clients pay professional fees for results. A firm should continuously show clients how they are helping the client achieve the best results. The benefits and improvements brought about through the use of the firm should be stressed. Yet, many professional firms still have the habit of doing the basic service, making out a bill, and sending the client on his way. A professional should be willing to look at his bill and be able to justify it by showing that the client has received greater benefit. He may even ask the client to ensure that the fee is satisfactory, acceptable, and justified in the client's mind. If it is not, the service level may be too low.

Follow-up

Many professionals are accused of being extremely technically oriented. They rush to get a job done so they can go on to the next. Professionals sometimes spend little time in reviewing files with clients. Yet that is the only way the client will fully understand the service rendered and the ways to apply the results. Many professional engagements may be broken down like this:

Initial client interview, taking instructions, etc.	1 hour
Doing the professional work in the office, without client contact	20 hours
Post-completion technical review of file with client	1 hour
Total time	22 hours

Only two hours, or 9 percent of the total time, were spent with the client. The post-completion review often consists only of a review of the technical aspects of the professional work. Little time is devoted to discussions about how those results may be applied by the client to improve his situation. At the same time, the client is faced with a bill for 22 hours, and he may have difficulty reconciling the amount of the fee with the two hours total time he spent with the professional. Only one of those hours, the post-completion review, provided the results the client originally sought.

A little more time might be spent on the total engagement. From the client's viewpoint, he might get double the results in direct time with the professional and a review aimed at improving his condition. For instance:

Initial client interview	1 hour
Doing professional work	20 hours
Looking for ways to improve client's application of professional work	1 hour
Post-completion technical review of file with client	1 hour
Showing client how to apply the results of professional services to improve his situation	1 hour
Total time	24 hours

The point is that from the client's perspective, the extra two hours spent on the file (which is double the time spent on it in the previous example) were applied to his direct needs, yet the total bill is only increased from 22 to 24 hours (9 percent).

Let's take a specific example. An accounting firm might spend the first 22 hours in providing minimum professional services requested by the client—specifically, the preparation of required financial statements and income tax returns for government reporting. The only reason the client initially chose the accounting firm and requested the engagement was to fulfill that government reporting requirement. This is negative motivation at best, because many people do not like to pay high taxes—but, to add to their frustration, they have to pay professional fees to have taxes calculated because of their complexity. They see no "pay value" to themselves. However, if the accounting firm spent part of the extra two hours on locating a $3,000 tax saving available to the client, the $2,000 professional fee would be more than justified in the client's mind. If the extra two hours were partially spent on analysis of profit improvement opportunities, leading to a $5,000 higher profit, the client might become positively enthusiastic about the professional service he received.

Follow-up and analysis of completed files to determine ways to help clients are possible in all professions, and may lead directly to further engagements with current clientele.

Expanding services to existing clients is usually the most effective marketing vehicle available to a professional firm. A full 70 percent of the firm's growth is often attributable to existing clients referring new clientele and to offering new services to existing clientele. The targeted marketing program should stimulate this. The message of the marketing campaign should stress that the firm cares about its clients and its personal and professional relations with them.

Potential clients are usually referred by existing satisfied and enthusiastic clients. Even if potential clients are exposed to the firm through a general advertising campaign such as newspaper, magazine, or TV advertising, they will rarely respond to that direct advertising until they have interviewed some current clients to ascertain that the actual professional services are in line with the impression given in the campaign. This, again, shows why timeliness, quality services, acceptable fee levels, and a general responsiveness to existing clientele are so critical to the firm's growth.

People who provide referrals are known in the professions as "feeders." Many professionals join clubs and attend social gatherings in the hope of gaining exposure and possibly referrals. The problem with this approach is that it is so nontargeted and general that it seldom brings the growth results desired. It also requires a lot of money, time, and effort. Every profession has a group of people, in addition to current clientele, who consistently provide and are a major source of referrals. Probably as much as 80 percent of all referrals, other than those from existing clients, come from only two or three identifiable groups—certainly not the general public. It is important to know who those groups are and aim the marketing program specifically at them. This program may simply include a letter directed at those "feeders" and outlining the specific services available. When referrals are made, a telephone call or letter thanking the person provides positive incentive to continue referring clients to the firm.

Luncheons, promotion expenses, travel, goodwill calls, memberships, and personal promotions are much more effective in terms of the results obtained if they are directed at the specific group of feeders who are known to be able to make consistent referrals.

For general accounting firms, the two largest referring groups are probably bankers and lawyers; for residential construction engineers, building inspectors and general contractors; for corporate lawyers, corporate bankers and auditors; and for medical specialists, general practioners.

Summary

In order to orchestrate a market for professional services, a firm must clearly define its objectives, know the mix of services it wishes to provide, and provide for compatability. Once those issues are addressed, it can design a marketing program targeted specifically to those individuals in the market who can most effectively help the firm in achieving the market objective.

14

Professional Marketing Tools

Without violating any professional ethics, we have many specific tools and techniques available to us in the application of many marketing, and specifically promotion, activities. Marketing as a function is new to many professionals. This chapter is devoted to providing many examples of appropriate promotion techniques. It will go from general "public relations" type programs to very specific techniques to generate new clients and expand services to existing clients. Chapter 15 will provide specific examples of comprehensive marketing programs for the firm.

Promotion means that we will use techniques to persuade clients and others to adopt our point of view—specifically, to acquire more of our professional services if we are trying to expand. It can mean much more than that—we may even "persuade" people to accept our professional advice. In this connection we must consider whether the act of persuading others to our professional point of view is even ethical. Many professionals look at persuasion as akin to manipulation. Perhaps one way of reconciling this disparity of opinion is to think in terms of whose best interest we are trying to serve. If we are trying to persuade someone primarily for our benefit, that is manipulation. Hard selling of services without subsequently providing timely high-quality services is an example. Attempting to get a client to accept our advice seems to be acceptable to most professionals provided that it is in the client's best interests. The problem is that it is often the professional who decides, sometimes erroneously, what the client's best interests are.

For persuasion to be effective, however, there must be empathy and effective communication skills. Empathy is the ability to be truly concerned about someone else—an ability to see things from their viewpoint. Effective communication requires an ability to present messages that will create an interest in or desire for our services, or acceptance of our point of view.

Even a professional image and demeanor may be thought of as a way to persuade clients to accept our professionalism—and point of view. In a personal sphere, the friends we make, and even our spouses, were initially attracted by the image we project and our ability to persuade them to "our side." A professional practice could not exist unless there was some persuasion which resulted in obtaining clientele in the first place. Professional advice is often not accepted by clients without a concerted effort at persuasion. The question does not seem to be whether or not we should persuade somebody to our viewpoint but *how well* we can persuade them.

A professional marketing program is critical in order for a professional to gain exposure and personal acceptance, as well as acceptance of his ideas and advice. The approach, however, must be very indirect so that the professional does not appear to put self-interest ahead of client interests. Obviously, nonsynergistic misplacing or misusing one professional marketing tool might have the devastating effect of destroying the entire marketing program. If any one of the tools is inconsistent with the firm's objectives or the self-image of the firm's professionals, the professionals would feel uncomfortable with the method and synergism would largely be lost.

Only when we can clearly define what it is we are trying to accomplish as a professional firm can we establish a marketing program.

This is most important. In order to create a successful external image, a firm must clearly understand whom it is trying to influence. It must establish empathy with those people who have the power to help it achieve its goals, and must design its image in response to *their* needs, wants, and expectations. That ability to put yourself in another's shoes goes a long way toward building your self-confidence, the confidence that others place in your ability, and in the long run, your ability to establish yourself as a successful professional.

We should be aware, too, that there are many underlying principles and values which are critical to establishing ourselves as preferred professionals, and even as friends of others.

We should speak and perform modestly. A quiet, conservative attitude can do much more toward cementing human relationships than self-aggrandizing statements. We all distrust and resist self-centered and opinionated individuals and professionals who seem to force their attention—and authority—on us.

A professional who says, "I did this tremendous amount of work for you," "I told you not to do that," or "My opinion is always better than yours" may remain an acquaintance, but he will seldom become a friend, and we will usually do everything in our power to resist his exerting any further influence on us.

Virtually all colleges and universities, and most night school programs, offer courses in communication skills, transactional analysis, assertive management, and "salesmanship." The main principle behind getting results and influencing others through human communication and interrelations is to listen as actively as, or more actively than, talking and to use positive, constructive "I" messages rather than an accusatory or "blaming message" when we want someone to do something for us.

Trying to build our own image by bad-mouthing other professionals has one of the most negative results in our efforts to influence others. Saying that other professionals don't provide a particular service being asked for, or that another has a poor professional reputation, not only sounds childish but also makes the listener think that we may be less than confident in our own abilities.

To gain the respect of others, we must be willing to accept the blame for our errors. We are all familiar with professionals who shift the blame. "I didn't do it because you never told me to," "My secretary forgot to mail that out for me," and "The receptionist lost the message, so I didn't know I was to call you back" are common. After a little while they become boring responses from professionals who consistently perform inadequately. Busy clients don't have time for excuses. They want action—now. It is surprisingly refreshing for a listener to hear, "Oh, that's my fault; I forgot to follow up." The listener usually knows that it takes a confident professional to admit his errors, and they usually are also warmed by the fact that the professional is human.

We should strive to be enthusiastic and aggressive, but not obnoxious. If we work in a firm in whose services we really believe, and, as important, if the senior professionals are dynamic and enthusiastic, this seems to filter down through the firm to dynamic bottom-line results. Obviously, the senior professionals must have vision and a clear sense of purpose if they are to provide the firm with a sense of self-worth, and they must be able to communicate that throughout the firm. They must develop the art of dealing with people to a finely honed skill.

One of the most effective means of projecting a professional image is to speak clearly to groups. People who have public speaking skills are often sought out to make presentations on behalf of their firm. Clients, employees, and others are proud of our ability to present ourselves publicly. Additionally, public speaking courses go a long way in building our own self-confidence as professionals.

Effective writing skills are also important in the development of the firm's image. Our ability to write letters, reports, and articles that get positive responses often leads directly to our being sought out for assistance by clients. Written briefs, presentations, and reports are becoming increasingly important in a complex society. Most colleges and universities offer courses to professionals, writers, and others who wish to learn effective written communication skills.

The clothes we wear, the cars we drive, the appearance and decor of our office, and our entire lifestyle should all inspire confidence, and those visual images should be consistent.

Promotional Decisions

Aside from the services the firm provides, its fee level, and its location, promotional tools will have a major effect on the success of a practice.

"Atmospherics," personal contact, publicity, advertising, and incentives are effective promotion devices that might be used by professional firms.

Atmospherics refers to the design of the premises or locations where professional services are purchased in such a way that there is a responsive and emotional effect on those we are trying to influence. Offices designed for client comfort, and professional demeanor and professional dress can be directed to provide the clientele with the visual impression that the firm is warm, stable, efficient, and concerned for its clientele. Alternatively, they can create an image of awe, remoteness, or even intimidation.

Personal contact between the firm's employees and clientele is seldom given the attention it deserves. Day-to-day personal contact is a most effective promotional vehicle, yet employees are seldom trained to use empathy and client-response skills. Telephone conversations, direct meetings, professional manners, and client responsiveness are critical. All staff can be trained to be more effective communicators and more aware of client feelings and needs, and to watch for areas where a client may need further assistance. Indeed, all meetings and direct contact with everyone should be planned for—professionals should know what they are going to say and what results they are going to achieve before meeting with anyone. Both the firm and its clients waste their time if discussions degenerate into boring platitudes or talk about the state of the weather. Objectives must be set out specifically before any personal contact is made so that results of those contacts can be measured.

Publicity is the use of a promotional vehicle without direct cost to the firm, as there would be in advertising. A publicity campaign attempts to build a professional image through news coverage. This might include the preparation of news releases announcing the opening of an office, writing controversial or topical articles that are newsworthy and would be published, and radio and television interviews or comments on aspects of the profession. The danger with this group of tools is that the media may either reject the copy or edit heavily, sometimes to the point that some items may be taken out of context or wrong, or else reach a market that was not sought. The news media have control over the message. The advantage of this vehicle is that it appears spontaneous and more dramatic, and will be read by people who read news but would not normally read an advertisement.

Advertising is paid-for media exposure that does not include personal contact. The media can include magazines, newspapers, radio, television, business cards, circulars, billboards, directories, and a host of other media. Institutional advertising is done to build the firm's name. Service advertising is used to build knowledge (and use) of a specific service of the firm. Announcements about office openings, new partnerships, and general matters are usually referred to as classified advertising. An important step in developing an advertising program is setting advertising objectives. Determine who is to be reached—the target market—the effect that the campaign is to have on that target market, how frequently the advertising should be run, and how much of the target range can be reached. No one could hope to achieve optimum advertising results without defining this, and without establishing an appropriate advertising budget. Media selection and copy theme are critical to a successful advertising campaign. Traditionally, professional firms often advertise only in their own professional journals or professional sections in newspapers. Their own professional journals seldom provide referrals, especially since they are often read only by other, competing professionals. The firm is advertised in a box, with hundreds of other competing firms being listed in similar boxes. No one has the time or interest to read all the little boxes—and little is done to distinguish one firm from another.

Incentives are a promotional tool whereby some value is added (or cost is lowered) to encourage client response. Incentives normally are financial. They may be as applicable in the professions as in commercial enterprises. The objectives of incentives normally are to use present excess capacity of a firm and to modify client behavior, usually in the timing of purchasing professional services, through fee reductions. Typically, an accounting firm might offer a lower fee for individual tax preparation if all the information is made available by March 15. This would allow the firm to better schedule the work load and avoid the sudden overtime and heavy pressures of the April 15 tax deadline. A medical clinic might offer some incentive by reducing the fee for annual medical checkups when all the checkups of a group of patients can be scheduled on the same day(s). Incentives can also be offered to introduce new services or to enhance goodwill—for instance, flat low-cost fees for will preparation, low-cost tax preparation for low-income pensioners, or low-cost medical checkups for the disadvantaged.

There are a number of decisions which must be made in the use of incentives or disincentives. The objectives should be clearly stated—to modify client behavior, create goodwill, or introduce a new professional service. The firm must decide which individuals or group should be the target recipients. Disincentives can also be used. For instance, taxpayers who bring in their return after April 1 might pay a 10 percent premium for tax preparation. Incentives can be financial or nonfinancial. Nonfinancial incentives might include the free use of a professional firm's library and inclusion of a client in some of the firm's training programs. Timing of incentives must also be considered. Finally, the amount of an incentive must be addressed. If it is too high, other clients might consider it extravagant, and if it is too low, it may be ineffective in bringing about the desired response.

Promotion Campaign—Building Credibility

Credible can mean trustworthy, believable, plausible, and/or honorable and estimable. As professionals we are trying to build our clients' and the community's esteem for our profession, our firm, and ourselves. We are trying to build our image in the eyes of others.

To do this, we must always remember a basic principle: it is difficult, if not impossible, to sell ourselves. Someone else's praise is always better. What we attempt to do, then, is to orchestrate the market "buzz." The things other people are saying about us should be positive and supportive. Our efforts, then, must be subtle and indirect. Our image enhancement program, or marketing thrust, must be aimed at creating positive comments from major target audiences—principally our own clients and people who make referrals—that can help us get the results we desire.

Professional writing can be a major source of exposure. Columns, articles, or books written for the profession, covering some aspect of professional service or concern, may assist in bringing about that indirect benefit. Clients take a great deal of pride in referring to their professional who has acknowledged credits for being a leader in publishing for the profession.

A weekly column in a local newspaper brings further exposure. Newspapers often prefer a local source rather than a syndicated column. Letters to the editor commenting on current events or practices pertinent to the profession reemphasize your concern, as a professional, for the community. Reprints are often available and may be distributed directly to clients and others after publication.

Holding seminars for other professionals is also a major way of gaining that credibility. It is also rather common to attain referrals directly from seminar participants. In addition, seminar brochures may be circulated to clients and "feeders" to determine if they are interested in attending and to indirectly reinforce their esteem for the firm.

Public speaking can be a rewarding form of professional exposure. There are currently many topical discussions in all professions:

Accounting:	"Saving Tax Dollars."
Engineering:	"Energy Conservation in the Home."
Law:	"Planning for Retirement."
Medicine:	"A Diet and Exercise Program."

Most groups and nonprofit organizations are always looking for interesting, informed, and dynamic public speakers. Consider women's organizations, Elks, Lions, and Kiwanis clubs, and other professions. Even though those attending may not require your services, they will know, and often refer, those who do.

Bulletins informing clients of new services or developments potentially valuable to them go a long way toward cementing client relationships.

Holiday cards keep your firm's name in front of clients at times which have special meaning to them. You are letting your clients know that you have a personal as well as a professional interest in them.

A *"spontaneous" letter or telephone call,* after reviewing a client's file, to determine ways you may be of assistance lets the client know that you have a continuous interest in his welfare.

Send *copies of letters* to "third parties" about clients to those clients. Keep them informed of what is going on and the work that you are doing on their behalf. They are naturally anxious about their professional affairs yet many professionals fail to keep clients fully informed.

A *library* can be built for *client* use, covering aspects and improvements of their operations or condition. Clients can be notified of its existence, free availability, and new additions as they come in.

If referrals come in, find out who made the referral and make a point of *letting them know that it was appreciated.*

Maintain *lists of contacts* of those people who can benefit the firm, and design a program to maintain positive contact with those people on a regular basis. Don't make contact so often that it is ineffective, or so seldom that the firm is forgotten. Let them know that they are important to the firm. It helps to make referrals to those people as well. Notify them that you have done so. They will generally appreciate the referral and your confidence in them.

Meeting dynamics can be useful in gaining clients' understanding and acceptance of professional advice. It has the subtle impact of letting the client know that he is worth the extra effort of a professional presentation in a meeting. Using blackboards, overhead projectors, color charts, slides, and useful examples, and paying careful attention to detail in gaining the client's understanding of often complex professional issues, have a dramatic impact, especially compared to a meeting with a professional who was not prepared or did not have an understanding of the principles of human communication.

Summary

A well-conceived marketing program requires that you know who you are trying to influence, how you are going to go about it, and the results you expect from your efforts. Planning, preparation, and clear objectives bring much more dynamic results from meetings and all other contacts than "goodwill" visits or letters. There must be a goal-directed purpose in all contacts or there is a strong possibility that everyone's time will be wasted.

15

Public Relations and Advertising

Traditional advertising does not work. Solicitation has negative results in a professional environment. Clients often feel that:

- It is difficult to obtain the services of successful professionals.
- All *good* professionals are also extremely busy.
- The *best* professionals—those who get client results—are also extremely expensive.

Whether those perceptions are correct or not may be the subject of much debate. The important point, however, is that those are often the market's *perception* of dynamic, results-oriented professionals. That is why a professional firm that solicits heavily is suspect. If the firm must solicit, it cannot be very good, in the market's perception. Clients and others may equate a direct solicitation advertising program with low-quality professional services or a self-centered interest of the professional. For instance, an attempt to obtain higher fees may indicate only a concern for revenue improvement of the firm, rather than a desire to improve client well-being.

The entire market-based approach rests on the foundation that concern for clients and responsiveness to their needs will ultimately lead to enhanced profitability and professional results in the long term—and to extremely well satisfied clients. The thrust of the public relations and advertising function should, therefore, be to improve results for the clients.

PUBLIC RELATIONS AND ADVERTISING

Efficiency and dynamic results are the services that a professional firm can sell. A willingness to change and respond to the marketplace are often more important, in the market's perception of a professional firm, than professional technical expertise. The thrust of a public relations and advertising program should be directed toward those client results and client concerns.

We had discussed marketing departments in Chapter 13. Two problems are immediately apparent with many professional firms, particularly smaller ones. First, many firms do not have the experience or education to engage in marketing activity, let alone a specific public relations or advertising campaign. Second, there has traditionally been no money or time allocated to market analysis and promotion in a professional environment. Even when the benefits of a marketing program campaign can be seen, the budget for the function, in all but the largest organizations, will be extremely tight. The smaller firms' marketing needs, however, are often less complex and may be obtained in a number of ways, including:

1. Hiring an advertising or marketing agency to assist in setting up an ongoing marketing program.

2. Hiring agencies to direct specific campaigns.

3. Obtaining the advise of a professional advisor from the governing professional organization. Many professional organizations are increasingly providing advice to their members on management and marketing. Often such advice is free or included in annual membership dues, whether it is used or not.

The professional advisor would also be cognizant of the ethics governing advertising for the profession.

4. Providing marketing and advertising courses for one or more professionals or staff members in the firm and making them initially responsible for the marketing and promotion programs.

Large professional firms may also hire marketing specialists to direct the marketing program. Before examining how the marketing function should be introduced and organized, we will examine the need for this more formal approach.

Every professional firm "markets" its professional services. It may perform the functions rather well. It should be considered, however, whether the program would be more effective if a formal, cohesive marketing department and program were introduced.

Organizational Considerations

Many firms would argue that *every* professional and staff member exposes the image of the firm and is, in effect, the marketing arm of the firm. They are trained and directed through policy statements to be responsive to client and community needs. Whenever there is a need to prepare circulation letters or advertising copy, the professionals are skilled enough in communications principles to obtain the desired response. Professionals and staff members are competent at interpreting client needs, whether discovered through client file reviews or client meetings. The professionals themselves are the market researchers and suppliers of quality services, and there is no need for a specialized marketing position. If specialized advertising campaigns are needed, the firm can obtain the services of an agency.

The opposite viewpoint is that a marketing position should be established as a senior, if not *the* senior, position in a professional firm. Many senior partners of even the smallest firm are known for their ability to obtain and retain clients. That is their primary function, and justifiably so, since the firm must have an adequate client base. The technical professional services are delegated throughout the firm, and the principal effort of the senior professional is to maintain and enhance client loyalty. The problem is that the duties and functions of that senior *marketing* position are often not clearly understood by the incumbent and may consist merely of client luncheons, goodwill calls, and meetings. Little effort may be made to measure tangible results of those activities. A dynamic senior-level marketing position, however, would include the following responsibilities:

1. Assessing the market. This includes developing formal reviews and obtaining statistics about client perceptions, market size, market share, segments and mix, fee levels, environment, client composition and attitudes, trends in professional services, marketing opportunities, and competition. These findings would be used by the firm to determine objectives.

2. Assisting in setting long-term and short-term objectives, particularly marketing objectives. Developing plans and implementing programs to attain those objectives (for example, increase annual gross revenues by 20 percent next year).

3. Managing the marketing program for the entire organization and responding to specific requests by other professionals and staff in the firm.

PUBLIC RELATIONS AND ADVERTISING

4. Acting as spokesman for the professional firm.
5. Acting as client advocate (or "market consciousness") for the firm—specifically, taking the client position when dealing with technically oriented professionals.
6. Handling all disputes between clients and the firm, including particularly concerns about the quality of professional work or the level of fees.
7. Mediating, arbitrating, coordinating, and handling all "public" responses and communications if the firm is subjected to bad publicity. Marketing professionals should be specifically trained to remain cool and level-headed during periods of crisis.
8. Providing marketing training to professionals and staff in the firm.

An organization chart for this type of position was shown in Figure 1-2.

There is a third alternative: The marketing position could be a staff position to support and make recommendations to professionals and staff members. The activities of the marketing function would be those requested by the firm. For instance, on request, special market research might be undertaken, a specific promotion program launched, or research undertaken to determine the viability of a proposed new branch office. The marketing function is set up as a service function to other positions in the professional firm (see Figure 15-1).

Marketing activities normally cover public relations, advertising, or specific research at the request of other professionals, but normally do not include ongoing research of client needs, accessability of professional services, development of new services, or attributes of existing services.

Public Relations

Public relations activities attempt to enchance the image of a professional firm. They normally include ongoing communications with clients and other regular publics, including people who make referrals. Generally speaking, these may take the form of bulletins, letters thanking people for referrals, entertainment, and visits to clients and others who can assist in the firm's growth. Many professionals feel that those are specialized staff functions and assign responsibility for these areas to a specific individual in the firm. Often the position is referred to as client services manager or client relations manager. Apart from managing the general

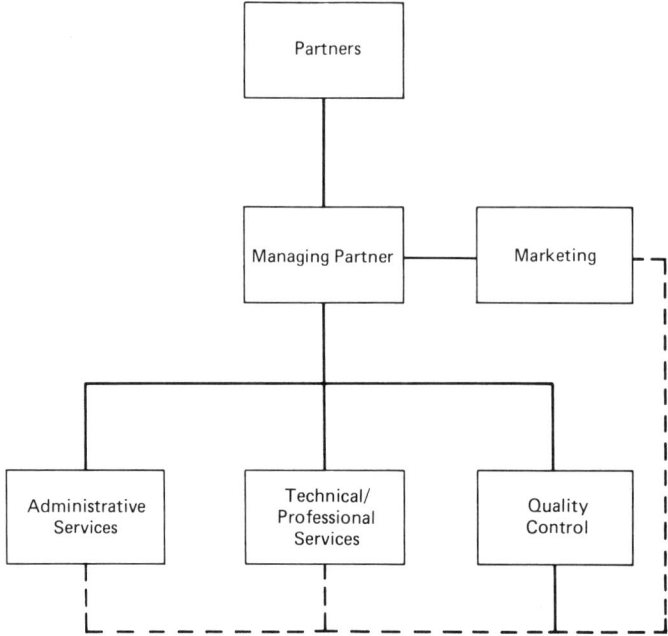

Figure 15-1.   Organization chart for a professional firm in which marketing is a service to other positions.

public relations efforts, this individual may also be responsible for handling client complaints. Seldom, however, do long-term market development plans exist, nor is a major effort directed at coordinating activities toward the long-term objectives of the professional firm. Little effort is directed at developing new professional services, raising the quality of professional services to meet continually changing market needs, assessing appropriate fee levels, or location considerations. The bulk of the effort is directed at promotion.

Advertising

Advertising is done to call attention to the firm's services. Expertise may be required in many applications. Mass media may be used, or there may be selective promotion and communication. An advertising specialist would usually be employed to design the message and direct its placement in appropriate media. Publicity for the firm would be carefully planned and orchestrated to estab-

PUBLIC RELATIONS AND ADVERTISING

lish it as a unique and preferred source of professional services. One of the major objectives of an advertising campaign would be to increase the market share of the professional firm.

In December 1975 a study was published by the Marketing Science Institute, Cambridge, Massachussetts, entitled "A Breakthrough in Strategic Planning." Although this was a study of commercial companies, the companies were from a wide variety of industries, and there is little reason to doubt that the findings are also applicable in a professional environment. The major conclusion reached was that profitability increased with increases in the share of the market. Almost irrespective of the size of the company, its net return increased dramatically with higher percentages of that market share (see Figure 15-2). Determination of market segment or "niche" is important, of course, but businesses with more than 36 percent of the market had a rate of return that was, on average, more than *three times higher* than that of businesses which had less than 7 percent of the market.

Particularly appropriate for smaller professional firms, however, was another conclusion that high quality can offset a low market share position. The rate of return was, in fact, similar where

Figure 15-2.   Net return on investment as a function of market share.

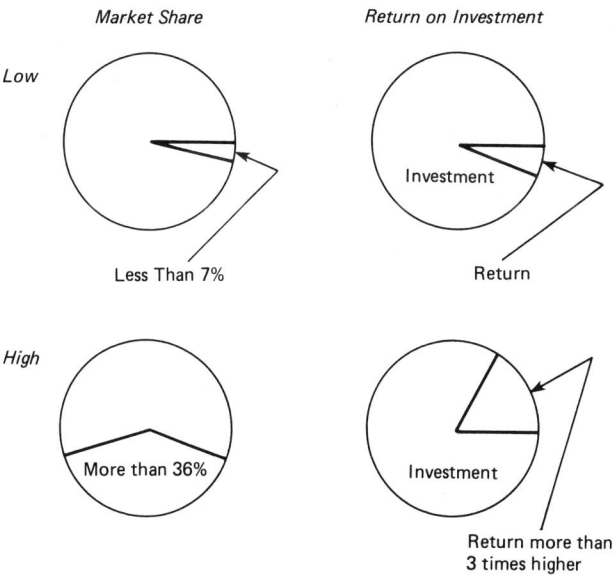

quality was superior but market share was low. Obviously, this implies that an objective must be built into the professional firm, and reiterated in an advertising campaign, to continually maintain and improve the quality of professional services. The advertising copy might show clients the tangible results of using the quality services of a specific firm.

An analysis of the target audience will assist the advertising professional in choosing appropriate media and techniques for the advertising program. Consideration must be given to advertising constraints imposed by the professional governing body, of course, but beyond that the professional should know whom he is trying to influence and how messages will be interpreted. He should know:

> The number of potential clients.
> Geographic location of clients.
> Client demographics, habits, and attitudes toward the profession.
> Client attitutes toward and responsiveness to various sales and promotion techniques.

Advertising and promotion can be tremendously expensive and considered wasteful unless tangible results can be seen. Advertising activities and results must be controlled.

A major constraint in developing an advertising campaign is financial. Specific budgeted amounts should be allocated for advertising and promotion purposes. These should be considered in terms of specific activities and results expected. A poor way to budget is to use a fixed annual amount for advertising expenses. Appropriate budgets should relate to proposed increases in revenues from offering increased services to current clients or from increasing the number of clients by some specific percentage. It is easier to set appropriate fee levels, coordinate advertising expenses, and establish a realistic goal for net income if there is a budget for the entire firm. Fixed advertising budgets often bring about inefficiency and waste. For instance, it is not unusual for a firm to find that 70 percent of a budget is unspent at the end of October and hurry to spend the allocation in November and December, the last two months of the fiscal year—sometimes without consideration of the advertising results. In many cases, furthermore, a campaign mounted in November or December is ineffective. For instance, accounting clients would be more receptive to a campaign during February, March, and April, because that is the time they are looking for tax advice.

Advertising results should be measured against specific objectives. Did the advertising campaign get 8 percent more revenue from existing clients through increased services? Did it bring in 10 percent more clients for engineering consultations? What was the cost of the campaign? Was it worth it, or could the campaign be more selective or otherwise improved?

The advertising strategy should be creative. Once a market niche is chosen, there should be consistency and continuity in the advertising theme. Again, this requires a well-defined target audience and a precise, short, simple, and memorable message.

The important criterion for advertising theme development is that it should provide the reader with immediate identification of the firm and its services. The advertising should convey a warm feeling and leave no doubt that the offering is true and genuine.

Themes should be consistently applied throughout the firm and in all advertising media. Exhibitions and/or displays during college career days, aimed at obtaining new professionals, should provide the same theme as newspaper copy. The literature in the reception area and discussions between clients and professionals should reinforce the theme.

Various media must be considered. Some professions are increasingly looking to television and radio as well as newspaper and magazine advertisements. Although the themes may be identical the individual advertisements must be clearly different for each medium. Target audiences must be considered. In relation to economic cost per coverage of a target audience, nontraditional forms of advertising may be considered. There has been research carried out to suggest, for instance, that it takes six or more regular insertions in business and professional magazines to obtain significant advertising results. These are for regular full- or partial-page advertisements, not an innocuous listing under a "professional directory" category with hundreds of other such listings.

Television is an increasingly important medium, for the obvious reasons that it provides tremendously wide coverage of a target audience and has great impact. Although it is costly, it may in fact be less expensive per target individual than repeated newspaper or magazine advertisements.

Direct mail, while much more expensive per thousands of target clients covered in an advertising campaign, can also be the most effective and cost beneficial medium. In smaller firms, tight budget constraints may make this the ideal medium. The major advantage is that it is targeted to the individual reader sought by the firm. Mass mailings may achieve the same sort of response that hundreds of other unsolicited mailings get; however they're often not read—and ultimately destroyed. There is evidence that a 3 percent response to a general direct mail campaign is high. This might be improved, however, when letters are specifically addressed and respond to specific needs of potential or current clients. Word processors and computers can facilitate this individualized and selective approach by allowing each form letter to be addressed and typed as an original. This might be particularly appropriate for announcing new services to existing clients, and the opening of a new office to potential clients. It may also be more effective than photocopied press releases to the media.

Opening a New Firm or Branch Office

One of the most interesting applications of the market-based approach is the opening of a new professional office. It is quite amazing that many professional firms start without any program or premarketing strategy. Occasionally, discussions are held with colleagues and other people in the same profession. These discussions form the only basis for a long-term commitment, and yet are the guides used to determine the eventual success or failure of the practice. Three days may be all the time taken by a professional to analyze the potential before going into practice. Yet it may take years to get out of that practice if the decision was wrong. The practice may go for years at subprofitable levels. Professionals may become dissatisfied and lose interest.

Professionals have suffered enormous financial hardship by giving little consideration to long-term requirements for opening an office. Certainly, a large potential client base is necessary—the market must be there. There are, however, many procedures that even the smallest professional firm might use to pretest and premarket the firm. These tools will not only help in determining the market but also provide exposure to critical factors and to people who can help the firm realize its potential. Assuming that the firm has no clients, the greatest potential for development will be those people who have the capability to refer clientele.

Here is an approach a market-oriented professional might use:

FIRST MONTH
I. Present a professional image. Know who you are and where you want to go. Approach people who can provide referrals (feeders) and request their advice on the potential for a new firm. For instance, other professional firms are unlikely to know about areas where there is need for service, specialization, timeliness, convenient location, or whatever. If they knew, they might be positioned there themselves. Feeders, however, will know what services, quality, fee structure, and timeliness of service are important to potential clientele. They are also likely to know who those potential clients are. If you are in the accounting profession, bankers and lawyers will be major informants on the quality and reliability of professional accounting firms. This approach allows:

> Environmental analysis.
> Analysis of the competition.
> To a certain extent, potential client analysis.
> Early identification of a "niche" with unmet demand.

Most important, it establishes initial contact. Ask these individuals to keep your discussions in confidence. Seek advice and guidance from as many of these professionals as possible. Find out who else could be of assistance in your decision. This is not in violation of any code of ethics—it is just good business sense. If opportunities are abundant, proceed to step II.

II. Approach leading people in the community in which you wish to provide service to obtain their perception of opportunities for opening an office. Again, ask for confidentiality. If opportunities are abundant, proceed to step III. If they indicate that there are no opportunities, reposition the firm or change location. These are potential clients saying *no*—so don't open.

SECOND MONTH
III. Approach those same people and ask their advice about the location of the office, the structure of the firm, and services to be offered. You are designing the firm according to their perceptions, and for their benefit. You do not solicit their support, but you are letting them know that you are concerned about being responsive.

Third Month

IV. Return to those same people and let them know you have *taken their advice* as to location, services, fees, and so forth, and intend to open the office at the beginning of the fifth month. You are letting them know that their input was important and had a bearing on your decision. Ask them to still keep the proposed opening in confidence.

Fourth Month

V. Organize work programs, office design, layout, library, reception area, professional support, image, and advertising campaigns, on the basis of that initial market research. Target for completion by the beginning of the fifth month. Include plans for an opening reception—all in confidence, if possible.

Fifth Month

VI. Give a reception in your office for the people who have given you that invaluable advice. For most people, a convenient time is 3 P.M. to 8 P.M. on a Friday evening. You will be surprised at how many will come because of an opportunity to obtain referrals for themselves, as well as to be welcomed in a professional environment. The decor, the library, the reception, the literature, and everything in the firm should suggest a dedication to client service. Possibly have the reception professionally hosted.

VII. Coinciding with the opening, provide mail notification and advertisements to target publics and specifically target clients.

What you may have done, in one well-designed program, that neither was too expensive nor violated any ethics, is to create a favorable market buzz. Clients and others will be talking about the new firm, because its opening is a newsworthy event.

There are three reasons for requesting confidence from the people with whom you have discussions:

1. So as not to provide advance notice to potential competitors —although you may wish to invite them to the opening reception.

2. To let those people know that their advice is important. Also, to allow them to be part of a conspiracy—we all love to be party to intrigue.

3. To release all marketing tools, advertising campaigns, and

strategy to gain maximum market impact and penetration. The opening of a new professional office will become newsworthy only if it comes as a complete surprise to the general public or, more specifically, key target clientele.

There are a number of other subtle benefits to this strategy of opening a new professional office, not the least of which is that you will be "known" where it counts, before the opening. Potential clients usually discuss a professional with a third party before approaching the firm. They want some assurance of professional quality and concern for their well-being.

Without a preopening strategy, the best assurance potential clients might get from third parties is "I don't know, I have never even met the professional." The worst would be "He must be a young upstart; we have been dealing with our friend Dr. X for years, and he has always provided satisfactory professional services."

If a premarketing strategy is used, the worse comment might be a neutral, "No comment—I have not seen the results of their work." More likely, the comments will be positive and even enthusiastic. "I met the professionals and they seem to know where they are going. They have a sense of purpose. They are concerned with the well-being of their clientele. They have good business sense (to pretest the market). They very carefully structured the firm to be responsive to client needs. (I know, they asked me how and then followed my advice.)"

Part II

Strategic Planning

16

Establishing Market-Based Goals and Objectives

In North America, less than 10 percent of our population has firm goals, and less than 3 percent commits its life-goals to writing. There is no reason to believe that professionals have a better record. Yet, current research in social sciences provides overwhelming case evidence that successful individuals are strong goal-setters—they know exactly where they are going. With this powerful tool they have a strong capability of searching out resources to assist them in the accomplishment of their goals.

Some of the market goals that might be set by a professional are: to have the ability to recognize clients' service needs and expectations and to meet those needs in a highly competent manner; to make a reasonable profit while doing so; to learn and grow in all respects, including resources, competence, and income; and to contribute to the growth of the total profession.

Most social scientists would recommend that when a person goes through a goal-setting process, he build a balanced set of objectives at a personal as well as professional level. For instance, you might at the same time plan the direction of your family relationships and social, religious, and health-related activities.

As with any program, the planning process requires thought and effort. Very briefly, the steps in goal setting are as follows:

Set objectives.
Plan how to attain them.
Accept feedback—monitor progress and be willing to change.
Review and revise goals constantly.

Rules for Goal Setting

1. Goal setting should be balanced between professional and personal goals.
2. Goals should be consistent and synergistic—goals that are set at counter-purposes would cause stress and conflict.
3. Goals should be constructive, building toward results. A goal-directed individual should see constructive and positive end results that have a value to him.
4. Once goals are clearly defined, specific programs to accomplish them should be implemented.
5. The goals should be something that an organization or an individual is comfortable with, because in the end that individual or organization must accept accountability.
6. Plan and allow for free time.
7. Keep personal goals confidential.
8. Goals should be reviewed and modified regularly on the basis of feedback obtained.
9. Goals should be written, particularly in an organization, so that the statement of main purpose, or mission, can be distributed throughout the organization to ensure that everyone will work in the same direction.
10. It is extremely important that goals be read and reviewed regularly.
11. Goals should be ordered by importance so that effort will be directed toward the major goals more than the less important goals.

Motivation

In his model of social hierarchical behavior, Maslow states that human beings respond first to physiological needs, second, to safety needs, third, to the need for love, fourth, as they mature, to the need for self-esteem, and fifth, the need for self-actualization. A person who has met his self-actualization need is assertive but responsive and in full control of his life. It is important to note that this level of maturity is not reached unless the more basic needs are met.

The same sort of conceptual model can be built for an organization. By way of example, a professional firm might start by going through what we have called the survival stage—a period of perhaps two years. When a professional firm or office initially opens, there is a period during which new clients must be brought in, administrative details organized, and an increasing profit and return to the principals or professionals shown. If, after that period, there is no adequate return for a professional, he will usually opt to leave the practice and return to a clinical environment or employment.

There are cases, however, where a professional stays on for years in a survival-type atmosphere. A very real problem for a professional working in this type of environment is that all effort and drive is placed on earning enough money to keep going. Little effort is directed at research, growth, and continued professional development.

The second level of development in a professional office is the comfort stage. The professional makes enough money to maintain a comfortable standard of living. He has an increased sense of self-worth, and the office is reflecting that mood. The professional feels that he knows his clients' needs and expectations.

His marketing methods may be based on the selling approach and be somewhat self-aggrandizing. He generally feels he has satisfied clients—they get what they pay for.

The third level might be entitled the control stage. The professional feels that he is now responsible for directing the growth and development of the practice, and he usually becomes more involved in planning the direction of the growth of the practice. There are usually steps taken also in budgetary areas. Interestingly enough, that difference in attitude comes through in other areas of the practice, including administrative areas. Lawyers and accountants often phone their clients to remind them of government filing deadlines for tax or legal purposes, and eventually this becomes an established procedure. Similarly, doctors and dentists often call their patients to remind them of annual medical or dental checks, and so on. The practice has an increasing income, and the survival of the firm is no longer a concern. The practice is earning a fair return on investment as well as a fair salary for the professionals—something beyond a comfortable level of earnings. The professional, as a businessman, recognizes that this is fair, since there is a risk involved in practicing any profession. The sense of self-esteem suffuses the practice.

It is important to note that the marketing effort has steadily shifted from one of selling to one of services. At the control stage the professional is concerned with his clients' needs. For instance, he is concerned that tax filings be done on time, or that a patient be reminded to have his medical or dental checkup. Clients and patients usually reinforce this change by thanking the practice for calling, and the staff of the professional takes pride in searching for new ways to help clients or patients.

These types of actions result in practice growth, in terms of new clients or patients as well as expanded services to existing clients. That is very interesting, because the services and concerns expressed for clients are very human-oriented rather than technically oriented.

The fourth level of practice development was the client-responsive practice. A professional practice at this level has fully adopted the marketing concept. The professional is inclined to discuss with clients and patients what their needs and expectations are. The professional often obtains the comments of clients or patients on many things concerning the practice. There might be discussions about developing the practice in an area of service which the client might like to see expanded, or about such simple matters as what periodicals and articles might be placed on the coffee table in the reception room.

What has happened, in effect, is that the practice matured over a number of years to become a progressive, dynamic, responsive professional organization using the marketing concept.

If a professional had decided, when starting his practice, to adopt the market concept and the concept of a client-responsive practice, the firm would have succeeded at this much earlier.

Inventory of Personal Characteristics

In the self-actualization process, it is important that the firm choose the type of clients it wants and the types of services it wishes to provide. We all know that we succeed best at those things which we enjoy doing. As a starting point in the goal-setting process, the firm should analyze its strengths and weaknesses. An individual professional might write a resumé of the work that he had done and the types of employers he had worked with. He should include his outside learning experiences as well, both formal and informal ones. He may have worked with small voluntary organizations or a church or a sport camp. If his daily activities somehow relate to those things that he has done successfully in the past, increased productivity and enjoyment from the profession should ensue.

In a professional organization that is goal- and results-oriented, the same principles apply. We should build on our strengths and remove problem areas. In his book *Management for Results*, Peter Drucker reinforces these thoughts in an organizational setting.

A word of caution. It is not too unusual for an individual who is going through a lot of introspection and planning and taking a fresh look at his career to decide to leave his profession totally, as he may discover that he has chosen it for the wrong reasons and may no longer be comfortable with it. Empirical evidence suggests that about 10 percent of the individuals who go through this sort of program leave their current position or profession. The other 90 percent, however, by the very process strongly reaffirm their personal commitment to the profession.

Planning for the Professional Firm

Three philosophies can be considered in a firm's planning, and these will reflect the attitudes of the professionals and their willingness to grow through the acceptance of challenge and change:

1. Satisfying planning—planning to achieve some level of satisfaction but not to exceed it. ("To do well enough, not necessarily as well as possible.")
2. Optimizing planning—planning to do as well as possible. This usually involves construction of models to simulate inputs and results.
3. Adaptive planning (often called innovative planning)—planning to develop and exploit the opportunities and potentials available to a firm.

In order to be effective, goals and objectives must be set at the top professional level and have the following characteristics:

1. Be stated in definite terms and as precisely as possible.
2. Reflect as much as possible the goals of the majority of individuals within the firm, with due consideration to "weighing" the value of the individuals to the firm.
3. Provide direction throughout the organization to maximize the utilization of resources.
4. Reflect a composite of personal, economic, and social considerations.
5. Be general enough not to require frequent revision, but not inflexible to new conditions.
6. Provide a clear basis for programs for their achievement.

The example in the Appendix to this chapter is for a professional firm; however, the same procedures for the establishment of goals and objectives may be applied in any organization. The goal-setting process can apply equally in a commercial or noncommercial (or even government) environment. The example is merely given to provide a practical example of a procedure that is usually addressed only in academic or theoretical terms.

This type of strategic planning is designed not only to forecast the future, but to control it—it must come from, be supported by, and be believed by the top professionals in the firm.

APPENDIX: SAMPLE GOALS AND OBJECTIVES FOR AN ACCOUNTING FIRM

BASIC OBJECTIVE (Main Mission):
 Our basic objective is to provide quality professional services for our clients at the lowest possible rates consistent with the maintenance of professional standards, fair compensation to our employees, and a fair return to those who have provided debt and equity capital necessary to provide the resources to operate our firm, maintain our jobs, and provide for the continuance of the firm.

This type of statement provides broad definition for management decision making. It is market-based, since it considers the interest of the clients (publics) first. But is must be made more specific to allow selection of specific targets, precise plans, and well-defined budgets. These subobjectives, or goals, might be stated as follows:

SUBOBJECTIVE 1:   Increased Public Confidence
 We strive to achieve the full confidence of our clients and the public.

This objective has been stated in very simple terms. However, the attitude and work toward obtaining confidence reach into every area of the firm. There is always the need to be courteous and professional in our relationship with everyone with whom we come into contact. This concern must be addressed in the way we answer the telephone, the appearance of our offices, the appearance and standards of our typed correspondence, the dress code of the staff, the use of modern, efficient office equipment, and the continued education of the professionals and staff to increase the quality and types of services to better respond to ever growing client needs and expectations. The firm must be willing to recognize those client needs and meet them in a highly competent and professional manner.

The area of building public confidence should also include outside activities. The firm, its professionals, and its employees should be encouraged to contribute time and/or money to projects that will improve the community served by the firm, including elected positions, provided these duties do not conflict with the firm's needs.

SUBOBJECTIVE 2:   Quality Professional Services
We strive to provide the highest-quality and most timely services to our clients, with a reasonable balance between the cost and value to our clients and to the firm.

We sell services, and this is done by providing quality and timely services and advice, as well as by the innumerable other contacts between the staff and all members of the public. "Highest-quality and timely services" refers to the kind of service which would be given if there were another firm across the street that was ready, willing, and able to take our clients away from us.

It is important to maintain a balance—good service costs money, and if we are to remain competitive, the costs of providing unusually demanding services must be considered.

SUBOBJECTIVE 3:   Lowest Possible Rates
We strive to charge the lowest possible rates for our services.

Competitive pricing will help ensure the maximum economic growth of the firm, both through increased value of services to existing clients and through increasing market share. Low rates can come only from increased efficiency coupled with aggressive marketing aimed at increasing the number of clients and the services offered those clients.

Low rates come directly from that high efficiency with the ability to delegate tasks and responsibility commensurate with the type and quality of work, reliability, promptness, and continuity. This largely comes from attracting, training, and maintaining competent, dedicated, and loyal employees (see subobjective 4).

SUBOBJECTIVE 4:   Fair Compensation to Our Employees.

We should provide wages, benefits, and a working climate which favorably compare to those of other local businesses and professional firms.

1. Our job is to operate as efficiently and effectively as possible.
2. High staff turnover is expensive in quality of service as well as costs.
3. We compete with other employers for competent staff.
4. The strength of the firm depends largely on our employees.

We believe that the continued efficiency and effectiveness of the firm requires the continued support of high-quality staff, and stability—and this requires fair compensation policies. Our objective is to be at the upper end of payment for wages and benefits in our community. Our job is to work efficiently so we can afford it.

In order to accomplish these objectives, we continually monitor wages and benefits in our community. We provide for regular salary reviews, at a minimum annually, with provision for merit increases as well as cost-of-living adjustments. There is also provision for bonuses for exceptional effort.

Major benefits include liberal vacation policies, group life insurance, and major medical insurance.

We also strive toward a sound and logical organization so that everyone understands his job requirements and can contribute to the overall objectives. We also expect and solicit open expression of ideas and opinions, free from unpleasant responses.

SUBOBJECTIVE 5:   Maintenance of Professional Standards

We strive to maintain our professional standards and to improve our competence to service our clients on a continuous basis.

We recognize that our profession is dynamic and that requirements and standards are in a constant state of evolution. The response to this environment must involve the continuing exposure and education of all professionals and staff.

Maintenance of standards requires continuous reading of new releases about and in our profession. It also requires attendance at various professional continuing education functions. This involvement should not be restricted to the professional staff but be extended, where practical and appropriate, to all staff. The firm facilitates this objective by paying registration fees for the professional educational needs of its staff.

We also recognize that the maintenance of standards extends to the continual review and updating of forms, office work flow, policies, procedures, standards, and so on.

SUBOBJECTIVE 6:   Effective and Efficient Operation
We strive to develop and operate our firm to provide reliable service, efficiency, and low costs of operation.

We must take full advantage of any improvement in administration, management, procedures, and technique. We will continually be able to originate and accept new ideas in operating methods and systems development and systematize and delegate these programs as soon as practicable. This requires devoting time and money to research and development of procedures that will improve efficiency.

SUBOBJECTIVE 7:   Change and Growth of the Firm
We must expand our firm if we are to remain dynamic and healthy. This expansion must include expanding services available to existing clients as well as attracting new clients. Our specific growth targets should be higher than our competitors'—we should strive to increase our share of the total market for professional services in our community.

In our marketing and promotional activities we must place emphasis on markets with the highest potential for the greatest profitability. This allows us to improve wages and profitability, and ultimately to maintain lower fees for our clients.

We must always be competitive, so meeting this goal requires constant vigilance for new techniques and developments to improve efficiency (see also subobjective 6).

SUBOBJECTIVE 8:   Improve Earnings (Profit)
We strive to continually improve earnings to provide a fair return to our professionals and debtors, to protect their investment, and to improve the value of the firm.

There is a need to show continuous improvements in net earnings if the firm is to keep pace with inflation, grow, and hold its own against competition. To provide a fair return to the principals and investors, the growth in earnings should average 20 percent [fill in as appropriate] over the next few years—10 percent to cover inflation, and 10 percent real growth through new services to new clients.

The principals expect an increase and continued growth in earnings as the firm grows. As a matter of policy, some of those earnings are retained in the firm to finance further growth and improve services. It is only normal for profits to be higher to cover that increased investment. The principals also expect to be compensated for the higher risk coincident with the firm's growth, since some of the growth may be financed by personally guaranteeing further borrowings from lending institutions. There would be little incentive to have the firm expand and grow without those increased earnings, and it would be increasingly difficult to finance expansion through borrowings.

17

Designing a Market-Based Professional Firm

In this chapter we shall discuss the development of the marketing concept, including an overview of the production attitude, the sales attitude, and the fully responsive marketing attitude. We will discuss an erroneous viewpoint that marketing is a tactical activity. Marketing is not necessarily a function or a department but an attitude which permeates the whole professional firm.

We will discuss the implementation of attitudinal changes leading to the development of a fully responsive professional organization. We will spend considerable time on staff motivation and involvement, as this may be the critical area needing the most improvement in many professional firms.

The Marketing Concept

The modern, progressive professional practice has passed through several stages in its development. Initially, professional practices had a production orientation (provision of service), subsequently a sales orientation (creating a demand for service), and more recently a marketing orientation (serving a need).

The marketing attitude began to come into prominence in the 1950s within industry with the advent of such techniques as market surveys through market research, market structure analysis, customer analysis, and service or product analysis, together with psychological pricing considerations.

Service Attitude

Prior to the early 1900s there was great demand in the marketplace for professional services and there were few professionals to meet the demand. Educational institutions were simply unable to supply enough doctors, dentists, lawyers, accountants, and so on, particularly in the remote areas of rural North America. At this juncture of development, potential clients needed the services and were willing to pay whatever "fair" fee might be required. In this type of scarcity economy, a professional might concentrate on finding ways to increase his services while maintaining or reducing his costs. The professional's effort to extend his services to more people and improve the efficiency with which they are given is known as service orientation. In this type of economic environment, there is little or no need for market research or advertising, as the service needs of clients are well defined.

There was little or no effort to measure client satisfaction, because professional services were kept simple. Occasionally the quality of the services was scaled down to meet the demand (that is, less time was spent on each client appointment, and spurious advice might be given, as there were always a number of other clients waiting to see the professional). Many professionals felt that this demand for their services would continue indefinitely and that there would be an ever increasing number of clients seeking their services. Often very little effort was taken to ascertain whether any client needs other than for the services requested were satisfied. Nor was any effort made to examine the growth of clients' needs and expectations from the profession.

Sales Attitude

The sales concept is the service or production attitude backed by promotion and selling, thus generating a higher client volume as the key to increasing practice income. It is based on the following premises:

1. The key to a successful professional practice is to obtain a sufficient number of clients for its services.
2. The client can be induced to obtain services through various promotion devices.
3. The client will probably return for repeat services. If he doesn't, there are many other clients waiting for the service.

As the North American economy grew toward affluence, clients were able to obtain sufficient professional services, because educational institutions provided professionals in ever increasing numbers. Also, clients had additional resources available to purchase professional services according to their needs and expectations. Professional firms facing uncertainty about the level of demand or needs for their services were anxious to use all of their productive capabilities. For the professions, this meant an increased investment in market stimulation, including advertising (where allowed), client promotion, well-appointed offices, and relatively easy credit terms for slow-paying clients. Efforts were made to get clients to accept the services the professional firm had available.

The sales attitude is well known among the professions. Management consultants, lawyers, and accountants spend vast sums of money on golf club fees, dinner clubs, travel, and client entertainment—supposedly to enhance "client goodwill." A great deal of time and effort are spent by the professional in these areas in order to obtain clients and keep them. There is little effort to measure what the client's needs and expectations are, and a lot of effort to get the client to accept the services offered by the professional. Professionals in this category spend a great deal of time not in listening, but in making self-aggrandizing statements.

The major risk that a professional organization takes in practicing with a sales attitude is that the service offerings will become outdated or their credibility strained. By not watching carefully the evolving changes in clients' needs, the professional services may become increasingly irrelevant and therefore increasingly difficult to sell. The professional will face the need to increase his investment in market stimulation still further, with diminishing results. Furthermore, the offering will not produce the expected satisfaction. Clients will increasingly distrust future messages. They will speak badly of the offering to others. They will see the profession as using them rather than serving them.

Marketing Attitude

A growing number of professions are beginning to perceive the limitations of the production and sales attitudes as stimulants for professional firms' growth. They are beginning to recognize that a professional firm would do better if it tried to serve a need rather than sell a service. They are beginning to see their clients as real people who are trying to satisfy real needs. The progressive professional firm's job is to find out these needs and organize its service lines and programs to satisfy these needs. It is easier to sell what clients want than to get the client to buy the services the firm wants to sell. Some professions have begun to invest heavily in client research to measure client needs and satisfaction.

In summary, the marketing concept for a professional is *an orientation to clients' needs, backed by integrated marketing aimed at generating client satisfaction as the key to satisfying professional goals.*

Obtaining and Developing a Client-Responsive Professional Staff

Any person may have a tendency to develop a complacent attitude, particularly if he has been at the same job, in the same firm, or with the same clients over many years. Quite aside from the prerequisite technical skills an individual brings to a position, he should develop an attitude of responsiveness if he is to be successful and, ultimately, happy in dealing with clients. This requires that a professional bring to each engagement or assignment:

A fresh viewpoint.
A "personal touch."
Responsive (active) listening skills.
Fast and reliable responses to information needs.
Interpersonal communications and skills.

Learning to be responsive to clients' needs is difficult in a changing environment when one is faced with the same routines, policies, and procedures year after year. When an engagement is first attained a professional brings a fresh perspective. He takes an objective, critical look at the entire problem of providing client service. Those reactions are immediate. However, a dynamic professional realizes that the client does not always recognize his needs for change. He should write his initial reaction in a file immediately. This is an invaluable future reference and may allow the professional to introduce change slowly in the future. If the firm's procedures, policies, attitudes, and systems can be improved, the "first impression" of a knowledgeable professional will often highlight this. If years are spent dealing with poor procedures, there is a tendency to lose the fresh perspective and view them as acceptable (they've always been used). A professional may lose a certain amount of healthy professional skepticism.

On analysis, there are many ways to bring a fresh viewpoint to an "old job." The following questions may be helpful.

1. Has a consultant been hired recently to give an objective, impartial, third-party viewpoint?

2. Has the professional involved had the opportunity to go to a retreat to allow rest to bring about a new perspective?

3. Is there a program for "working sabbaticals" so that the professional can look at the other firms in a similar profession, but in different departments, jurisdictions (often different countries), and "noncompetitive" businesses as well as libraries?

4. Is job rotation in effect? Some larger firms grant fully or partially paid sabbaticals for six to twelve months every five, ten, or twenty years. Job rotation of employees can provide a veritable gold mine of new perspectives.

5. The professional should always look for effective time-saving techniques, "shortcuts," and more efficient operating procedures.

6. How often are client services reviewed? The chief executive officer of a large organization is often so involved in day-to-day activities that he does not have the opportunity to provide a remote and objective approach.

Attendance at continuing professional education seminars, for both staff and the professional, can also often provide fresh insights into procedures that would result in a more profitable and/or efficient professional firm. Finally, staff training and staff input can provide an invaluable source to meet client needs and examine procedural effectiveness. Some professional firms conduct detailed surveys among their staff to allow this invaluable feedback.

In order to be responsive, a professional must keep ongoing contact throughout his firm and with clients. This involves not only personal contact with personnel but also getting acquainted with all facets of the client's operation. Initially, it takes a great deal of time to establish personal contact and become familiar with client procedures. However, once this is done, it is not too difficult to maintain contact and be up to date on all relevant aspects of the client's business.

Some larger firms are now assisting in establishing initial contact and structuring dialog between their own and client personnel through training programs. Very often these seminars initially deal with organizational behavior, leadership, or communications —general topics to allow wide participation. Participation, however, is restricted so that there is only one participant from each department in the firm. The program is not dominated by one group, which enable participants to learn about other services offered by the firm and to develop a team approach to overcome client problems. This often leads to the "multidisciplinary" approach as a tool for overcoming client problems in the longer run through the subsequent use of a task force consisting of staff of both the professional firm and the client organization. In addition to that possible benefit, the training programs also help build a team spirit between the firm and its clientele—an "esprit de corps," which many trainers feel is even more important than the learning of the seminar topic itself.

Another vehicle is an interdisciplinary in-house training program. This requires that the firm's staff, even though not involved in an operating facet of a client's operation, attend programs on that facet. For instance, the head of the client firm's department could give a talk or lead a workshop on major administrative facets of his operation and provide an overview of his department's *technical* programs. He may mention areas, in a constructive fashion, in which he is having problems with the professional firm. This may be his only chance to complain directly to those who may help in overcoming the problems, since some of the participants would be from the staff of the professional firm.

Quite aside from the above-mentioned programs, a professional should use his own initiative in keeping up with other departments if he is employed in a large firm, and keeping up with changes in his client's affairs. This involves simply keeping in touch to learn about the client's problems. A short meeting, luncheon, or telephone call is often all that is necessary. However, since it is easy for this to slip off a "priority list" with the pressures for short-term job results, it is important to schedule these contacts well in advance and give them priority once they come due. This should be done at appropriate intervals, say every two to three months.

This form of developing interpersonal relations is a major ingredient in building a successful professional firm.

Acting as a "sounding board" for client problems may be one of the biggest needs that can be met by a professional. In professional practice, a client often has no one other than his professional with whom to discuss business or personal matters.

Sometimes professionals give the impression that they are interested only in the technical aspects of the job—in the case of accountants, for example, financial statements and their analysis, or specialized tax matters—and not in the client's other problems. This is unfortunate, since it does not allow the professional the opportunity to assist the client in other areas. It can be an interesting challenge to range far afield from the traditional professional service functions and get interested and involved in all aspects of a client's organization or life.

Professional firms, over time, often develop elaborate and cumbersome policies and operating procedures. These may result in higher professional standards because of the control placed on staff and professionals in the firm. The problem often is that by the time reports are available to clientele, a lengthy period has elapsed during which corrective action could have been taken. Lost opportunities and lost profits if the client was a business client, lengthy suffering for medical clients, and the worry of waiting for a legal opinion add to the client's burden when he deals with tardy professional firms.

A professional might review his client's needs for quick information—those areas in which fast corrective action is important—and introduce procedures to get that information out to clients as fast as possible. For example, clients are not as interested in receiving full typed statements late as they are in getting operating information early—a quick telephone call or penciled draft will allow them time to make operating decisions. Similarly, in a computerized environment, a vast amount of information is usually available fast—but there is often so much that there is an information overload, and by the time the reports are digested, several days (or weeks, or even months) may have elapsed, during which corrective action might have been taken. A professional might review a client's information need with the client's managers to develop key information packages—brief, often one-page, summaries of key information on which immediate action can be taken.

Some professionals are criticized because information is entered in the firm's files and little thought is given to the client's information needs. A quick telephone call to a client immediately the information is available and fast response in providing professional services can go a long way toward cementing client relations.

A professional essentially deals with people and their problems. To be successful, he must learn the "art of dealing with people" as well as the "art of the profession." Shying away from personal contact with clients does not allow the professional to develop so that he can better assist the client. A professional should be a keen observer of human nature, truly enjoy helping people with problems, and be willing to accept and deal with people as they are.

Marketing Departments

To attain a professional firm's marketing objectives, a marketing mix must be struck so that there is balance between the major program components—types of services, location, fee levels, and promotion activities—for major clientele segments.

Many firms would argue that each of their individual professional and staff members should be sensitive enough to client needs and expectations so that there is no need for a formal marketing department in the professional firm. Other firms would argue that marketing is such an important and sophisticated function that responsibility should rest with an entire department under the direction of the senior partner. The major proponents of this point of view would argue that:

1. There is the tendency for other professionals and staff to become so engrossed in the function of providing professional services that they lose their objective view of major market changes and directions.

2. Staff must be trained, and the marketing function must be managed and coordinated so that it is cohesive and consistent throughout the firm.

3. Only a senior partner, responsible for marketing, could assist in determining marketing objectives and strategies and have the authority to redirect the firm and/or its staff and other resources.

4. Only a senior partner might have the experience and knowledge to ascertain major relevant facts about the market environment, mix, segmentation, and patterns of change. Only a senior partner could convince other partners of the need for new directions and changes within the firm.

A third alternative—a balanced approach—is to set up a marketing department as a staff service function, charged with providing market research support to the firm and assisting in the development of promotional campaigns. The department might also assist the firm in making the other professionals and staff aware of the value of client relations, as well in providing a review of client problems.

Most professional firms operate without a marketing department, or without making any individual partner responsible for the marketing function. Most often the function is but part of the many activities of the managing partner. The pressure of other duties, plus a lack of marketing expertise—the managing partner was often trained as an accountant, engineer, lawyer, or doctor—may result in the entire function not being effectively managed.

Even those firms which employ partners whose major responsibility is client relations do not manage the entire function. "Client relations" partners are responsible mostly for maintaining a positive image with existing clients and for professional development or exposure of the firm to potential clients or those who can make referrals. There is little attempt to measure client needs, expectations, or preferences. Little attempt is made to introduce new, or change existing, professional services. The function is often designed to mollify clients who are unhappy with the existing level of service.

Still, many large professional firms do set up a marketing function. For instance, in the July 17, 1978, issue of *Fortune* magazine, an article appeared titled "Competition Comes to Accounting." The discussion centered around the development of marketing activities of the then "Big Eight" accounting firms—Arthur Andersen, Arthur Young, Coopers & Lybrand, Deloitte Haskins & Sells, Ernst & Ernst, Peat Marwick Mitchell, Price Waterhouse, Touche Ross. No doubt the article was the cause of considerable controversy in the accounting profession, particularly when the competitive tactics used by some firms appeared to be very traditional selling approaches rather than market-based approaches.

Certainly, large professional firms have the resources to establish a marketing department. There may be more consistent demand and need to coordinate marketing activities because of the firm's size. However, even the smallest firms are beginning to recognize marketing as a separate function. Even though no department as such may exist, marketing will be assigned to the managing partner and become an increasingly important part of his responsibilities.

A professional firm must consider the effort, ability, motivation, and morale of staff and professionals in dealing with client needs. It may consider staff training in these areas.

Marketing is a "specialized" function and should be organized along the lines of the specialized types of services or clientele that the firm hopes to attract or retain. Only then can target objectives be set for specific segments, and programs to evaluate accomplishment be introduced. The firm would also consider whether its marketing effort and client-oriented services are sufficient to obtain the results it desires.

Staff Motivation

One of the most surprising facts in many professional firms is their lack of understanding of the importance of the staff and employees in the firm.

"Partners say hello and acknowledge my presence for about two days. After that they simple ignore me.... I feel like a piece of furniture.... I don't know whether that is a result of their professional training, or simply conceit. To be honest, after those two days I lose interest in the partners and the firm. However, I try very hard to maintain an empathy for the firm's clients, even though I don't feel supported in this by my [professional] bosses."

That quote is from a secretarial employee of a professional firm whose professionals pride themselves as leading consulting psychologists.

Every professional firm must obtain certain results. Certainly, profitability is one of the most important if a firm is to remain viable and in business for a long period. In the final analysis, those results in profits can be achieved only by the firm's employees. The firm therefore has a vested interest in seeing to it that its employees are motivated to create the desired profitability.

Perhaps the most difficult question to answer is, how do we motivate? There is no simple, clear-cut set of guidelines or rules. Motivation deals with what it takes to create a desired action, even when many factors are unknown. Emotions, short-term or long-term requirements, personal preference, the weather, how someone is getting along with his spouse, and other seemingly unimportant factors could play a very important role in how a person achieves results himself or through others. What a professional perceives as important to an employee may differ from what the employee considers important.

This often means that the professional has to learn new skills if he is to effecitvely motivate his employees. Social sciences address some of the problems which people have in communicating and in managing group relationships. Seminars and night school programs abound on such topics as assertive management, transactional analysis, employee communications, successful contract negotiation, time management, and achieving human potential. The topic of group dynamics dominates many management education programs.

One motivator that might be used with the new generation of employees is to make jobs worthwhile so as to build the self-esteem of the employee. *Job enrichment* is a deliberate effort to restructure the job to give an employee more variety, challenge, and a sense of accomplishment. Not all jobs can or should be enriched. This concept involves bringing the job content up to the ambition and skill of the worker hired to do the job.

The employee must derive a feeling of achievement or accomplishment from the work he is doing. He must feel that the job he is doing is worthwhile, interesting, and challenging. Finally, the employee must receive recognition for a job well done.

If work becomes engrossing, pleasurable, and interesting, positive motivation will occur. These conditions don't come easily. They can be enhanced by a supervisor who is trying to increase an employee's job responsibility. The professional will ultimately develop productive and satisfied employees through job enrichment, but it can pose problems. It requires considerable planning and in some cases is feared by professionals who see it as a threat to their own security and status. Also, some employees may resist it because they actually prefer very simple, repetitive tasks. It is important, therefore, to give adequate consideration to individual differences, as this is the key to getting along with and motivating individual employees.

One of the dangers of job enrichment is that a professional may think of it as job *enlargement.* Enlargement involves assigning more duties, in the belief that a greater variety of tasks will make the job more interesting. Unfortunately, simply expanding the number of tasks done in a job does little or nothing to make a job more enriching. After an uninteresting job is enlarged, the employee no longer has a small boring job, but instead a rather large boring one. It takes just a little longer to get bored by a large, involved (but routine) job than it does to get bored with a small routine job.

Job enrichment and the idea behind it require that the employee actually experience a feeling of satisfaction from doing the job. Needless to say, productivity is far higher in an enriched job than when every duty is treated in an automatic way and every employee is expected to behave mechanically.

Unfortunately, it is not always possible to make all jobs highly satisfying. We must recognize that some dull, boring jobs will simply be that, no matter what we do with them! Some people will be saddled doing jobs that are not intrinsically enriching or rewarding.

Many professionals will accept this as an excuse for not trying to enrich jobs. However, it must be recognized that practically all people have some need for an enriching experience at work—otherwise they will soon become dissatisfied and less productive.

Management by objectives is a technique in which professionals and subordinates set mutually agreed-upon goals and then periodically meet to evaluate progress in obtaining these goals. In essence, each employee is made the manager of his own work. What is accomplished and how it is accomplished depend on the employee's own efforts. Determination of the objectives and how the employee intends to achieve them is subject to final agreement with the supervisor, of course. The employee's efforts are evaluated by comparing what the employee planned to achieve with what was actually achieved. Self-control, responsibility, and accountability for accomplishing stated goals are emphasized. This challenging and self-motivating technique places the employee in a position to realize his strengths and minimize his weaknesses.

MBO aids motivation of all participants by carefully defining common goals and ensuring concerted action toward those goals. When people can see their goals and how fast they are progressing toward them, they are motivated. By coordinating personal goals with the firm's goals, participants gain added incentive to improve work performance.

MBO helps many firms to achieve excellent results. However, it isn't a panacea. A great deal depends on the employee's desire to have MBO as part of the work experience. Also, it is a time-consuming process and must have genuine support from all levels to be most effective.

Job rotation involves the orderly movement of personnel from one assignment or job to another, consistent with an overall objective. Unlike job enrichment, it requires no redesigning of jobs. It is an effective motivator and an excellent way to develop employees by helping them to increase their potential through gaining knowledge and experience in different areas of the firm. It is also helpful in that it introduces new personalities into different areas, which may have a positive effect on attitude, leadership, and approved ideas and, in fact, may lessen the rigidity of the present structure.

There are disadvantages to job rotation. Some jobs may require a specialist, and some inefficiency and increased costs often accompany the moves. The program should be suited to the firm's needs. The employees must understand and agree with the basic goals of the job rotation effort.

Being consulted and knowing that their suggestions are considered in arriving at decisions that affect them have high motivational value to employees. Employees feel that they are part of the firm. Their basic needs to belong and to feel important are satisfied in part by participation. Their sense of responsibility and desire to gain adequate knowledge about the subject at hand are stimulated by participation and, in turn, contribute to employee motivation.

Providing opportunity for positive criticism—for suggesting specific methods for improvement and ideas on what corrective actions are needed and what past actions should be eliminated—is extremely effective in motivating people. This approach must be constructive and the suggestions offered compatible with the firm's objectives. The professional must get an exchange of beliefs, with the employee offering suggestions.

The professional and the employee must stress immediate and realistic personal plans and actions and agree on a specific schedule for improvements. The agreed-upon plan of action must be clearly understood by all parties. The professional must be genuinely interested and supportive and follow up on the process to ensure its success.

One of the ways to motivate an employee is to find out what his or her personal goals are or to get the employee to accept a goal you wish to achieve, then help the employee achieve that goal. This requires that the professional know the employee as a distinct person and be able to identify the employee's personal goals. It is important that the achievement of the employee's personal goals tie in with the goals of the firm—there must be a correct combination.

Since most personal goals are individual and dynamic, motivating professional employees is an ongoing process. It requires much thought, creativity, and skill. A professional must recognize that what is effective at one time for a specific person is not necessarily effective for another, or for the same person at another time.

There are six key factors in motivating an employee:

1. The employee must be convinced that he is performing challenging work.
2. He must be capable and operate with a highly positive attitude toward the work and environment.
3. He must have the respect of his supervisor for his skills, knowledge, and understanding.

4. He must be enthusiastic about the firm's goals as well as his personal goals.
5. He must participate in formulating objectives, policies, and general directions relating to his work activities and environment.
6. He must clearly see that a specific action will satisfy his needs.

Eighty-two percent of employees are less than fully satisfied with the jobs they are in. According to an article appearing in *Psychology Today*, when employees were asked what they wanted, they simply stated "more."* But they wanted more satisfiers in a psychological sense, not just more money and benefits. Forty-three percent felt that they may have been victims of some form of job discrimination during the past five years. Forty-four percent felt trapped in their jobs. However, 78 percent would like flexible working hours. Most people would continue to work in the jobs they enjoy, even if they could afford to live comfortably for the rest of their lives without working.

Judging by that sort of response, we may be in for a period of increasing instability, because of the turnover of those who can find better jobs and the turnoff of those who can't. Particularly disturbing is the fact that these data come from a sample that contains *mostly professional and managerial employees*—who are essential to any large organization or professional firm and who have traditionally had a lower rate of turnover. Equally unsettling is the discontent among the critical groups—supervisors, clerical personnel, and skilled and unskilled workers.

There is only one thing that professionals can do, and that is to learn about employee needs and satisfiers. Understanding the new job values and practicing responses to them are critical. Otherwise the firm will have problems with its most important resource—people. And without qualified and motivated people a firm cannot provide dynamic and high-quality professional services.

*Patricia A. Renwick and Edward E. Lawler, "What You Really Want from Your Job," *Psychology Today*, May 1978, p. 59.

18

Defining Internal Resource Needs to Accomplish Objectives

The formulation of general policy to guide the firm toward achieving objectives should begin with an examination of the existing resources. The central objective of the management function in a professional firm is to optimize the use of those resources. Resource planning inherently involves considering methods to use, modify, or redeploy resources to attain objectives in a more efficient way.

Resources are both tangible and intangible. Resource planning should encompass nonhuman resources (capital, office and equipment, and materials and supplies) and human resources (personnel).

These resources must be provided if the professional firm is to accomplish its intended purpose. The firm must (1) determine the amount and timing of resource requirements, (2) establish plans to acquire or generate the resources, and (3) allocate the resources.

Nonhuman Resources

Capital

Budgeting and financial resource planning are understood and used in many professional firms. However, many firms equate financial planning with the total planning concept, when in fact it is only a small, though important, part of the total planning process.

Financial planning provides the communication link in ascertaining the utilization of nonhuman resources. A financial model (plan or budget) provides the ability to forecast the financial position to future periods. The model must be flexible enough to allow the application of different assumptions and environmental conditions.

The financial model is used as a tool in the planning function. The model projects the sources and application of monetary resources of future periods, on the basis of the firm's plans. It is therefore able to predict the surplus or shortage which must be expected unless there is planned intervention.

Financial planning thus allows intervention to generate or acquire additional resources if there is a predicted shortage. This may be done well ahead of time through additional investment by professionals, borrowings, sale-and-leaseback agreements, cost reduction, raising fees, and so on. Financial planning allows time for a thorough, systematic evaluation of the alternatives—there is usually no panic financing with the often extremely high interest costs resulting from it.

Financial planning further allows the planned deployment of surpluses on a systematic basis, which would accrue to improved efficiency and profitability. Equipment replacement, distribution to professionals, expansion, reduction of bank borrowings, and effective interest generation on unused cash are but a few of the alternatives. Obviously, this requires the extension of financial planning to all facets of the firm—there must be not only an operating budget (income statement) but also pro forma balance sheets, a statement of changes in financial condition, and cash flow budgets.

Some of the major management problems center around the efficient use of assets. These problems can be somewhat ameliorated—or at least alternatives chosen before a crisis—with effective financial planning. Major asset areas of professional firms and some associated problems include:

Cash
   Cost of acquisition
   Care and custody
   Determination of amounts needed
Receivables
   Client relationships
   Excess levels

DEFINING INTERNAL RESOURCE NEEDS

    Collectibility
Inventories
    Care and custody
    Optimum quantities
    Efficient use
    Purchasing alternatives
Investments
    Care and custody
    Approrpriate levels
    Costs
    Profitability
    Security
Fixed assets (largely, office, buildings, and equipment)
    Types needed
    Timing of need
    Availability
    Size
    Costs (incurred and projected)
    Operational benefits expected
Other assets (prepaid expenses, deferred items, goodwill, etc.)
    Level of investment
    Standards of valuation
    Impact on profitability

Planning of financial resources involves not only budgeting for balance sheet items but also considering their effects on liquidity, soundness, and profitability of the firm.

Office and Equipment

Planning for facilities, including equipment and premises, includes not only the purchase of new facilities, but planned replacements, optimum maintenance policies, and planned obsolescence.

The planning process should address the size of the office premises for optimum efficiency. There are alternatives of opening branches or expanding existing facilities, and so on. Alternatives can be built into models so that appropriate choices can be made.

Location of facilities is often critical. Convenience to clients may be of paramount importance. The business location will directly influence the cost of operation and the types of clients who are serviced in those premises. Once location is decided, it can be changed only at substantial cost in relocation expenses, interruption of professional services, and possible loss of clientele. If the premises are located at a distance from the market, clients often have to go out of their way—or, alternatively, the business must go to them, which is costly and time-consuming.

Similarly, referred professionals, sources of materials, and suppliers should be conveniently located in relation to the firm. The firm should be relatively close to trained personnel it wishes to employ.

It is also important that the professional firm examine recent trends in the area in which it will operate. These trends include population shifts, orientation of development (industrial or consumer), traffic flow, property maintenance (what impression does the neighborhood give?), and registered permits for rezoning. These and other considerations were discussed in Chapter 11.

Once facilities are chosen it is important to schedule and allocate work programs, to determine what level of professional service will be needed, and what materials and staffing will be required so as to minimize service and/or transportation costs. Sources of supply must also be considered.

There are many techniques that are relevant to planning for facility and equipment utilization, including CPM, inventory theory, mathematical programming, PERT, queuing theory, replacement and maintenance theory, and sequencing and coordination theory.

Materials and Supplies

There should be procedures for checking levels of inventories for future use and making sure that supplies will be available in sufficient amounts at acceptable costs. If there is heavy reliance on a specific material or supplier, the planning process should include consultation with the supplier to obtain assurance of future deliveries. Even when supplies are available, there is the possibility of significant changes in prices, which may lead to a search for alternative suppliers or the use of alternative materials.

Human Resources

Staff planning involves allocating people with the proper skills to implement the organization's plans. It presupposes that the total number of personnel will be kept to a minimum to enhance efficiency and the firm's total profitability.

DEFINING INTERNAL RESOURCE NEEDS

Skills

A properly designed organization chart, backed by thorough job descriptions, job analysis, and evaluation, will assist in identifying the skills needed by the firm at various levels. Of necessity, personnel planning cannot be considered in isolation from total planning for the firm. The previously determined goals and objectives of the firm, and the strategic plans for their accomplishment, will identify needs for new staff and new skills.

Staff Size

Personnel stability is a prerequisite to the efficiency of a professional firm. Staff cannot be drastically cut back without negative effect on future recruiting efforts. At the same time, it is generally held that it is necessary to keep the number of staff to a minimum. The personnel planning function, however, is designed to minimize the cost of staffing, not necessarily the number of staff.

It is advisable to determine optimum staff size with the help of a staff response function (see Figure 18-1). This method attempts to weigh the costs of increasing staff against the incremental benefits derived.

When more staff is added, professional services and fees may be increased—but only to a resistance level. Beyond that level additional staff does not result in increased services and fees. A saturation point is reached when added staff actually reduces the *rate* of increase of services and fees. A supersaturation point is reached when adding staff results in decreased services and fees at an increasing rate. More time is spent on internal administration and concerns of communication and organization.

The theory is that a certain amount of activity will be required before any professional service output is generated. Once this process starts, it continues to improve at an increasing rate (lower variable costs of staff than revenue generated, and so on), until a resistance level is reached when costs start to rise in relation to output of professional services. The point when staff or facilities are used to capacity, or when increased activity is unlikely to lead to commensurate increases in services (and profits), is called the saturation point. The model becomes supersaturated when increased staff and the push for more professional services result in equipment failure, overworked staff, or reduced client loads because of market resistance. In such a situation, clients often feel offended by the indifference they are shown.

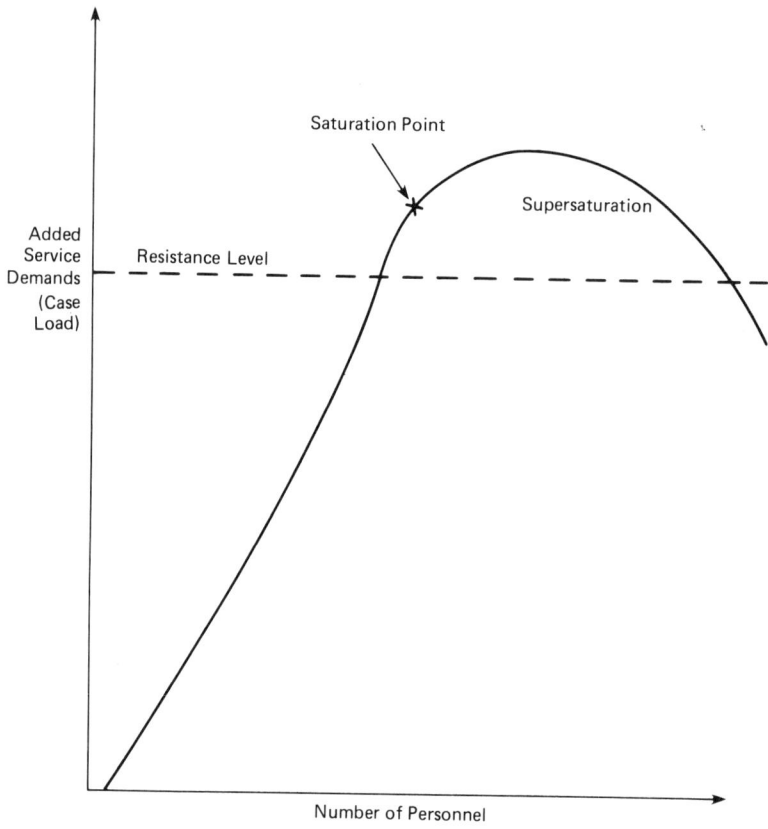

Figure 18-1.   Staff responsiveness as a function of staff size and service demands.

Allocation for New Staff

A firm must often recruit new staff, either because it needs more personnel or because existing staff is not qualified and must be replaced. This is sometimes brought about by the firm's failure to train and develop its existing staff. The recruitment process involves consideration of likely sources, which might include placement agencies, professional organizations, government agencies, universities, high schools, and trade or vocational schools. Direct newspaper advertising may also be used. The process involves screening of candidates and selection of new staff after weighing personal attributes and skills. This is done to ensure that the right people are chosen—people who fit in well with the firm and who will respond well in their positions. Obviously, the firm must have a clear definition of itself. Whichever method is used to obtain personnel, job descriptions are imperative.

Salaries and Benefits

In order to draw bright, efficient people into a firm, and keep them, consideration should be given to offering them salaries that are equal to, or higher than, what they would receive elsewhere. An alternative is to offer other than monetary incentives through benefit programs. These might include:

Definite personal growth plans.
Development programs.
Flexible or shortened work week or hours.
Fringe benefits (for example, extra time off in slack periods).
Life insurance plans.
Medical and/or dental plans.
Pension plans.
Savings and investment plans.
Training programs.

In large firms, jobs should be classified and rated within ranges in order to provide a consistent demonstration of fairness and continued sensitivity in the administration of the wage and benefit system. The danger here, however, is that a "system" will become too mechanical, which could remove employees' motivation to enhance their efficiency.

Predetermined salaries kept to minimum levels will directly limit the quality of personnel. For example, a minimum salary would usually draw applications only from inexperienced staff or from those who have difficulty in obtaining employment.

The single largest cost component in most professional firms is the cost of salaries and related staff benefits. Next to delivery of professional service, most professionals consider staff salaries and benefits the second most difficult area to address. The complexity of the payroll administration function is brought about by a proliferation of diverse positions and specialized areas, which is unavoidable in most larger professional firms. This has been further compounded by government intervention, minimum wage laws, tax laws, and unemployment insurance and worker compensation legislation, together with myriad demands for cost-of-living and staff benefit adjustments in an inflationary economy. In addition there are changing social values and attitudes of staff and potential staff, who have much greater expectations for high pay, partly as a result of higher education levels.

Obviously, in all but the very smallest of professional firms, a well-formulated salary and benefit program is essential. Although such a program will not be a substitute for sound judgment, it will assist in providing consistent and more objective salary decisions. A structured program is more likely to appear fair in the eyes of the staff and has a greater chance of gaining their acceptance than three other possible approaches, including individual bargaining, collective bargaining, and the "market approach."

An individual bargaining approach often results in disparate internal pay relationships and leaves the employer firm with the greatest bargaining strength, which could result in unrealistic wage levels, staff apathy, and, ultimately, frustration. Collective bargaining is increasing or threatened in many professional environments. Although it may equalize bargaining strength, it does not reduce prejudice or result in objective solutions, particularly where negotiators are under the emotional pressures of the negotiation. This may be somewhat ameliorated by adopting formalized techniques prior to negotiations for wage and benefit programs. The "market approach" may be workable in very small firms; however, with the increased complexity in the structure of larger professional firms, undefined staff markets, and the specialized skills required for unique positions, it is often inequitable to pay the "going rate" for comparable staff categories within the community.

A formalized salary and benefit program does not necessarily mean a complex program. It is usually wisest to develop the simplest program necessary to meet the firm's objectives. Various concepts and techniques can be used to form an integrated compensation program compatible with the overall objectives of the firm, rather than operate case by case without predetermined objectives or policies. The objectives of the wage and benefit program may be to (1) contribute to the development of the firm, (2) provide a vehicle to contribute to the strategic achievement of the firm's objectives, and (3) overcome existing problems with salary and benefit administration. In order to accomplish these objectives, the salary and benefit program should:

1. Motivate staff members to perform their duties in such a way that the achievement of the firm's objectives is enhanced.
2. Provide opportunity for every staff member to achieve his in-

dividual goals, insofar as they reinforce and contribute to the firm's effectiveness.
3. Be competitive with pay levels in alternative employment, so as to attract and retain staff members who are required to help the firm accomplish its objectives.
4. Avoid placing the firm in a noncompetitive position because of excessive costs.
5. Be acceptable to staff members—they must understand the policies and procedures and view the program as being fairly and objectively administered.
6. Minimize the administrative time and expenses and the amount of professional time needed for administration and negotiation of the program.
7. Be acceptable to others with whom the organization works, including partners and other investors, clientele, government agencies, and the general public.

Obviously, there is no one right way to design a salary and benefit program because of the number of variables which must be considered, including the type of profession, the services being offered, the firm's structure, policies and objectives of the firm, economic factors, and the attitude of partners. However, techniques may be developed for the individual firm which will assist in program development. Basically, positions should be grouped on the basis of shared job characteristics and training and experience requirements. Position grouping will assist in many personnel functions, including communication, recruiting, training, and the administration of a salary and benefit program. The steps necessary for this classification and subsequent administration of the program include:

1. Obtain position information to determine the job requirements and provide a basis for job evaluation.

2. Determine the relative worth of the position.

3. Translate the relative worth of the position into monetary value.

4. Allow flexibility for individual adjustments to reward staff members for high productivity or to reflect increases in pay levels. This should allow for general salary adjustments, merit increases, promotion increases, or a performance pay increase system.

5. Communicate with staff members, providing information necessary to gain an understanding and acceptance of the program.

6. Maintain currency of information about all aspects of the program, comparative salary analysis, and current operating statistics to assist in providing guidelines for individual salary packages.

7. Maintain control over salary and benefit costs and ensure that the program is consistently and equitably administered.

Job groups can be set up to reflect the range of salaries in a firm. In Figure 18-2 there are 12 specific groups. This breakdown facilitates the introduction of across-the-board increases to reflect inflation rates and yet allows for flexibility within categories to allow for differences in specific jobs.

Figure 18-2. *Salary levels for staff and professionals by job groups.*

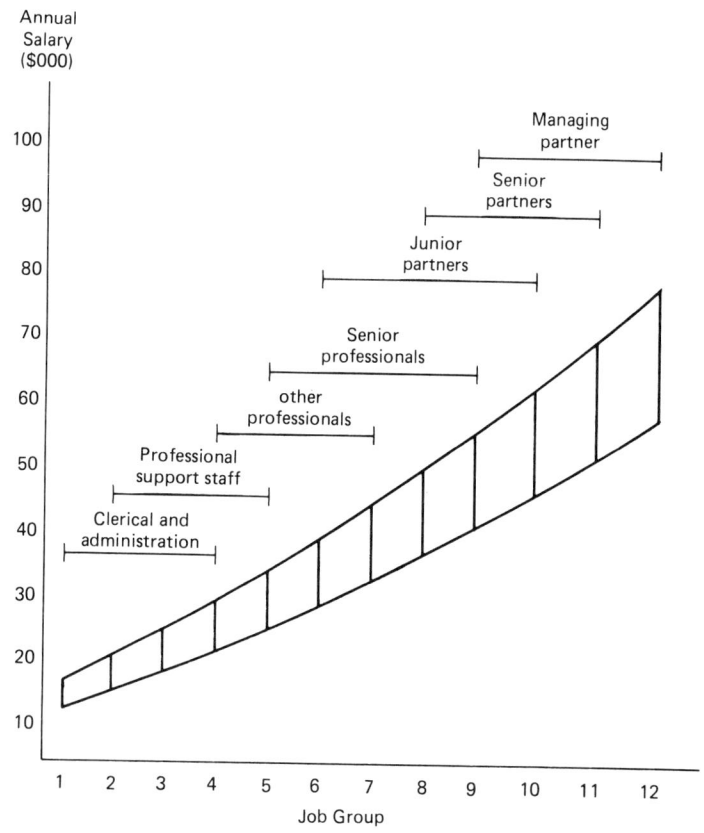

Fringe Benefits

In the past, this area was belittled by being called "fringe benefits." However, it has grown to such an extent that it now accounts for between 30 and 40 percent of most firms' payroll costs. Here is a typical breakdown, accounting for 39 percent of payroll costs:

Legal requirements (unemployment insurance, Social Security, etc.)	10%
Pensions, group insurance, and other agreed-upon employer payments	12%
Paid rest periods and similar benefits (coffee breaks, etc.)	4%
Payments for time not worked (annual holidays, statutory holidays, sick leave, etc.)	10%
Other	3%
Total	39%

Legally required payments are payments which are wholly or partially financed by the employer and are required under state or federal statute.

Insurance benefits are those which are financed on a group basis for employees of a firm. They generally include a pension plan, a medical insurance plan, life insurance, temporary disability insurance, long-term disability insurance, and travel accident insurance.

Paid rest periods would include formal work breaks, such as coffee breaks and time off for personal reasons for which there is provision for payment.

Pay for time not worked includes such items as annual holidays, which may vary from two to four or more weeks with pay; paid statutory holidays, which may vary from eight to fourteen days annually; and sick leave payments while employees are absent due to illness.

Other benefits might include pay for time lost due to jury duty, pregnancy, sick leave, or other personal reasons.

In addition to these, one might consider the following as fringe benefits: overtime premiums, profit sharing plans, employee savings plans, free professional services, cafeteria, employee activities, and perquisites such as company cars, parking, staff counseling, and housing assistance.

Obviously, with the amount and increasing importance of

fringe benefits, the program should be designed with extreme care, and policies should be established to govern the fringe benefits available to all staff and professionals. This is necessary not only to maintain control over what may be a major expense area but also to ensure that there is equitable treatment of staff members and professionals.

"Cafeteria" Benefits

With the advent of computerization in payroll administration, there is increasing consideration of a "cafeteria benefits concept" in staff benefit planning. This approach recognizes that each staff member within a firm has unique needs for varying degrees of coverage in the overall benefit packages, and allows the staff member to choose custom-tailored benefits which meet his needs. Younger staff members, for instance, might choose higher life insurance coverage and lower pension contributions, as opposed to an older employee, who might choose high pension contributions and capital accumulation over the increasing premiums of term life insurance. This approach allows flexibility and the integration of personal financial planning with the firm's benefit packages. Major problems associated with the cafeteria concept are the complex administration required and the complex tax rulings pertaining to the various employee benefits offered.

Personnel Management

Management of the staff function is critical in helping the firm obtain and retain staff to assist it in accomplishing its objectives. Irrespective of the size of the firm, it is crucial that a professional firm be aware of:

1. Its compensation policies in comparison with other organizations and within a geographic area.
2. Market values of various position categories.
3. Educational, training, and experience requirements for staff.
4. Changes in labor legislation.
5. The availability of government assistance for staff members, particularly in areas of recruitment and training.
6. The availability of qualified potential applicants for future openings within the geographic area.

DEFINING INTERNAL RESOURCE NEEDS

Environments That Motivate

Apparent irrational behavior of staff, on close examination, is often not irrational at all but a response to an irrational environment.

A professional firm should endeavor to attract staff who are motivated by a commitment to personal and professional achievement. These highly motivated individuals hopefully will realize their goals, at least partly, through the achievements of the firm. However, they will excel only in certain environments. Specifically, they need a high degree of autonomy; clean, comfortable, and attractive surroundings; prompt and specific feedback; and an atmosphere of cooperation and "esprit de corps." Staff members who perceive that they are working with a dynamic and successful professional firm usually have a feeling of well-being, which reflects back on their work, their standards of professional service, and their efficiency.

This atmosphere would be reinforced by providing effective professional leadership and by allowing staff members to participate in the planning process and rewarding them, through an incentive system, for their achievements which have a direct bearing on the accomplishment of the firm's objectives.

Education and Training

The whole process of education and development of staff in a professional environment should be geared toward the improvement of professional efficiency. A further objective is to close the gap between the firm's expected needs and the training and experience of existing staff. Intense training may be needed if the firm is experiencing major growth or changing its strategies. Normal training would be required in the case of staff turnover or changing professional needs. The following points should be kept in mind in designing training programs:

1. There must be staff participation.
2. Staff members must be receptive to training.
3. The training program must have a recognizable level of quality.
4. The program must provide for immediate positive reinforcement.

5. Managing partners should participate in and provide input to training programs so that all participants are aware of the senior professionals' clear interest in the training process.

Summary

We have examined the major nonhuman resources, including finance, facilities, and materials and supplies, and the human resources available to a professional firm. Of necessity, we have examined the human-resources aspect of the planning process in greater detail. Professionals responsible for planning must consider human resources, since it is only through people that a firm will accomplish its objectives. People have the ability to sabotage the entire plan and expected results—or to magnify the benefits of the planning process. The kind of staff a firm is able to recruit, motivate, and retain will largely determine the success and growth of the firm.

19

Determining Organizational Structure

Once the firm has developed its plans, it is important to structure the organization to respond to clients' needs. Organizational structure cannot be planned without identifying resource needs or defining of work programs and policies to accomplish the firm's objectives. The entire planning process may require that the professional firm reorganize itself.

Organizational planning requires that tasks necessary to accomplish objectives be identified, grouped into jobs, and assigned to a specific individual or group. It also requires:

1. Identifying the decisions to be made at different levels in the hierarchy of the professional firm.
2. Modeling the decision-making process—that is, determining the effect of alternative decisions made at each level.
3. Designing a management information system that will provide necessary information for decision making at appropriate levels.
4. Designing individual jobs by grouping decision-making duties at various levels into job descriptions.
5. Designing information systems that will measure performance.

Professional firms tend to resist reorganization, primarily because it changes individual job requirements and necessitates the learning of new skills. Some jobs may even be canceled, with layoffs involved. In an ever changing environment, however, such resistance to change may lead to a lost opportunity to substantially improve performance. Possibly, the tool with the most potential to improve the firm's effectiveness is reorganization.

Identification of Decisions

Essential to a discussion of the decision-making process is a clear understanding of how decisions are made. Webster's New World Dictionary, Second College Edition, defines decision as "(1) the act of deciding or settling a dispute or question, (2) the act of making up one's mind, (3) a judgment or conclusion, (4) determination; firmness of mind."

Decision-flow analysis assists in the identification of the types of decisions and actions which have an effect on the operation of, or results achieved by, a professional firm. This type of analysis is usually best accomplished by flow-charting decisions, actions, and relationships.

If the professional firm has adopted a market-based approach to its development, the decision process can best be analyzed by:

1. Determining client needs and expectations. This identification has two important components: first, the types of clients to whom the organization can respond, and second, the types of services that might be needed. This phase is known as market identification.

2. Determining how those needs and expectations are communicated to the professional firm. Communication may be through a response to specific requests from clients for information or through a survey of client requirements, a basic form of client or market research.

3. Determining how the information on needs and expectations of the market is recorded, processed, and communicated within the professional firm.

The last point may best be illustrated by an example from the provision and billing of professional services. Invoices are usually prepared with several copies, and each of the firm's copies will be processed for either eventual destruction or entry in a permanent file. At any point, two things can happen to the information. One, it may be transformed to codes, summaries, analyses, or the like, usually to assist the firm with the production of a new report. (These reports, too, should be traced to their ultimate destination.) Two, at some point, information from the original documentation or from report summaries and analyses will be used to make decisions and issue instructions. Once these decisions are made or instructions issued, they too should be followed to their ultimate execution.

This type of analysis is usually done by a *systems analyst* and can be broken down to show the flow of work (or materials), instructions, and information. Copies that do not produce decisions or actions but serve only information purposes need not be traced to ultimate disposition. The objective of the analysis is to identify decisions that should be made at each level in the firm.

Modeling

The ultimate objective of decision-flow analysis is to design the decision-making process and ascertain what kind of information is necessary for the support of the system. Decision-flow analysis thus provides information to allow the design of integrated management information systems.

Some types of decisions cannot be modeled; other types can be modeled but not solved; and still other types of decisions can be modeled and solved. The last type can be routinized and/or delegated by professionals to much lower staff levels. This type of analysis can result in greatest efficiency improvement and cost savings. The other types of decisions will, to a greater or lesser extent, require some level of professional judgment, usually by senior professionals.

The example of a flowchart model in Figure 19-1 segregates the work (materials or services) flow from the flow of instructions and the flow of pure information.

Information Systems

The major danger of most professional information systems is that they supply more (often irrelevant) information than is needed to make a decision. The use of models (provided they are correct) ensures that only information that is necessary to make decisions is provided. Information overload would result from supplying too much information, and there are serious dangers in supplying irrelevant information.

Planning the information packages is closely related to the design of information systems to control operations. Information systems must be designed to allow:

1. Identification of the need for a decision.
2. Information to support the decision.
3. Evaluation and control of the decision once it has been made.

(This type of feedback is necessary to allow the decision maker to modify a previous decision or take other corrective action.)

As the design and implementation of management information systems is a topic in itself, this area will be left for a fuller discussion in Chapter 20.

Designing Jobs by Decision-Making Duties

The decision cycle consists of four steps: decision, implementation, evaluation, and recommendation (see Figure 19-2). Each of these steps requires internal and possibly external information input.

When information needs for managing and operating the professional firm have been clearly delineated, one of the objec-

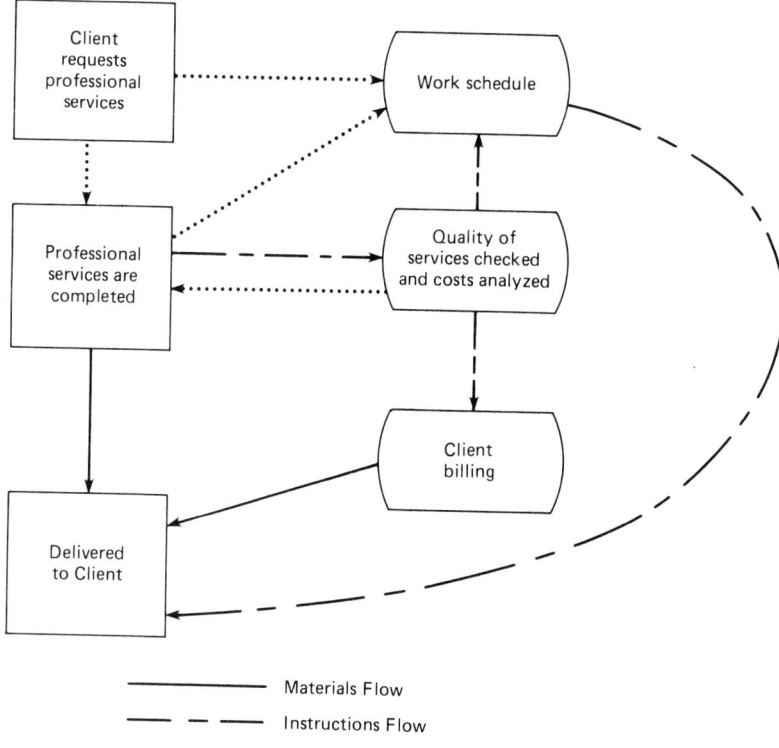

Figure 19-1. Example of a flowchart model.

DETERMINING ORGANIZATIONAL STRUCTURE

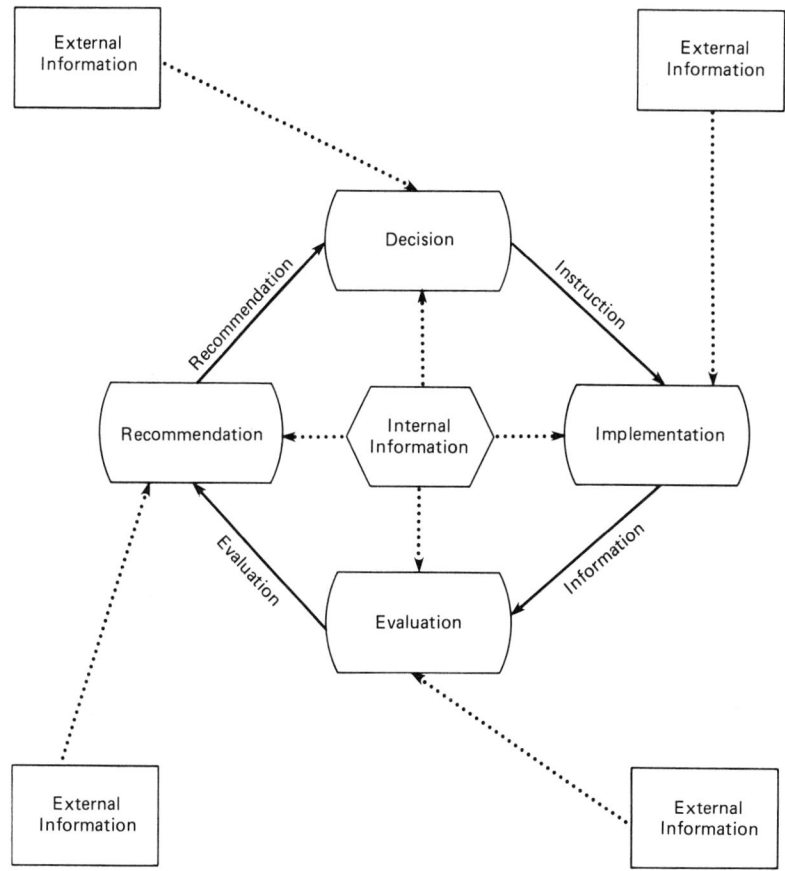

Figure 19-2.   The decision cycle.

tives in organizational design is to allow the grouping of decisions so as to minimize the amount of information needed. Decisions that use the same or similar information can be grouped into specific jobs or job groups.

Professionals are called upon to make recommendations to others, make decisions themselves, implement decisions of others, and evaluate decisions made by themselves or others.

An organization chart, then, is an end product of organizational planning. Once the four steps in the decision-making process are specified, lines of authority and responsibility will become evident.

Measures of Performance

Professionals will try to maximize their results in terms of standards and specifications of predetermined measures of performance. For instance, if the only measure of performance is to attend two court cases per day, this is what a lawyer will strive to achieve, without too much concern for other considerations unless they have a direct bearing on those results. This type of restriction, for instance, might mean a lawyer places little emphasis on other legal services he could perform to increase the firm's profitability. The measures of performance must, therefore, be carefully considered to enhance the firm's ability to attain its objectives.

Principles of Organization

There are several traditional principles that must be considered in designing organizational structures, including:

1. The need for objectives. Each individual, unit, and department should be organized in such a way that it will contribute to the achievement of the firm's objectives. The objectives should be broken down to show how each individual or unit is expected to contribute to the overall objectives.

2. Each job confined to specific function. This requires that each position be filled by a specialist and that specialties that are similar report to the same group.

3. Coordination of activities. There should be one plan, and one individual professional responsible for activities with the same objective. Each individual should be accountable to, and receive instructions from, only one direct superior. The senior partner should not instruct a staff member without transmitting the instruction through the staff member's direct superior.

4. Span of control. No supervisor should be responsible for more than a specific number of subordinates. At the same time it is important not to "layer" by creating too many levels. Major advantages of increasing the span of control are that it improves the ability to delegate and increases revenues and profitability. However, major disadvantages appear as costs are increased and more time is wasted in administrative detail. Professionals must realize that they cannot forever exceed emotional and physical limits, and they should be prepared to delegate responsibilities and the necessary authority to assist in achieving the firm's objectives.

Popular organization theory states that the number of subordinates who can be effectively supervised (span of control) varies from three or four to seven or eight.

5. Authority. If an individual staff member is being held responsible for achieving a specific result, he should have the authority to assure that achievement. This is important in enhancing efficiency, because when a subordinate needs advice, he can go to his direct supervisor rather than to a senior partner. It thus avoids delays in the decision-making process and reduces expenses. Removing senior professionals from many small, often trivial problems usually allows more effective and significant decisions at the senior level and on more important matters.

6. Delegation. The decisions in an organization should be delegated to the lowest level at which staff members are capable of making those decisions.

7. Chain of command. Every professional firm has a hierarchy of authority (layers) extending from the managing partner down to the clerical staff. This should be as direct and short as possible to allow easier communication and faster decision making. It is not unusual for even the largest organization to try to restrict the number of layers to seven.

8. Balance of functions. Emphasizing various functions, units, or departments at the expense of others could lead to organizational imbalance. This is one of the dangers in internal promotion to a managing-partner position, since there is a tendency to continue emphasis on old functions. A managing partner of an accounting firm who was promoted from the tax department, for instance, might place a great deal of emphasis on taxation at the expense of market research or staff development. Similarly, a managing partner promoted from auditing might place great emphasis on this function at the expense of the administrative and taxation departments. This may be true, as well, for a newly hired managing partner who has obtained a preponderance of knowledge or experience outside the firm—but only in one specific function.

9. Foresight. Any organizational change will have an effect on the professional firm. Some effects will be positive, others negative. When organizational change is being considered, it is important to model possible results in an attempt to foresee all possible effects and ensure that changes are in the overall best interests of the firm.

Organizational Groupings

There are six major groupings basic to organization design:

1. Functional groups—administration, professional services, quality control, and so on. Control is maintained by department heads. (See Figure 1-1.)
2. Geographic groups—applicable where the organization is designed to cover all functions at regional or geographic centers.
3. Service groups—usually for larger firms in which the organization chart is based on service group lines. In a large integrated law firm, for instance, there might be a conveyancing group, a litigation group, an estate group, and so on.
4. Process groups—used where services are broken down into various stages of development or distribution. A medical facility might be broken down into a research group and a second group for distribution of professional services.
5. Client groups—applicable where the firm is designed to respond to various client needs and expectations. A large legal firm, for instance, might be organized into groups responsible for criminal law and corporate law.
6. Matrix or combinations—used where the firm is organized along functional lines (see 1 above) and, usually, along service groups (see 3 above).

Almost every professional firm is organized by functional groups. This is because of the traditional task or service orientation, specialization, and advanced education of most individuals in a professional environment. The organization is structured in terms of jobs to be done, not in terms of the clients to be served. Unfortunately, that type of grouping often detracts from a professional firm's ability to respond to the variety of client needs. For instance, a client may be referred to three individuals in a professional firm in order to have his needs satisfied—in an accounting practice, to the accounting department head to obtain his financial statements, to the audit department head to obtain an audit, and to the tax department to file the necessary returns. In a law firm, the professional responsible for obtaining a divorce for a client will refer the client to another professional in the firm to have wills changed. The concept of "one-stop shopping" definitely does not exist in most large firms. The result, often, is client frustration.

A second major problem is that no one individual in the firm is responsible for ensuring that the broad needs and expectations of

DETERMINING ORGANIZATIONAL STRUCTURE

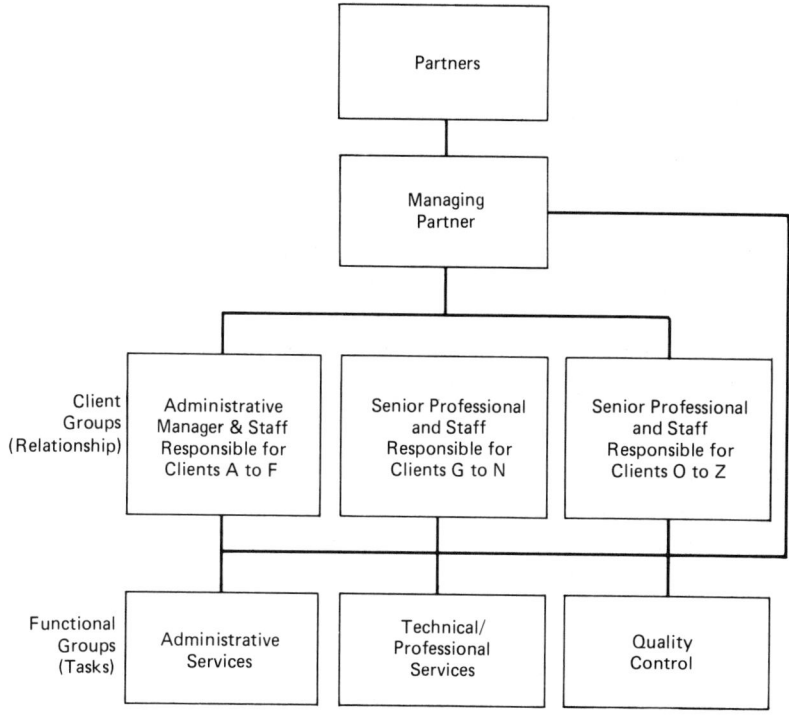

Figure 19-3. Matrix organization chart.

a single individual client are met. However, with the complexity of professional services, some specialization by function must exist.

Matrix Organization Chart

The use of a matrix organization chart along both functional and client group lines (see Figure 19-3) would overcome some of the imbalance of functional groupings. For instance, each professional and staff member in a firm would be responsible not only for the performance of a function but also for ensuring that the needs of individual clients (or groups of clients) are being met by the firm. The individual in the firm who is responsible to each client would also ensure that the firm is responding to that client's broader needs.

The staff at the client-group and functional-group level are the same people. However, they all have two jobs: (1) client relations and (2) the provision of functional professional services.

Summary

The objective or organizational structuring is to give the firm an opportunity to exploit its strengths. Coordination and control of the firm are important, but consideration should be given to advantages of specialization, individual development, and lower costs. Attention should be given to ways in which a firm can recognize and respond to local (geographic) opportunities and client needs. The organizational structure should be designed with emphasis on important activities—those which will be most efficient in obtaining the firm's goals. This requires:

1. The establishment of objectives.
2. Identification of major obstacles.
3. Identification of major opportunities.
4. Consideration of alternative structures.
5. Selection of the structure which will work best in accomplishing objectives.

20

Strategic Planning for Management Information Systems

Management information systems (MIS) for professional firms are not accountants' information systems. Only when accounting reports and summaries are concurrent with other data and systems do they become an overall MIS. This means that the design of the overall system should be the responsibility of top and senior professionals who have knowledge of their world, and not the responsibility of technicians who know only their speciality.

A comprehensive MIS provides all the information needed to make informal decisions. Historical and current information as well as forecasts of anticipated results are organized suitably for the professional firm.

This expanded definition relates to the need to provide both external and internal information. Externally the professional firm must have information of environmental forces: demand, opportunities, and problems. These include economic considerations, technological advances, social advances, political inputs, competition, and social responsibility. Internally the professional firm must have information which affects its markets (revenue forecasts and professional performance); materials and supplies; personnel (recruiting, payroll, personnel practices, and skills inventory); provision of service, routing, and scheduling; and finance (budgets, cash flow, forecasts, general ledger, money markets, payables, and receivables). All this information may be necessary to allow professionals, as managers, to make informed decisions.

The design of a total management information system obviously requires a great deal of data for input. It is important that the system provide relevant information to professionals. At the same time—and this may be more important—it must not provide an overabundance of irrelevant information.

This chapter will discuss these underlying assumptions, principles, and expected results, because these must be defined at the outset, well before a decision for manual information reporting or computer-based systems can be made.

Strategic Planning

To reiterate, planning has four major components:

1. Defining what is to be achieved (objectives).
2. Deciding how to accomplish those objectives (action).
3. Defining subordinate goals needed to accomplish major objectives (goals).
4. Designing procedures to monitor results by specific measurement of performance (control).

This is summarized in Figure 20-1.

Strategic planning is the process by which realistic objectives are set, recognizing demands, opportunities, and problems (threats) from external and internal sources, and actions or methods of achieving those objectives are determined. To assist in setting objectives for the MIS, the following items should be determined:

The objectives and philosophy of the firm.
The desired annual growth rate.
Desired return on investment.
Future demands for alternative professional services.
The position within the firm to which the MIS should be responsible.
How the MIS will affect the image of the firm.

There is a specific series of steps for the development of management information systems:

1. Initiate the effort. The user recognizes a need for information to assist in the decision-making process and prepares or obtains a feasibility study. A cost/benefit analysis is conducted to determine whether the benefits and results of a new system would offset the development and operating costs.

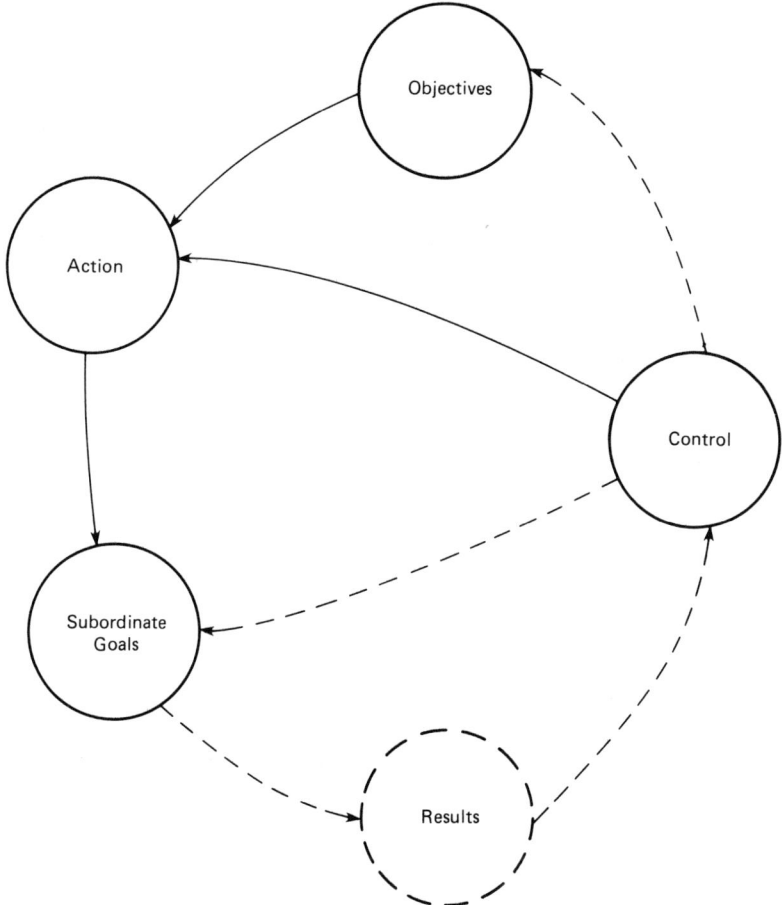

Figure 20-1. The planning and control cycle.

2. Analyze the old system. Provide a functional description that the user can understand. Concurrently, prepare a description of the proposed benefits, capabilities, and results of the new system, again in terms the user can understand.

3. Design the new system. Detailed specifications are prepared for the new system. This should include systems flowcharts, definition of input/output needs and the data base needed, and program specifications.

4. Develop the system. Once detailed specifications are pre-

pared, these are translated into specific work programs or, in the case of computers, into computer programs.

5. Implement the system. This phase often requires the training of users. More important, it might be defined as a testing phase, during which the new programs are run through to ensure that they achieve their objectives and are compatible with existing programs. This is usually done by making several runs of both old and new systems to allow comparison of output results.

6. Operate the system. This phase entails not only day-to-day use but also evaluation of the new operating system against original functional descriptions and specifications.

In designing the MIS, consideration must be given to controlling the decision making within planning, operations, and management. The management system consists, in part, of control, decision making, and management information, and these cannot be considered in isolation. Control involves:

- Determining the expected outcome of decisions in terms of specific measures of performance.
- Gathering data on actual performance.
- Comparing expected outcomes with actual performance.
- Where decisions are shown to result in variance from expected outcomes, taking steps to correct the consequence of those decisions, correct the procedures that produced the variance, and provide feedback for setting future expectations.

A comprehensive MIS provides the following external and internal information necessary for making informal decisions:

External	*Internal*
Competitive factors	Finance
Economics	Inventories
Political factors	Markets
Social advances	Office and equipment
Social responsibilities	Personnel
Technological changes	Production
	Research and development

External Information (Strategic)

Changes in technology, legislation, or social demands may affect entire professions dramatically. For example, socialization of medicine has significantly affected that profession.

One problem is that there are so many environmental factors—for example, domestic and international economy, competition, technological developments, government, legal and political changes, and social issues. It is necessary to determine which are the most significant and to spend time and effort in analyzing them.

A discussion of the major areas on which an individual firm may focus follows.

Economic Considerations

There must be a thorough understanding of the effects of the economy on the profession and the firm. This provides a distinct advantage over competitors. In addition, one must also distinguish between long- and short-term factors.

Points to consider:

1. How does the course of the economy affect revenues and the services of the firm? Are short-term or long-term economic effects more important?

2. Are economic effects direct or indirect? What is the timing of these effects? Do they lead, coincide with, or lag behind economic trends?

3. Are these economic effects real or perceived? Can perceptions be altered before economic effects take hold?

Technological Advances

In this context, *strategy must be flexible.* We are living in an age of rapidly advancing technology. Professional planners must have a clear understanding not only of the present state of technology affecting the firm's services but also of potential future advances.

They must also be able to consider the effect that seemingly irrelevant technological changes may have on the firm. Many professions have found, to their dismay, that technological events in seemingly unrelated areas have shattered supposedly carefully planned strategies. An example is the effect the development of fluorides had on corrective dentistry.

Points to consider:

1. How are new service methods, new materials, new equipment, new products and/or services (for example, automatic data processing equipment, plastics, data transmission, in-home computerized libraries, and information retrieval systems) likely to affect the firm?

2. What use should be made of technological forecasts?

Social Influences

Societal composition and thinking, values and demands, education and access to information, leisure, mobility, and definition of market(s) must be addressed.

Points to consider:

1. How are the size, location, and age makeup of the population changing?

2. How is the educational level changing?

3. How are the values and norms of the population changing?

4. To what extent are such changes and other social changes likely to have an impact on services of the profession?

5. To what extent and how should forecasts based on survey research be formulated and used?

Political Inputs

There are very few government actions that come as complete surprises to the economy. Foreknowledge of these actions can often give a professional firm the added competitive advantage it needs to create and implement a successful strategy.

Points to consider:

1. What agencies now hold some type of regulatory power in the profession? Is there leeway in the interpretation of these regulations? Are the agencies receptive to innovation in the profession?

2. Who are the individuals involved in setting regulations or legislation in our future areas of competition? What might be their personal and professional views on our projected moves? Are these individuals likely to be replaced through electoral or other means? What other pressures or groups must they face?

3. Are there indications of wholesale changes in the government process? What are the possible predictors of change? Can these predictors be spotted well in advance of changes? How can they be measured?

4. Are government assistance programs available?

Competition

Other professional firms face the same environmental issues. Their reactions to these inputs must be considered if a strategy is to be feasible and well-rounded. The firm needs to know their possible reactions to the firm's strategic moves. Thus, an analysis of the strengths and weaknesses of other firms is extremely useful.

Points to consider:

1. What is the competitive environment of the profession? Is competition concentrated among a few firms or is it spread over many firms?

2. What policies and strategies are followed by individual firms in the profession? Do they lead the profession in developing new methods and fees? What are their strengths in research and development, marketing, promotion, and so on? What are their professional service strengths?

3. What is the financial condition of the various other firms? Will they be vulnerable to strategic moves because of lack of financial resources?

The human, material, and financial resources available to the other firms must be analyzed so the firm can formulate contingency plans in its strategy against any moves initiated by those firms.

Understanding the constraints imposed by the external environment provides the basis for redeveloping objectives for the organization. It also enables the professional to formulate alternative plans for achieving those objectives.

Social Responsibility

This issue must be faced in a society that places increasing emphasis on the responsibility of the professional firm toward its environment. The question arises as to whose evaluation of social responsibility the firm should follow. A strictly rational evaluation would lead the firm to choose strategies that will improve both the services to its clientele and its own viability.

If the environmental actions are not required by law, the question arises as to the competitive position a firm might find itself in if it were the only firm taking environmental action. The professional must question whether the gains, if any, in image, personnel, and professional service will overcome potential cost disadvantages.

Internal Information (Resource Development and Operations)

Recognizing the firm's need for a range of information is difficult for anybody but a senior professional. One problem is that a firm has broad and general information needs, whereas the MIS planner may have been educated or gained experience in only one professional function. Information is needed on financial matters, of course, but also on inventories, markets, offices and equipment, personnel, service, and research and development. Here again it is important to determine the most significant areas which can bring substantial results and, possibly, prioritize the amount of time spent in analyzing information needs before developing the management information system for each function. Activities would focus on areas or variables that are deemed to be most critical to the organization at that time.

Finance

The financial reporting system should provide clear information on revenues, expenses, and profitability and allow comparisons to prior periods, standards of other professional firms, and plans. There must be a clear understanding of relationships between profit margin and turnover, of variable and fixed costs, and of corrective actions—such as cost reduction programs—which could be used to effect change.

Points to consider:

1. Is the financial reporting system clearly understood by the user—the professional who is in a position to affect or change the operation of the firm and its financial consequences? Are short-term profits more important than long-range viability? Is the system designed to provide the information professionals need?

2. What has been defined as an adequate profit?

3. Are variable and fixed expenses clearly segregated and understood? Is variance reporting in effect, and is it understood by the professionals? Are cost, volume, and profit relationships analyzed and understood? Are breakeven analysis reports or charts prepared?

4. Is there provision for control through comparison to previously determined plans or budgets?

5. Does the reporting system provide enough information for detailed future planning and budgeting purposes—by center, by client, by type of professional service, by employee, and so on?

Inventories

The management information system must identify responsibility for and costs and flow of services and materials. Purchase orders and store requisitions should be designed to provide continuous information to maintain effective inventory control. This may be particularly appropriate where holding costs are high,

MANAGEMENT INFORMATION SYSTEMS

especially with current interest rate levels. Maximum and minimum inventory and economic order quantities should be identified.

Points to consider:

1. Are there adequate records and controls?
2. Are purchase orders, change orders, and requisitions designed to forecast residual inventories?
3. Are there reports and procedures for disposal of slow-moving, obsolete, and scrap items?
4. Has supplier credit been used to the maximum economic level?
5. Are inventory purchases analyzed to determine economic order quantities?

Markets

There should be a clear understanding of the expectations and needs of the market—and the firm should learn to respond to those needs. The firm will better serve its clientele—and be better able to achieve its objectives—if it responds by fulfilling needs rather than hard-selling its services. Surveys and reports should be an integral part of the management information system to establish the type of client who would be attracted and the type of services and level of fees which would respond to their needs.

Points to consider:

1. Has a "market audit" been conducted of the microenvironment—the total market environment and external considerations, including evaluation of markets, clients, and competitors?
2. Has the firm identified the market segment to which it wishes to respond—both the clients it wants to serve and the types of services (based on clients' needs) it wants to provide?
3. Has a "market audit" been conducted of the microenvironment? That is, has the marketing system currently being used by the professional firm been evaluated and have internal goals been established and/or reviewed, current services analyzed, and new services that might be offered planned?

Office and Equipment

Expenditures covering acquisition and disposition of fixed assets, maintenance of fixed assets, and operating costs should be included in the management information system. Reports covering efficiency, productivity, and downtime should be considered.

Procedures should be implemented for early identification of obsolescence and recognition of the need for an "abandonment" decision. Capital expenditures or abandonment should be considered in relation to long-term growth, reduction, or change in service or revenue capacity.

Points to consider:

1. Does the firm require that pro forma statements be prepared comparing alternatives, on a discounted cash flow basis, prior to commitment to capital expenditures?

2. Are market growth or decline and market share growth or decline carefully considered before making the capital expenditure/abandonment decision?

3. Are procedures in effect to compare costs, productive capacity, and efficiency of assets of various ages—possibly with those of competitors—to determine areas for improvement?

4. Are procedures in effect to evaluate, on a planned and periodic basis, all office and equipment installations to determine if there are better alternatives? This evaluation may consider efficiency, location, and size of office or equipment. By the time there is *obvious* need for change, many months or years may have passed during which the firm accepted a low profit when an alternative may have led to improved results. This area requires continuous vigilance.

Personnel

Procedures and professional management information should be available to assist the firm with recruiting, screening applications, interviewing, testing, reference checks, evaluation, salary and promotion policy, and salary levels paid by competitors and others. Human resources are critical to the firm if it is to attain its objectives.

Points to consider:

1. Are training programs in effect? Is there effective delegation to ensure lower costs and improved efficiency? Growth necessitates delegation.

2. Are incentive programs considered at the professional level? Achievement bonuses, financial security, job security, and salary levels can be important tools in personnel motivation.

3. Is information available to determine competitive salaries, appropriate fringe benefits, bonuses, and job description changes?

Are there regular reviews with personnel regarding performance and salaries?

Production

There must be thorough internal understanding and reporting of the efficiency in providing professional services. This provides knowledge and distinctive competitive advantages. There should also be a clear understanding that short-term pushes for higher capacity may result in long-term losses from equipment breakdown (due to inadequate maintenance and higher production than equipment was designed for), earlier obsolescence, and increased staff inefficiency and resistance because of long work hours.

Points to consider:

1. Are staff productivity reports prepared regularly? Do they compare results with previous periods and predetermined standards?

2. Are staff overtime reports prepared regularly, not only listing total overtime paid, but broken down for each staff member?

3. Is consideration given to writing off equipment on the basis of usage rather than time?

Research and Development

Economic and environmental forces bring about a need for continuous investment in effort, money, and time to maintain markets and market shares in increasingly competitive professional environments. This brings about the requirement for continuous vigilance and research to ascertain ways of improving effectiveness in all areas, including the external environment, finance, inventories, markets, office and equipment location and productivity, personnel selection and skill needs, and efficiency of professional services.

Points to consider:

1. Has the firm considered obtaining government assistance in its research and development efforts? There are numerous programs available.

2. Has the organization prepared MIS studies of the long-term benefits of obtaining or retaining a research capacity?

3. Does the MIS respond to all areas of research needs rather than just those of the traditional professional service and/or marketing function?

Forms and Procedures

Various forms and procedures may be used to assist in comprehensive MIS design and development in a larger firm. The following are some that were identified by Norman L. Enger:*

1. Initiation—user request, user proposal, feasibility study, and project plan.
2. Analysis—functional description and data requirements.
3. Design—system specifications, data base specifications, and program specification.
4. Development—program documentation.
5. Implementation—test and implementation plan, test analysis report, and user manual.
6. Operation—operations manual, maintenance manual, and evaluation report.

Summary

A professional firm's management information system should generate timely, clear, and consistent information to provide a basis for informed decision making.

Strategic planning includes the selection of a firm's objectives, goals, and policies and the identification of resource needs to accomplish objectives. The professional's function is to use those resources to attain objectives. The management information system must be flexible and generate information which the professional user needs to make informed decisions. It must provide managing partners with control to ensure that the firm's goals and objectives are being achieved.

A professional staff member is usually restricted in his ability to consider broader issues and long-term commitments because of a concern for day-to-day results. This reinforces the concern that the design of the management information system be understood

---

*Management Standards for Developing Information Systems, New York: AMACOM, 1976.

by the firm's senior and managing partners and that the parameters of the system be assigned by them.

The best features of responsibility accounting must be incorporated into the system. The system must be tailored to a specific profession. Reports must be prepared promptly, and be kept simple so that trouble spots can be located quickly. It must provide for a guide at the time of decision making and for control once the decision is made. It must be tailored to meet the needs of individual professionals and staff at all levels.

21

Market Planning, Information, and Control

A professional firm's main effort must be directed toward attaining, maintaining, or improving its ability to serve its markets in order to improve its viability and profitability. No matter what other lofty goals a professional firm may have, without economic profitability it will eventually fail—and with that failure all other objectives will go unfulfilled. Irrespective of the current profitability of a firm, and without attempting to define what it should be, most professionals would agree that they could or should do better. Most professionals would also agree that the environment, markets, and professions are changing so fast that it is no longer enough to drift from year to year hoping that the firm and its operation will improve. However, it will not improve without a thorough analysis of the firm's markets, plans that are responsive to market demands, and control of marketing and operating results. Of course, some might argue that improvement or success of professional firms is a matter of luck or fate. But the success of the firm is too important to allow a guess or hope to intervene in the decision to be in the right location, at the right time, with the right professional services, at the right price, and with well-considered marketing strategies. Yet many, particularly smaller, professional firms do not even prepare a budget. If budgets are prepared, they often simply reflect projections based on last year's revenues, expenses, and profitability. Often, little is done to analyze the firm's strengths and weaknesses, the long-term market

MARKET PLANNING, INFORMATION, AND CONTROL

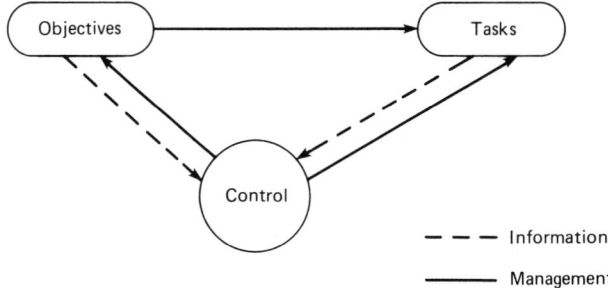

Figure 21-1.   Interaction of control, objectives, and tasks.

demand for professional services, future client levels, long-term fee levels, or even potential problems that the firm may encounter, let alone the range of opportunities it has available. All too frequently there are no clearly stated objectives in the program, let alone plans and programs to accomplish those objectives. For instance, there may be an object to "grow"—but in which direction? at what rate? how much? Unless objectives are stated in specific terms, the control of the firm is at best ambiguous. The planned management process requires that we determine objectives first, then decide on the tasks necessary to do the job. Control involves measuring the results of our actions against those plans, taking corrective actions to get back on target, and/or modifying the plans so that we know more precisely where we are likely to be (see Figure 21-1).

Growth Planning

In the corporate business world, at least, there have been studies conducted to determine the main criteria of success. In a study* of more than two hundred companies with a history of profit growth, four common characteristics were found:

1. Such companies have organized programs to seek and promote new business opportunities.
2. They operate in growing fields and markets.
3. They have proven competitive ability in present fields.

*P.J. Lovewell, "The Key Factors in Successful Growth," Management Report No. 3, *Planning Ahead for Profits*, American Management Associations, 1958.

4. They have courage and energy—they are willing to take carefully considered risks.

Change is coming at an ever increasing pace. Certainly technological advances, even in the professions, have been staggering in the past few years. The implementation of advanced computer and communications systems will bring even faster changes throughout the 1980s and beyond. Higher education levels, faster information retrieval, clients' knowledge and awareness, increased professional competition, and lower costs through automation will dramatically affect all professions. Professional firms that do not grow or are unresponsive to rapid change will surely not survive.

If they do not get new clients, no one will replace clients who die, leave the firm, or go out of business.

If they work in professional fields that are not growing, they will be increasingly subject to obsolescence and have fewer clients. In many cases, technology may provide lower-cost alternatives to the services offered. For example, once-in-a-life corrective eye surgery will replace the need for repetitive replacement of some types of eyeglasses. Some other examples of threats to traditional professional services are legal "self-help" books on incorporation and divorce, computer packages for financial-statement analysis, and computerized drafting services.

If the professional firm is stuck with old-fashioned attitudes about marketing and client service, it will lose clients to aggressive and competitive professional firms.

If the firm is complacent and extremely conservative, it may be unable to learn new techniques quickly, and unwilling to spend resources or take any risks in developing new clientele or new services. If a firm is doing things because "that is the way they have always been done, and it's safest," the world and its rapid changes and new methods will quickly pass it by.

Growth, and planning for growth and change, is necessary to long-term survival.

Responsibilities of Senior Professionals

One of the problems of professional firms in the 1980s and beyond is that senior professionals are trained only as professionals—that is, they are only trained to complete the technical professional functions of the profession. They are often not trained to develop vision. They are trained to offer quality professional services today, rather than to think about what the future might bring. In addition, it seems a natural human condition that we accept change as final rather than continuing. We all know about major changes in our profession in the last twenty years; we accept them—but we still have difficulty understanding that those changes are *not* final. Even all those innovations will be improved upon, be changed, become inappropriate or obsolete.

Unfortunately, senior professionals who manage firms sometimes have relatively closed minds on new concepts and change, or do long-range planning perfunctorily at best.

Change is inevitable. We may choose not to plan for it, and hope that change will pass our firm by, leaving it relatively unscathed. At the other extreme, we may plan to change too quickly without the experience or resources required to be successful in implementing the change. There is no doubt that either extreme has tremendous risks.

Professional firms usually do little planning other than through informal meetings at best when certain new steps are considered. This usually brings unsatisfactory results, so there is often a stage where a firm does more formal annual planning and budgeting. It soon realizes, however, that even annual planning is difficult unless it is done within the framework of comprehensive long-range objectives. Eventually those long-range objectives will be identified by meaningful segmentation of the types of services and clientele the firm wants. This will make it possible to develop the firm and its people and organize its resources to be responsive to those segments.

The senior professionals in the firm may initially be the only ones who perform, or even perceive the need for, long-range planning. They set objectives and targets for everyone else in the firm. This form of top-down planning is relatively autocratic and largely ignores input from junior professionals and staff members in the firm, who are typically told what to do and handed budgets or professional performance standards that they are expected to meet.

Some firms attempt a democratic planning process, in which juniors in the firm plan their own objectives from the bottom up and seek higher-management approval. The psychological theory behind this approach is that people will be more enthused about and committed to goals they have set for themselves. Unfortunately, this humanistic approach, while working well for the employees in a professional firm, may not bring the most positive results attainable for the firm as a whole. Individual goals are often fragmented and set too low.

A third alternative is a compromise: the participative approach to planning. Senior professionals initially review the market and the environment of the firm and establish parameters and broad objectives for the firm as a whole.

The senior partners, for instance, might decide that the firm should grow by 20 percent per year, but individual professionals and staff members in the firm might best decide how that is to be accomplished—by type of service, fee schedule, type of clientele, or some other means.

A marketing plan should contain the following sections:*

1. Overall objectives and a marketing mission for the firm.
2. A description of the current and forecasted position of the firm.
3. A listing of alternative strategies available to the firm, and the reasons for choosing the particular alternative.
4. Specific actions to be taken by specific personnel during the period to accomplish objectives.
5. The budget of resources (money) needed to carry out the tasks.
6. A list of target variables, such as revenue, growth, expenses, and so on, which should be reviewed every month or so to ensure that objectives are being achieved.

Optimum Market Service/Pricing Decisions

Marketing costs money. Research, planning, advertising, and promotion are all extremely expensive. Presumably those expenditures will increase revenue. Yet one of the objectives of a firm must be to optimize the return on those expenses. Providing various services, at particular levels of fees, and marketing those services, should generate a higher return to the firm than if some of those services were not offered, fees were not adjusted, or the costs of marketing were not recovered. All this work and expense should result in optimum benefit to the firm and its clientele. Presumably these expenses will enhance the firm's ability to service its clients. If the costs of marketing were too high to be absorbed by the market, then one would have to question the viability of the program.

The market response function is the relationship between the

*Adapted from John M. Brian, *Corporate Market Planning*, American Management Association, 1967.

market response, including increased revenue and public awareness, and the costs and expenses of the marketing and promotion function. The objective is to allocate enough resources to marketing and promotion to maximize the services offered by the firm and/or the net income to the professional firm.

Too little money, allocated to marketing would not improve revenue and, hence, net profit. For instance, two percent of a professional firm's revenue budgeted for marketing activities would probably have little impact on the firm's growth—only enough money would be available for an occasional newspaper insertion announcing the opening of a new office and to buy current clients and people who make referrals an occasional lunch. If 20 percent of the firm's revenue were spent on marketing, this might stimulate a great deal of new business initially, but revenue might drop off over time as clients realize that they are required to pay high fees, not just to obtain quality service, but to support the professional firm's expensive marketing program. The trick is to find a balance—a level of marketing expenditure that is high enough to stimulate sustained growth, yet low enough to maintain reasonable fees with maximum provision of quality service. This should result in maximized return, or profitability, for the firm over the long term.

Market Share

One of the objectives in comprehensive market planning is to control the market share of the professional firm. If your firm is one of twenty other firms evenly offering essentially the same services to the same (potential) clientele, competition is going to be exceedingly difficult. The firm may not be able to expand at a rate faster than the average expansion in the market, almost irrespective of the amount spent on advertising and promotion. There is full supply, and many of the services of the twenty firms (each with 5 percent of the market) may be recognized as of similar quality. Clients may be predisposed to choose a firm primarily because of lower fees. Generally, lower fees can be obtained by reducing expenses, including marketing expenses. This is one of the reasons it was important to segment the market—to allow the firm to spend time and money in analyzing a particular segment's needs and expectations through market research so that it can concentrate on becoming a dominant factor and needs satisfier in that submarket.

Analyzing the Cost-Effectiveness of the Marketing Program

Before embarking on any program, a professional firm must weigh the benefits which will result from that program against the costs of mounting the program. A firm may wish to decide between alternative services to offer or alternative promotion vehicles. It may measure the benefits to costs by many criteria: the time it will take to earn back the revenue to pay for the expenditure (payback period); the return on investment (essentially, the net income that will be generated by the expenditure); or a simple ratio of benefits to costs.

Promotion costs money, and controls should be established to ensure that the benefits (revenues) are greater than the costs (outlays). A professional firm with limited resources might have to choose between two marketing methods: it can either visit people who might refer clients and promote the practice, or it can use letters and direct mail to existing clients to show them ways it can help extend the services (and benefits) to those existing clients. A comparative analysis of these two alternatives is shown in Table 21-1.

Such a simple analysis of alternatives may indicate which has the most beneficial short-term economic benefits. However, it does not measure the quality (value) of long-term contacts. The visitation program may result in long-term referrals over many years, while the direct mail program may increase only current revenue. Costs and benefits should therefore be projected over long periods of time, and spin-off benefits considered (see Table 21-2). A personalized visitation campaign in year 1 may lead to referrals over a number of years.

Budgeting and Forecasting

The planning process prescribes the direction of growth and change, and the best methods for obtaining objectives, in qualitative and quantitative terms. The budget process, which is part of short- and long-range planning, expresses in quantitative terms (dollars and units) those plans for a specific period of time, usually one month, one year, or five years. The very process of budgeting and planning will provide a means of reconciling conflicting efforts within the professional firm and coordinating activities to serve the best interests of the entire firm. An example of this type

Table 21-1. Cost/benefit comparison of two alternative marketing programs.

	Alternative 1: Visit People and Establish Contacts	Alternative 2: Write to Existing Clients
Estimated revenue (increase)	$5,000	$5,000
Less: Cost of providing services (staff time, labor, etc.)	3,000	3,000
Gross margin	2,000	2,000
Less:		
Direct travel and entertainment costs (20 visits)	800	
Professional time (40 hours to make appointment and visit, 20 hours to draft letters) @ $50/hour	2,000	1,000
Typing and mailing costs (20 letters)		200
Expenses	2,800	1,200
Net income (loss)	$ (800)	$ 800

Table 21-2. Long-term cost/benefit comparison of alternatives.

	Alternative 1	Alternative 2
Revenue: Year 1	$ 5,000	$ 5,000
2	3,000	—
3	2,000	—
4	1,000	—
	11,000	5,000
Less: Costs of providing services	6,600	3,000
Gross margin	4,400	2,000
Less: Expenses	2,800	1,200
Net income (over 4 years)	$ 1,600	$ 800

of conflict is where professionals want "state of the art" professional services, yet the firm wants equipment that can be used for a long time, is simple to operate (and thus avoids training costs), maximizes the professionals' efficiency, is not overly expensive, and earns a maximum profit for the firm.

The budget should not be prepared by simply extending the operating revenue and expenses from previous periods. This approach totally ignores the external and internal environments, which are in a constant state of change and flux. It also totally ignores programs for the achievement of the firm's objectives. Altogether it is a rather myopic approach to budgeting and does not address major opportunities for improvement.

Once the firm's objectives are clearly stated, it can start the process of budgeting (up to one year) and forecasting (one to twenty years). This involves determining:

1. The level of acceptable profit—a reasonable return on investment.
2. The best methods to achieve that profit level.
3. The resources needed to reach that profit level.
4. Whether the resource needs—capital, staff, marketing capability, professional service capacity, and so on—can be met from within the firm or must be obtained from outside.
5. The most effective use of all resources so as to attain the firm's objectives.

Flexible Budgeting

Relationships between cost, volume, and profit must be clearly understood by professionals at all levels. This is particularly important if there is uncertain demand for the services being offered by the firm. A clear distinction should be made in the budgets and financial reports between variable, semivariable, and fixed expenses so that alternative budgets and plans can be quickly introduced if there are variations in fee volume. A flexible budget will reflect the results of different levels of fees and revenue.

A simple breakeven chart is shown in Figure 21-2. It identifies such fixed expenses as depreciation, office, rent, and administrative salaries of $80,000; variable expenses, such as labor and materials used in the provision of services, of $20 per (billable) hour; and semivariable expenses such as supervision and office maintenance costs. Assuming the average "charge-out" rate is $30

MARKET PLANNING, INFORMATION, AND CONTROL   247

per hour, the "breakeven" point—the point at which there will be neither a profit nor a loss—is $320,000 in revenue on 10,666 billable professional and staff hours.

Flexible budgeting is useful to senior professionals for checking efficiency against plans and budgets. It allows the development of cost analysis to determine reasons for variance from plans. The determination of such items as staff cost variances per hour, billable hour variance, volume variances, and expense and fee variance will allow the firm to take intelligent corrective action, say, by changing overtime policies, reducing fixed expense items, or reconsidering fee policies.

An analysis of the items which went into the breakeven chart and the budget itself could be prepared to identify different levels of activity (see Table 21-3).

Figure 21-2.   Breakeven chart.

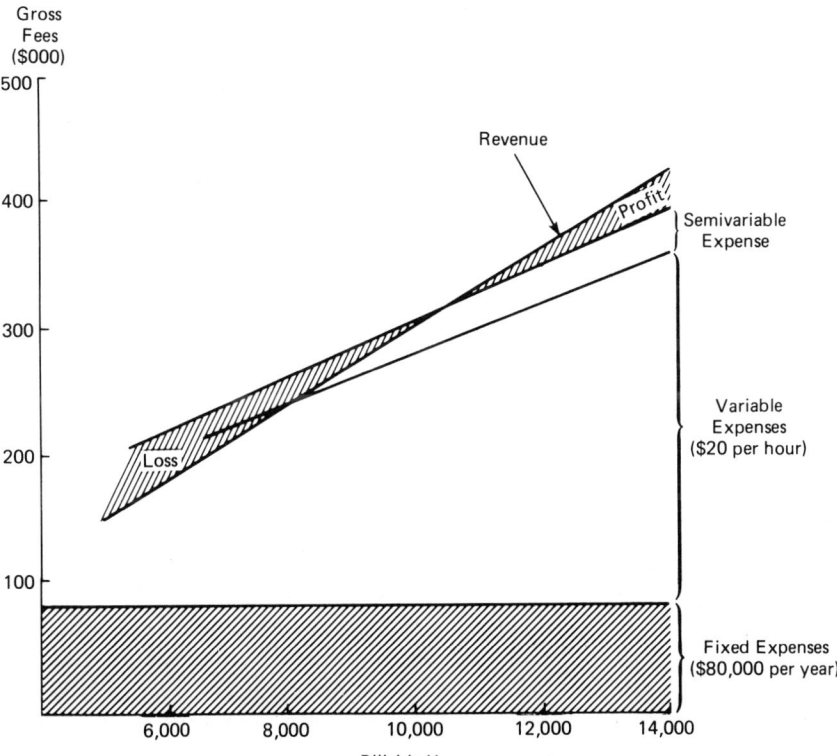

Table 21-3. Analysis of breakeven data at three levels of activity.

	Level 1	Level 2	Level 3
Number of billable hours	8,000	10,000	12,000
Expenses ($000)			
Variable (with amount of work)			
Staff salaries ($20/hour)	160,000	200,000	240,000
Semivariable			
Supervision, office maintenance	20,000	25,000	30,000
Fixed (amount per year—does not change with amount of work)			
Depreciation, rent, administrative salaries, etc.	80,000	80,000	80,000
Total expenses	$260,000	$305,000	$350,000
Expenses per billable hour	$32.50	$30.50	$29.17

Actual results and budgets should be presented and analyzed in a format that is consistent with the way authority is delegated.

Responsibility Accounting

For a larger firm, budgeting and forecasting should involve the lowest level of supervision responsible for obtaining results toward the achievement of objectives. Statement formats will vary depending on the size of the firm, the profession, and whether functional, service, matrix, or other organizational groupings are used in the design of the firm's structure. The important point is that the budgets and statements clearly show that the individual professional or staff member who makes a revenue or expenditure decision is accountable for that action.

Management by Exception

A large portion of senior professionals' time should be devoted to planning for the future, no matter what daily problems there are. This can be accomplished only by having carefully prepared plans in advance and then managing the exceptions and problems emanating from variances to the plan. Operating reports that compare results to plans, that are kept brief, and that point out why there are any significant deviations, will result in much more effective corrective action being taken—and sooner. The alternative to developing the budgeting, forecasting, and planning function to a high level can only be continuous management by crisis and short-term firefighting. Effective corrective action cannot be taken if the firm does not know the immediate overall effect of those actions and if it still does not have clear direction as to the long-term objectives it wishes to obtain.

Profit Centers

In larger firms, profit centers have important advantages in the control of the firm's operations. One, they allow an easy way to report, analyze, and control the effectiveness of these departments within the firm. Relative profitability of these departments is an important criterion for senior partners' decision making and the allocation of the firm's resources among departments. Two, they provide high motivation to individual professionals, who are held accountable and responsible for an individual department's results. Professionals clearly understand what cost, profits, and revenues are, and dynamic professionals appreciate being measured against common yardsticks.

The best way to measure individual financial performance in a firm is to design profit centers which reflect the firm's objectives and the nature of the profession in which the firm operates (to allow comparisons to other firms in the same profession), and which are modified to allow for special needs of the firm where the firm has unique competitive ability or resources.

At the same time, profit centers must provide for goal congruence. In any firm, each individual department is competing with other departments for profitability and resources. The profit centers should be designed so that financial operating and marketing objectives are fairly assigned to each managing professional in each department. This assignment would ideally allow each professional to take actions which would benefit not only his department but the organization as a whole. This takes a great deal of effort by senior partners. The design of profit centers should not allow individual professionals to work at cross-purposes in their attempts to obtain the best *overall* results in relation to the firm's total objectives.

The budgeting and reporting systems must appear appropriate

and fair in the eyes of the professional who is being reported upon. This means that there must be consistency, that only those items over which he has control be included, and that positive decisions which he has made are reflected in the reports.

Classification of Financial Responsibility

We have discussed the profit center concept without defining its meaning or discussing other ways to distribute fiscal responsibility. Fiscal responsibility centers can be classified as:

Discretionary expense centers. These are most applicable in administrative departments in which there is no practical measure of productivity, efficiency, or results. Judgment is used to determine budget amounts and how much money will be spent in providing quality services.

Investment centers. These are most applicable where a managing partner is being held responsible for the amount of resources used. This is appropriate where maximization of rate of return, or profit after cost of capital, is used to determine investment alternatives. This is an important criterion where there is a choice between maximization of short-term branch or department profits and the maximization of long-term profitability.

Profit centers. These are most applicable where there are definitive units of service and the trade-offs are between costs, productivity, and revenues to allow profit maximization. However, it is still important to make each managing professional responsible for only those costs and revenues over which he has authority and control.

Revenue centers. These are usually most applicable in revenue departments, particularly where no authority is delegated to the individual professionals to change the level of fees (which would or could affect volume). The objective of this type of organization is to make the individual professional responsible for the budgeted expenses, which will generate maximum revenue, but not for the fee changes, which could affect revenue volume.

Standard cost centers. These are usually most applicable in professional (operating) service departments. Standard costs and quantities—particularly variable direct salary and materials costs and variable overhead expenses—are specified during the budget process for each service produced or hour billed. The objective of this organization is to make the individual professional responsible for minimizing variances between actual and budgeted (standard) costs.

There can be other forms of profit centers, depending on the type of profession and the critical functions that could be managed and controlled by introducing centers for marketing if marketing is the major activity for a firm, or multiple profit centers where there are two or more integral functions and activities within a firm. For example, in individual high-volume tax preparation there might be a case for a firm to establish tax preparation and marketing profit centers with both branch and marketing managers responsible for part of the profit earned by the branch.

Budgeting Problems*

Budgeting might be referred to as a planning and control system. It is a system, which implies that it is subject to continuous review and revision throughout the budgetary period. Budgeting covers three fundamental functions of management: planning, actuating, and controlling operations. Despite the importance of budgeting in the planning, and indeed, the total management function in a professional firm, there are many problems:

1. *Budgets are not prepared.* Many firms, particularly small firms, do not prepare budgets or financial plans. In some firms the budget is looked at askance as a necessary evil—something to keep senior partners or lenders happy. Where this occurs, the major advantage of the function—the critical control of the firm—is totally overlooked. Other firms budget effectively for only parts of their operation and either ignore other functions or place such little emphasis on them that the budgeting process is ineffective as a control vehicle for those functions. For instance, a legal firm might place a great deal of emphasis on costing and analyzing lawyers' direct salaries, materials, billable hours, and entertainment expenses while ignoring or skimming over such functions as administration, reception, and advertising, possibly in the erroneous belief that these are somewhat uncontrollable.

2. *Budgets are not reviewed and revised.* If budgets are set only annually and not reviewed and updated from the most recent information available, they will lose much of their effect as a con-

---

*See also R.L. Jones and H.G. Trentin, *Budgeting: Key to Planning and Control*, New York: AMACOM, 1971, and *Management Control for Professional Firms*, New York: AMACOM, 1971.

trol vehicle. When a professional says, in July, "I know I am way off budget, but there is nothing I can do about it, because it was caused by the six-week postal dispute last spring," we know we have problems with the budget. A revised budget should have been prepared immediately after the extraordinary or unbudgeted occurrences. The new budget would reflect, despite the occurrence, what can be done by the professional *now* to work toward revised objectives. That is the only way the professional will feel that the budget (as revised) is fair, will reflect his current and future efforts, and be attainable—and, one hopes, will motivate for achievement.

3. *Budget allocations are not changed* when pressure is put on a department or branch to increase productivity.

4. *Analysis of results is poor.* Variance analysis should pinpoint the causes of variances and the individual professionals or staff members responsible for controlling the variances. Too often financial analysis is so general and vague that it is useless as a control tool.

5. *Budgets are cut arbitrarily.* Arbitrary "across-the-board" budget cuts determined from "above" despite the detailed, dynamic, and constructive efforts of individual professionals and staff members to maintain minimum budgets and costs will quickly erode anyone's enthusiasm and initiative to serve, especially if it appears impossible to stay within such reduced budgets.

6. *There is no dynamic forward planning.* Where alternatives may be implemented to improve efficiency and reduce costs, historical data are simply reshuffled as the basis for budgeting the alternative.

7. *Allocation of higher overhead costs and head office expenses* because of an extraordinary service or marketing effort may result in the appearance of reduced profitability at a branch or department level.

Nonfinancial Criteria

Managers in large professional firms are not, or should not be, judged solely on their financial results. These, after all, can be the result of many external and possibly internal forces over which the manager has no control. He can be judged more fairly for financial results over which he can exercise control; however, another criterion is often much more important, namely, his ability to manage a professional firm.

Increasingly, large firms are turning to management performance appraisal to measure the ability and effectiveness of professionals as managers. If these performance appraisals can be prepared objectively, they can be important tools in the control of professionals and, hence, the entire management function within a firm. These appraisals or reviews often take the form of interviews in which the capabilities of professionals are measured in broad terms and objectively compared to objectives and responses obtained from others. The areas commonly measured are:

1. *Planning*—budgeting, establishment of written objectives, forecasting, involvement of subordinates, scheduling, time management, work programs to accomplish objectives.
2. *Organizing*—assignment processing, clarity of subordinates' duties and functions, delegation and routing, staffing, work environment.
3. *Supervising*—action, communication skills, decision making, encouraging cooperation and exchange of ideas among subordinates, resolving conflict, management by principle.
4. *Motivating*—attitudes and esprit de corps, appraisal and coaching, encouraging subordinate development, using abilities of subordinates.
5. *Controlling*—corrective action, measuring results (scope and ways of measuring), utilization of the firm's objectives, planning, and policies as a criterion in measuring results.

Summary

There are many methods of measuring the effectiveness of a professional firm and its management, controlling the results of management actions, and controlling professionals themselves. Effective planning, budgeting, and analysis of marketing and financial results are one effective form of that control. In addition, comparison of actual results with plans allows feedback for the successive refinement of the entire planning process—and that is the key to making the professional firm's plans become reality.

22

Determining Policies to Attain Objectives

The one constant in the life of an individual or a professional firm is that there will be change. Technological and competitive factors certainly affect this need for change, but the personal and professional growth of individuals within the firm will also result in change. There is a tendency for dynamic and enthusiastic professionals to leave static organizations. Stating the objectives of the firm in clear terms will tend to attract professionals and staff who fit into the firm and the position. Given that the professional firm's policies and work programs are definitive and organized in such a way that they allow each individual to perform to his maximum capability, it will be possible to reconcile the individual's objectives with those of the professional firm.

It would seem a natural law that there cannot be inertia in human organizations. There will be growth or decline, but nothing will remain the same. Given this scenario, it seems prudent for the professional firm to plan, organize, and even encourage change—but to do this in such a manner in the statement of objectives and policies that the direction in which the organization wishes to grow (or decline) is identified. That is, the firm must try to *manage* change.

Once a firm's goals and objectives have been identified, statements of policy are written to reflect the philosophy and direction of the organization. When policy is carefully prepared and administered, it will form the base for decision making at all levels.

DETERMINING POLICIES

Written policy statements tell each individual in the firm what he is expected to know and do. The policy is a general type of rule which usually deals with recurring events. It allows the senior professional to delegate routine decisions. He still retains the right to change or manage the process by the simple expedient of changing the policy.

If there are no written policies in a firm, there are still policies. These are informal, have been developed implicitly by philosophy and precedent, may be subject to many variations and changes at the decision-making level for the sake of expediency, and do not form a base for consistent decision making. In addition, it takes a great deal of time for a new staff member in a firm to assimilate this informal policy—it may take years of individual experience to understand the basic direction, thinking, and philosophy of senior partners, let alone other professionals, clients, and other external groups which have a major impact on the firm. An alternative to "assimilating" informal policy is to let the new staff member spend a great deal of time with a knowledgeable professional in the firm in the hopes that the professional will cover all areas of importance and that the new staff member will learn and assimilate the information that is passed to him. This process presumes that the experienced professional is an effective teacher and that the new staff member is an effective learner. Obviously, these methods of educating new staff members—hoping that something will "rub off"—are difficult, expensive, impractical, and time-consuming. Furthermore, the new staff member may leave the firm after months or years when he has finally determined and assimilated informal policy—and found that he and the firm were at variance in philosophy or intent.

A policy is a general rule or operating principle designed to aid in achieving the firm's objectives. It acts as a guide in consistent and continuing decision-making processes. Policies differ from objectives in that objectives are specific goals, and from procedures, in that procedures are methods of performing something. Policy provides direction in the sense that it shows *why* something should be done, whereas procedures explain *how* to do something. Unless there are clear and formal (that is, written) policies, it is difficult to control the operation of the firm. It is recognized, however, that in certain confidential or extremely competitive areas policy cannot be formalized.

Policy statements should be written holistically, that is, for the entire organization. In line with objectives, statements of policy should address advertising policies, client relations, debtor relations, finance, government relations, inventories, markets, partner relations, personnel relations, office and equipment, public relations, purchasing, research and development, and revenues. Obviously, this is not the job of just a specialist but should involve the senior professional of each department who is most experienced in that area.

Once policy statements are prepared in draft form, they should be circulated to all professionals who would be affected by the policy, to elicit their opinions before seeking approval and acceptance by senior partners. Only senior partners or the managing partner can coordinate and integrate the policy-writing effort—and policies must blend with and reinforce one another. This might be accomplished by a policy committee of senior professionals and/or senior partners. Since the world in which a professional firm works is continually changing, policies must be periodically reviewed, revised, or canceled, depending on changing circumstances.

Characteristics of Written Policy

A policy is a guide to individual action, designed to assist in the attainment of an organization's goals and objectives. As such, written policy statements should be:

1. *Long-range.* Policy is a statement which is expected to be used as a guide to management action in the foreseeable future. Operating practices and procedures are by their nature short-range. In relation with the setting of goals and objectives and long-range planning, policy is the result of senior professionals thinking through to the actions that will assist in meeting the objectives established for the firm.

2. *Approved by top management.* Policies are usually developed by most or all of the professionals in a firm. In order to provide stability and continuity, however, they must be approved by senior partners. If senior-level decisions continuously override policy, the policy obviously does not reflect the thinking of senior professionals and should be rewritten or dropped. Policy must be agreed to at the senior level, usually by partners, to ensure that continuity, and the actions of everyone, including the managing partner, are subject to guidance. If this precept is not followed, policy may change or be overridden at a senior level and be subject to change at the whim of a senior professional, or the

DETERMINING POLICIES

direction of the firm may totally change when those professionals change positions.

3. *Firm.* Policies should be capable of standing up under scrutiny or crisis. They should provide guidance through all circumstances, without exception. They are subject to laws and ethics which control the actions of the profession. Such items as legislation regulating hours of work and minimum wages, or client confidentiality, would not be overridden by establishment of policy.

4. *Expressed in general terms.* Policies should be written in broad terms so that they express a principle, but allow flexibility for individual professionals and staff members to choose among various courses of action the one that will best accomplish a desired result.

5. *Brief.* Policy statements should be brief and avoid detail. The reason for the policy is to clearly convey the *intent* of senior partners, not to dictate how to do the work.

6. *Capable of acting as guidelines.* When policy is written, it should be clearly understood that senior partners are not trying to make all decisions for professionals and staff in advance. Decisions will be made by professionals and staff as circumstances change, but they will be able to follow policy guidelines which express the senior partners' intent.

There are many advantages to all levels of professionals and staff members in developing written policy, and firms are increasingly finding it worthwhile to develop basic policies. Advantages to various levels in the firm are:

Professionals and staff members—provide direction, educate, inform, and provide a basis for satisfaction and security. People usually feel better when they know where the professional firm is, in which direction it wishes to go, how it intends to get there, and what is expected of the staff.

Senior professionals—provide direction, make decisions easier, provide consistency in decisions, ease transfers and promotions, save time, and allow freedom of action.

Senior partners—provide continuity, provide a form of control and profit improvement, support the professional firm if there are arbitration decisions involving unfair hiring practices and the like, provide a high form of professional development, promote cooperative effort and increased capacity for professional service, and assist in the firm's growth and development by stimulating effective communication.

The effectiveness of a professional firm depends heavily on the amount and quality of coordination and teamwork—or on synergism. The activities of each professional and staff member in the firm are those which the senior partners are willing to delegate. Policy statements help the staff understand the intent of the managing partner and the senior partners and provide a vehicle to coordinate and complement activities.

Some sample policy statements follow.

SAMPLE POLICY STATEMENTS

The following policy statements are but a few examples of what a professional firm might devise. I have included 100 separate policy statements to provide an understanding of the intent and content of formal written policies. Many large firms have more than 100 policy statements because of the diversity of functions and professional services offered. At the same time, however, policy makers should be aware that the number of policies directed at any *one individual or group* of professionals or staff members in the firm should not be excessive; usually it should not exceed 30. If there are more than 30, they often start stating how a job should be done, rather than *intent*, and may not be remembered.

The policy statements convey the intent and beliefs of the firm, often as reflected from clientele.

One of the things you will note, if you are familiar with the policy writing process, is that many of these policy examples are somewhat different from others you may have encountered. Traditionally, policies in professional firms have been written from a tactical perspective. They are written at the policy-making level—by the executive committee and the managing partner—and are directed to convey intent of that group down through the firm. This sometimes results in no policy guidelines being written for the policy makers. Yet, under a holistic approach, policy guidelines should be written from an external, strategic (client) perspective and guide the actions of the entire professional firm, including most important, the policy makers themselves.

A. ENVIRONMENTAL RELATIONS

A.1 *Economic Considerations*
The firm will control its growth and development through careful examination of the effects of the economy on the profession and the firm.

A.1.1 Major economic cycles and trends and their potential effects on the revenues of the firm, or on the types of professional services

DETERMINING POLICIES

	to be provided, will be examined before any major growth or decrease decisions are made. The executive committee/managing partner are responsible for performance of the firm in relation to those economic considerations.
A.1.2	Local economic conditions, cycles, growth trends, competition, population shifts, and other indicators will be used by the executive committee/managing partner in determining office location and size, fee structure, types of professional services to be offered, and the types of promotional activities appropriate for the firm.
A.1.3	The executive committee/managing partner are responsible for preparing contingency plans in case of major economic changes (for example, inflation or recession).
A.2	*Research and Development*
	The research and development goals of our firm are to avoid obsolescence in professional services or types of clientele and to seek opportunities for long-term growth and viability.
A.2.1	Market research will be carried out to determine the demand for professional services before major resources—money, time, or effort—are expended in developing new services or new clientele.
A.2.2	Market research of existing services and clientele will be carried out, at a minimum annually, to determine changing client perceptions and needs, to determine new services or clientele, or to determine dropping old services and/or clientele.
A.2.3	Each new development or divestment area or project will be examined for the potential effect on other services/clientele of the firm and its effect on the firm's profitability and viability.
A.2.4	The priority of our research and development efforts will be to: 1. Improve the effectiveness of our professional services to existing clientele and maximize the utilization of existing resources in present locations. 2. Provide new related services which are in demand by existing clientele, and which we are, or can become, qualified to perform. 3. Provide existing services to new clientele. 4. Provide new related services to new clientele, provided that we can become the leading professional firm in that market segment. 5. Consider acquiring other firms, provided that they will (a) complement and improve the capability of the firm to provide professional services and (b) improve the financial viability of the firm. 6. Consider new locations.

A.3   *Societal Relations, Influences, and Responsibility*
       The firm will respond to the needs of society and maintain a high standard of moral conduct at all times.
A.3.1 We encourage our professionals and staff members to take part in public debate on today's leading social issues. We recognize that as employees we do not speak on behalf of the firm; but our professional views and opinions are often needed in discussing complex social issues.
A.3.2 The firm, its professionals, and its staff members are encouraged to contribute time and/or money to improve the community we serve. This includes seeking elected positions.
A.3.3 No partner, professional, or staff member shall engage in any activity which is, or appears to be, in conflict with (or contrary to) the firm's interest in the well-being of its clients or of the firm itself.
       This includes the acceptance of "kickbacks," loans, payments, services, gifts, travel and entertainment expenses, or any other items that are clearly not beneficial to the firm's clientele. It includes investment in the client's or a client's competitor's business, or even a seemingly unrelated business investment if clients could have a potential interest. The firm and its professionals and staff must at all times remain objective in protecting the client's best interests.
A.3.4 The firm will monitor environmental and social perspectives and demographics including population shifts, educational levels, values and norms of accepted social behavior; and, it will be responsive to environmental and social considerations (i.e., in 1982, professional offices should be effective leaders in the energy conservation efforts of the nation).
A.3.5 The firm will promote and invest in constructive actions which will improve the economic climate of the communities we serve —for the benefit of the general public, our clientele, and ourselves.

A.4   *Legislative Relations*
       The firm will obey the letter and intent of the law.
A.4.1 In the long-term, the firm and its professionals will succeed only if it obeys all laws governing its existence and actions, and the existence and actions of its clientele. At no time would it be legal or ethical for the firm to engage, or to counsel its clients to engage, in illegal activity.
A.4.2 The firm recognizes that new laws seldom come as a complete surprise, and believes that its clients and the firm itself are important parts of the community. The firm feels, therefore, that it has the right and duty to provide input into the legislative process

DETERMINING POLICIES

insofar as this is in the best interests of the general public, clientele, and the firm.

A.4.3 The firm feels that the general public believes government taxation and intervention has reached excessive levels. Where we obtain revenue from taxation sources, we will do our utmost to improve our efficiency and effectiveness to minimize the burden on taxpayers. Within the parameters of the law we will minimize the level of taxation on our clients and the firm and seek out ways to lessen government taxation at all levels in the economy.

A.4.4 The priority of ethical considerations that the firm will normally follow are to:
1. Obey the laws of the land.
2. Obey the rules and ethics of the profession.
3. Follow clients' directions.

(It is recognized that the law profession's ethics code stresses "client privilege"—client confidentiality and concern are recognized legally as coming before the law, and a lawyer will not divulge privileged information about a client even to the courts or the professional governing body. Other professionals are increasingly seeking this privilege to allow "the client to come first"—for example, the accounting profession is seeking the right not to testify in court against its own clients in tax avoidance cases.)

A.5 *Quasi-legislative Relations*

The firm will obey the letter and intent of the by-laws, rules of professional conduct, and codes of ethics of the professional organization.

A.5.1 In the long-term, the firm will become successful, viable, and recognized as a leading professional firm only if it follows the dictates of its own profession.

A.5.2 The firm recognizes that those rules and ethics should continually be questioned, however, given continuous changes in environmental conditions and client needs and expectations. The firm, therefore, feels that it has a duty to challenge the rules governing the conduct of the profession and to provide input for change where this is clearly in the best interests of the general public, clientele, and/or the firm.

A.5.3 The firm feels that the general public perceives the profession as a "closed shop," and professional organizations as set up, basically, to govern and protect members. The firm feels that it has a duty to help open communication and understanding between the profession (organization) and the general public, and that a major purpose of a professional organization should be to help the general public and help members help their clientele. Major resources of the professional organization should be directed to that purpose, as well as to governing and administering the activities of the membership. The firm actively supports its professional organization in bringing about improved public and client services.

A.6   Relations with Competitors
Our relationships with other (competitive) firms should be cordial, cooperative, and professional at all times. Within those parameters, however, we shall be competitive in quality of services, types of services, and fees, and responsive to client needs.

A.6.1   One of our objectives is to have our firm grow. Other than by increasing services to existing clients, or winning new clients who are entering the marketplace, the major source of that growth will be by increasing our market share. Basically, that means obtaining clients from other professional firms. Because we are a market-based, growth-oriented firm, one of our objectives is to increase our share of the market by 5 percent per year. We do, however, recognize the other firms as professionals first, and competitors second.

A.6.2   When a new client comes from another firm, we will write to that firm advising it of the change and querying if there are any professional or ethical reasons for not accepting the engagement.

A.6.3   The executive committee/managing partner, during an annual strategic planning session, will study and analyze the strengths and weaknesses of competing firms. They will analyze competitors' resources, including their financial and staffing capabilities, service and leadership capability, and marketing strategies. This is seen as being done in the (potential) clients' best interests, since the firm is looking for ways to better meet their needs and expectations. It is also a defensive strategy in that it will enable our firm to better understand the reaction of those firms to our strategic market moves. In addition, it will allow us to provide contingency plans in our strategy if those firms make strategic market moves.

B. CLIENT RELATIONS

We are a market-based firm. Our clients come first. We believe we must always be responsive to our clients' needs and expectations, and that this leads to a secondary result: that the firm will be successful, profitable, and viable in the long term. We believe that to be *the only way*. If we place self-interest ahead of client-interest and responsiveness, we may lose clients (market share) to other firms and/or have clients who are dissatisfied with fees and services. Ultimately, the very survival of our firm will depend on our ability to maintain our clients' confidence and goodwill. We must continually attract and retain increasing numbers of service or fees. Our policy is to encourage legitimate complaints or client concerns so that we can better satisfy those clients. We will make adjustments where legitimate complaints are encountered, with the objective of attaining clients' long-term goodwill.

C. OBJECTIVES OF THE FIRM

We are a goal-directed firm. We believe that if we are going to be more dynamic and successful in practicing our profession, we must have a clear sense of purpose in response to client needs.

C.1   Our basic objective will be stated in market-responsive terms.

C.2   Our basic objective will be reviewed periodically, at a minimum annually.

C.3   Subobjectives, goals, and policies will be subject to questioning and challenge by everyone in the organization. They will be reviewed and updated in their entirety, at least annually, to reflect changing conditions and environments and to ensure that they are cohesive and congruent.

C.4   Every professional and staff member will be involved in the objective-setting process and will be responsible for determining specific targets for improved services and revenues or reduced costs in his area of influence. Targets should be tight but attainable. We expect that, with increased emphasis on planning, variances between one-year plans and budgets and actual results will be ± 3 percent within five years.

D. QUALITY OF PROFESSIONAL SERVICES

The very reason for the existence of our firm is the provision of top-quality professional services. Our services are designed to provide client satisfaction. We strive to be the acknowledged leading firm in the provision of quality professional services. The quality of our professional services cannot be compromised.

D.1   Quality control procedures are employed to ensure that poor-quality services never reach our clients. Every professional and staff member in the firm is dedicated to maintaining and improving the quality of service.

D.2   We constantly review clients' changing needs and expectations, and pay attention to detail in providing professional services, so that we will obtain recognition as the leading firm.

D.3   Our objective is to lead the profession in providing quality professional services that are needed by clientele. This includes not only providing professional services where needs were unmet, but also improving the way we provide existing professional services.

D.4   In the provision of professional services, we should be different

DETERMINING POLICIES 263

clients and provide increasing services. If we did not, client and service attrition (the loss of clientele through death or business closure, or their learned ability to perform "professional" services themselves, or other causes) would eventually mean that few professional services could be supplied by our firm. We must always hold our clients in high esteem and act with integrity toward them if we are to continue to deserve their loyalty and patronage.

B.1   We will always be courteous and professional in our relations with everyone.

B.2   We will assess the clients' perception of the profession and our firm in order to determine clients' needs, wants, and expectations. This includes the clients' perception of our fees, convenience of locality and services, quality and timeliness of work, and so on.

B.3   The growth of our firm will depend on high client satisfaction. We strive to ensure that clients are not only "satisfied" but enthusiastic about our firm and the support it provides. Efficiency, promptness, courtesy, and clear concern for our clients and their well-being are the evidence which clients look for in determining if they are satisfied.

B.4   Our firm is client-oriented. Everything we do should respond to known client needs, wants, and expectations.

B.4   Every client will be treated as though the existence of the whole firm depended on him.

B.6   Our goal is to ensure that a client gets the best professional help and support available, rather than to try to get the most out of him.

B.7   We encourage warm and friendly relations, and open communication, between the firm and all clients. This can aid in maintaining a cooperative atmosphere and lead into other areas where we can assist our clientele.

B.8   We discourage undue familiarity (sexual relations and so on) between clientele and members of the firm. This could lead directly to a breakdown in the client–professional relationship. Personal considerations could outweigh professional objectivity in responding to our clients' professional needs, wants, and expectations.

B.9   We will not downgrade the qualifications of other professionals in discussion with anyone. Negative comments about other (competing) professionals' character, quality of professional work, or fees do not enhance our esteem in the eyes of clients. They only lead to a client's perception that we lack confidence in ourselves.

B.10 Even when we attempt to be totally responsive to clients' expectations, there are occasional complaints about our professional from all other professional firms. The quality, uniqueness, and types of our services should cause our (potential) clients to prefer us, as the leader in the profession.

E. FEES

We establish our fees on the basis of the costs of operating our professional firm. We feel entitled to a fee that is high enough to allow principals a return on their investment in the profession and the firm, in addition to adequate professional-level salaries.

E.1   In order to obtain fair and adequate fees we will differentiate client services, maintain a high volume of services (client base), and maintain high-quality, prompt, efficient, and courteous professional services.

E.2   We will not stint in providing quality professional services, even in low-fee areas.

F. LOCATION

We will maintain our offices in locations which are most convenient for the majority of our clients.

F.1   We will use the type of office space that provides the most comfortable surroundings for our clientele. A balance, based on client preference, will be struck between ostentatious and purely functional facilities.

F.2   We will be concerned about obtaining and maintaining lower-cost office facilities within the guidelines set out above. This will help us in maintaining lower fees to our clientele.

F.3   Office facilities will be designed to provide (1) for client convenience and comfort, and (2) for efficient low-cost deployment of professionals, staff, and supplies in providing professional services.

F.4   We will keep our offices and facilities neat, tidy, clean, and orderly. We know that the appearance of disarray and untidiness may give clients the impression that our professional services are equally unorganized.

G. PROMOTION

One of our basic goals is to attain leadership in our market segment.

G.1   Market trends and techniques will always be under review. Markets and client needs and expectations are undergoing continuous changes and flux. These changes provide tremendous opportunities for responsive firms to grow and prosper. Our objective is to be first in responding to opportunities presented in new market developments.

G.2 Our promotional objectives are aimed at providing new services to existing clientele and offering professional services to new clientele, to increase our revenues and our capability to provide low-cost quality services, and to stabilize our income throughout the year.

G.3 Our employees are encouraged to participate in community activities. The firm provides nonpartisan assistance in areas which will benefit the general public and the community at large.

G.4 Every professional and staff member must consider himself a marketer at all times. The firm exists in response to market needs. Our existence depends on meeting market (client) needs effectively and efficiently every day. Our future depends on the ability to ascertain demands and develop new services to meet those future demands.

G.5 All our promotion and advertising efforts should establish our firm as client-oriented—we are here to help. Our promotion efforts will be in the form of providing clients with information and assistance that they need and that shows that our firm is progressive and responsive to client needs. Advertising and promotion activities should also be well-targeted, show that we are different from other firms, and show that we are more responsive, so that clients will prefer our firm and the services it has to offer.

H. RESOURCES—FINANCE

We are a fiscally responsible professional firm. We believe that in order for our firm to grow and prosper, we must plan and control our financial resources.

H.1 The firm will prepare an annual budget, broken down by month, for all revenue sources, expense categories, and net profits. It will project its financial position (balance sheet) one year into the future. This will alleviate the necessity of panic financing and help control the financial aspects of the firm. Monthly income statements will be prepared, comparing monthly results to the budget for the month. Year-to-date statements will also be compared annually.

H.2 In addition to annual budgets, forecasts of growth, income, expenses, and profitability will be made for an additional four years (thus the total is a five-year budget). This will help the firm assess all its resources in making long-range plans.

H.3 Major expansion, new branch offices, equipment, and other long-term capital expenditures will be carred out only if they have maximum potential to attain a significant rate of return, thereby improving the long-range profitability and viability of the firm and its ability to provide quality low-cost professional services to its clientele in the long-term.

H.4 The firm may attract liability for an individual partner's failure to pay his income taxes or other liabilities. Each partner is expected to maintain his income taxes and other liabilities current at all times and/or to disclose to the other partners the potential liability to the firm.

H.5 The firm actively pursues methods of improving efficiency and reducing the costs of providing professional services. All professionals and staff members are expected to be "cost conscious" and continually look for ways to eliminate unnecessary expenses and improve efficiency.

H.6 Financial reports for the firm will be prepared promptly and supplied to all partners, banks, and other interested parties. We strive to maintain superior relations with our creditors. Growth will be financed from internal revenue whenever possible. We strive to keep borrowings to a minimum level. We expect prompt collection of client accounts to assist in this objective.

H.7 The firm will maintain sufficient cash and credit reserves to meet unforeseen circumstances.

H.8 The firm follows sound, conservative accounting practices and principles. The accounts and financial statements of the firm will be audited annually.

I. RESOURCES—OFFICE AND EQUIPMENT FACILITIES

The firm uses modern and efficient facilities and equipment at all times.

I.1 We are aware that the use of modern equipment and facilities enhances our image—it shows clients that we are modern and efficient professionals. The firm constantly searches for new facilities, equipment, technology, and methodology and keeps current with modern developments.

I.2 All office and equipment facilities are insured and safeguarded against loss.

J. RESOURCES—MATERIALS AND SUPPLIES

A main function of those professionals and staff members who purchase materials and supplies is to attain and maintain suppliers' goodwill. Suppliers are essential to the firm's well-being, and in the long-term, good supplier relations will enhance our ability to obtain supplies in periods of short supply, obtain preferred financial and credit arrangements, and ultimately reduce costs and enhance ongoing client services.

J.1 We survey the suppliers periodically to determine the best and stablest sources of supply with the lowest prices. We establish and maintain relations with as few suppliers as possible.

J.2 We treat all suppliers in an ethical and professional manner. We do not take unfair advantage, and will correct supplier errors in our favor, avoid cancellations and returns, not request bids unless a supplier is known to have a fair chance at supply, and not exaggerate our long-term requirements or otherwise erode our suppliers' confidence in our integrity. We expect our suppliers to be equally professional and ethical.

J.3 Costs of materials and supplies are next to salaries in terms of total expenses to this firm. Our objective is to choose the most appropriate supplies and be economical in using them.

J.4 Professionals and staff members are expected to maintain a cordial and cooperative relationship with suppliers at all times. Personal obligations, such as gifts, "kickbacks," or donations, should be avoided so that individuals in the firm will be objective in always choosing quality supplies at the most favorable prices.

K. RESOURCES—RELATIONS WITH PROFESSIONALS AND STAFF

The most important resource of this firm, and the source that is fundamental to the firm's success, is its people—the professionals and staff members employed by the firm. The firm is, in fact, these people.

K.1 Our objective is to recruit, select, develop, and retain the best qualified, client-concerned professionals and staff available.

K.2 To retain the best qualified people, we pay salaries that are competitive, or higher than they could attain elsewhere. Our job is to be efficient so that we can afford it.

K.3 We provide all professionals and staff members with opportunities and an environment that give each individual a rewarding and satisfying sense of achievement.

K.4 Each individual's rights, professional standing, and ethics will be respected, by everyone, at all times. There will be equal opportunity. Our policy is to select the best possible person for a job irrespective of age, color, creed, national origin, religion, or sex.

K.5 Our objective is to minimize staff turnover and build staff enthusiasm and morale.

K.6 All professional and staff members are encouraged to make comments and recommend changes which will improve our capability to service clients. In no case will a suggestion put forth receive an unpleasant response. Communications, dialog, and discussion are to remain open at all levels in the firm in order to develop high morale, esprit de corps, a sense of belonging, and high individual self-esteem in a group environment.

K.7 All professionals and staff members should expect cooperation,

DETERMINING POLICIES

encouragement, constructive assistance, and confidence in their abilities from their supervisors and all others in the firm.

K.8 This firm has established salary levels to ensure that fair, equitable, and impartial consideration is given to the salaries of all employees. The levels take into account the complexity and scope of various positions in the firm and the education and experience needed to fill those positions. All salaries reflect, as objectively as possible, the relative worth of those positions, compared with other positions in the firm and with comparable or higher salary levels outside of the firm.

K.9 Our salary policy is designed to:
1. Attract and retain people who can immediately perform required services and who have the capability of assuming greater responsibility with experience.
2. Develop a dynamic and cooperative attitude, enthusiasm, loyalty, and high staff motivation.
3. Balance the salaries to ensure that they are fair and equitable.

K.10 We will automatically review every salary at least semiannually. It is the firm's responsibility to initiate discussions, since it is usually embarrassing for the staff to do so. The increase will include a cost-of-living increase and a merit increase for increased efficiency and value to the firm and its clientele.

K.11 In cases where no salary increase is justified, immediate termination must be considered. This must be thought of as in the best long-range interest of the employees and the firm's clientele.

K.12 Our firm delegates as much professional work as possible to the most junior level in the firm capable of doing the work. This is done for a number of reasons:
1. To ensure lowest costs to clientele.
2. To develop professionals and staff members, allow them to learn new skills, increase their responsibility, and, ultimately, increase their salaries.
3. To improve the firm's efficiency in providing professional services.
4. To allow senior professionals time to plan further ways to provide professional assistance needed by clients and improve the firm's efficiency in meeting clients' service needs.

K.13 All professionals and staff members are expected to perform to the limit of their professional capabilities. Cooperation, teamwork, constructive attitudes, and enthusiasm about the profession, the firm, and its clientele are the keys to a happy and successful practice. Performance evaluations will be used to determine individual salary levels, since there is a definite relationship between the entire firm's performance in these areas and its ability to earn fees.

K.14 Whenever possible, it is the firm's policy to promote professionals and staff members from within the firm. This will help improve efficiency and retain increasingly experienced professionals and staff. We will:
1. Assist all professionals and staff in choosing appropriate career paths, and offer definite promotion opportunities.
2. Advise all staff when a position is open and offer the position to qualified existing staff.
3. Offer positions to those with the greatest experience, if qualifications are identical.
4. Hire from outside the firm only as a last resort.

K.15 We are concerned with the advancement and psychological and physical well-being of all professionals and staff in our firm. We want to ensure that everyone earns the maximum salary and derives the maximum satisfaction possible. We believe that environment will best help the firm reach and maintain the level of efficient, high-quality professional services expected by our clientele.

K.16 To encourage all professionals and staff to improve their professional competence, we offer assistance through the payment of tuition fees for professionally related education. We pay all costs of part-time undergraduate courses leading to a professional designation and all continuing education costs of professionals.

K.17 Our firm has a policy of not establishing a uniform retirement age. Some professionals and staff members may wish, or have the need, to retire at an age earlier than 65. Others may have the ability and desire to continue well beyond that age. However, we appreciate discussion and notification, preferably one year ahead of the retirement date, to enable the firm to plan succession and promotion opportunities for others in the firm. This policy applies where there are no laws governing mandatory retirement ages.

K.18 Professionals and staff may accept outside assignments which do not conflict with the professional services of the firm, or for which the firm cannot be held liable. Such items as consultative services, speaking engagements, and writing assignments which are not the normal activities of the firm are encouraged.

K.19 Professionals and staff who cannot have problems resolved at their direct supervisor's level are encouraged to seek assistance from higher authority.

K.20 The firm discourages the employment of close relatives or intimate relationships in a close working environment. The firm is concerned that emotions and misunderstandings among staff and clientele may lead to embarrassing situations and less than objective professional services.

K.21 We encourage participation, fairness, and teamwork so that professionals and staff will not feel the need to obtain third-party support on their behalf. Our objective is to remain non-union.

K.22 Our best professional results will be attained through outstanding professionals and staff.

L. TARGETS

We believe that we must carefully plan our growth, and that growth is basic to maintaining a dynamic and healthy professional environment.

L.1 We strive to increase revenues by 24 percent this year, accounted for as follows:
Ten percent inflationary increase.
Eight percent by offering new services to existing clients.
Six percent by increasing our market share (obtaining new clients).

L.2 We strive to increase our gross billings to $2 million in five years by providing quality professional services based on client needs and expectations. This represents a minimum increase of 18 percent per year, averaged over 5 years. Revenue sources will increase by 8 percent per year; the balance (10 percent) is the estimated inflationary rate.

L.3 We strive to grow not only in size but also in the quality of services we offer.

L.4 We strive to improve client satisfaction. We believe that growth is necessary if we are to achieve a steadily improving level of professional service that is in line with our clients' needs and wants.

L.5 Our target objectives are designed to encourage:
1. Growth, education, and experience of all professionals and staff members.
2. Willingness to keep current with technical and professional changes.
3. Anticipation of and adaptability to change.
4. Active search to find and provide new services needed by clients.
5. Improved efficiency and service to all our clients.
6. Search for new clients who have an expressed need for professional services of our level of quality.

L.6 Providing quality professional services has inherent high fixed administrative and overhead costs. As our volume of professional work increases, however, those costs remain relatively stable. This is why it is important to increase volume to the maximum level, while sustaining quality of services. It improves our ability to offer cost-effective additional services, or lower overall costs per client, in the long run.

M. MANAGEMENT OF THE FIRM

Every human organization must have effective leadership. Our partners elect a managing partner at an annual meeting. That partner is charged with the firm's leadership for the ensuing year.

M.1 The partners, at regular monthly meetings held at 9:00 A.M. on the last Thursday of every month, discuss the strategic planning, policy, and marketing strategy of the firm. Day-to-day operations are delegated to the managing partner.

M.2 The partners may appoint an executive committee, consisting of three partners, to assist the managing partner in policy decisions between meetings.

M.3 The partners may appoint a strategic planning committee, or other special committees, to be responsible for making specific recommendations to the next general partners' meeting.

M.4 A managing partner is elected at an annual meeting of all partners. He is the chairman of all subsequent partners', the executive committee, and special committee meetings. A deputy managing partner, also elected at the annual partners' meeting, assumes all of the managing partner's duties when the position is vacant, or as assigned by the managing partner from time to time.

M.5 The firm evaluates the performance of every partner, professional, and staff member on a consistent basis, at least annually.

M.6 All people in the firm are encouraged to contribute to the firm's planning and growth.

N. OTHER

We are a firm that strives to grow and be dynamic and vital in an increasingly competitive professional environment.

N.1 We devote time and resources to research to determine new ways to efficiently and effectively offer quality professional services to an expanding client base.

N.2 We research and develop ways to better satisfy the needs, wants, and expectations of our clientele. In this way we are better able to supply them with a quality of professional service they desire, and our services are designed specifically for our clients and are of value to them.

23

Summary

Professional firms are resource converters. Resources include not only supplies, capital, finance, facilities, and staff, but many intangible resources such as time, professional education, knowledge, and experience. Only when all these resources are brought together to efficiently meet market demands can a firm become successful and efficient.

The successful firm continually assesses its environment and markets, sets objectives, and designs strategic plans and efficient work programs to achieve results. Planned management in a professional environment begins by determining market needs and stating desired results, then designing tasks to accomplish those results.

There are many methods of measuring the effectiveness of a professional firm, controlling the results of professional actions, and controlling the professionals and staff members themselves. The model of planned management rests on market-based strategic planning, which is designed not only to forecast the future but to help control it. The success of the professional firm will be based on its ability to respond to the needs and expectations of the marketplace. Client satisfaction or enthusiasm is the key to achieving professional goals.

Senior professionals and partners formulate general policies to assist in the accomplishment of the professional firm's plans. Daily decisions must be made at every level in the professional firm, and a "planned management" model assists everyone in his decision-making efforts. A central management objective in a professional firm must be to optimize the use of all resources. In every decision, and particularly expansion or reduction decisions, consideration must be given not only to marketability of professional services but also to financial capability, professional service capacity, availability and cost of facilities, equipment, and supplies, and the most critical response of all—qualified professional and staff personnel—not to mention that the firm's owners expect a profitable return on investment.

Using a market-based approach, Figure 23-1 shows what a "planned management" model in a professional firm would consider.

Most professional firms should have a "planned management" model to help coordinate the firm and its operations. Models vary from firm to firm, but the essential elements of management planning, organizing, initiating action, and controlling results are central to a sophisticated management style.

We had stated that planning takes a great deal of time, effort, and money. There is little doubt that no other organization function can provide a greater return, not only financially, but in terms of building a personally rewarding firm and professional career. With no other function can omission prove more costly to the professional and his firm. Without planning, a firm may drift aimlessly and without purpose.

We have provided a planning model to assist in the development of a desired future and establish policies and programs to bring that future about. There must be collaboration, cooperation, and effective and open communication between all partners, professionals, staff members, clients, and creative experts. Not only must complex problems be overcome, but opportunities must be explored for their potential.

Professionals must be knowledgeable not only in their profession and specialty but about the world. They must be men of vision. Some of the more sophisticated techniques to accomplish this arise from the application of third-force psychology, including a technique known as constructive synthetic visualization, whereby professionals will actually visualize the complete firm and its operations and client relations five, ten, and twenty years in the future, in order to decide what must be done *now* to accomplish that goal.

Professional success can only be described as the meeting of

SUMMARY

some professional goal. Motivational psychology suggests that there are three criteria for the success of an individual: (1) he must have a goal, (2) he must have a plan about how to accomplish that goal, and (3) he must be committed to that accomplishment.

In a professional firm, the planning process consists of:

1. Stating desired results first (the vision).
2. Deciding how to go about it—what work must be done and what resources must be utilized.
3. Organizing the firm so that it is responsive to its clientele and so that there are clear-cut lines of authority, responsibility, and decision-making capabilities at appropriate levels in the firm.
4. Designing a management information system to control the firm and its operation.

Even in the smallest firm, senior professionals must be concerned with *market planning* and *strategic* planning. There must be long-range, results-oriented planning besides tactical planning, which is very short-term. Although short- and long-range plans interact, there is the possibility that the word "planning" may mean only tactical planning in a professional firm and that only short-term plans (for one to three years) are made. Directing all effort toward improving next week's quality of service or next month's gross fees, or next year's net income, and totally ignoring the longterm effects of such actions will not necessarily improve, in the long term, the professional firm's effectiveness in providing quality professional services or enhance its profitability and viability. Market reactions certainly must be considered. Increasing clientele by 10 percent next year could result in staff shortages and untimely services. Opening a new office may strap the financial resources of the firm. Those resource limits would have been previously analyzed, and the use of resources optimized, through strategic planning. Conceptual models like the one in Figure 23-2 can be devised to show the allocation of resources.

In order to attain viable long-term results, there must be (1) consistent (full) market demand, (2) a determination of the amount and timing of resources needed, (3) efficient allocation of resources, and (4) plans to acquire or generate the resources.

Financial resource planning (budgeting) is clearly understood and used in many professional firms. Yet, it is only a small part of the total strategic planning process for resource allocation. Financial planning allows the projection of sources and applications of monetary resources and can predict a potential surplus or short-

Figure 23-1. Planned management model.

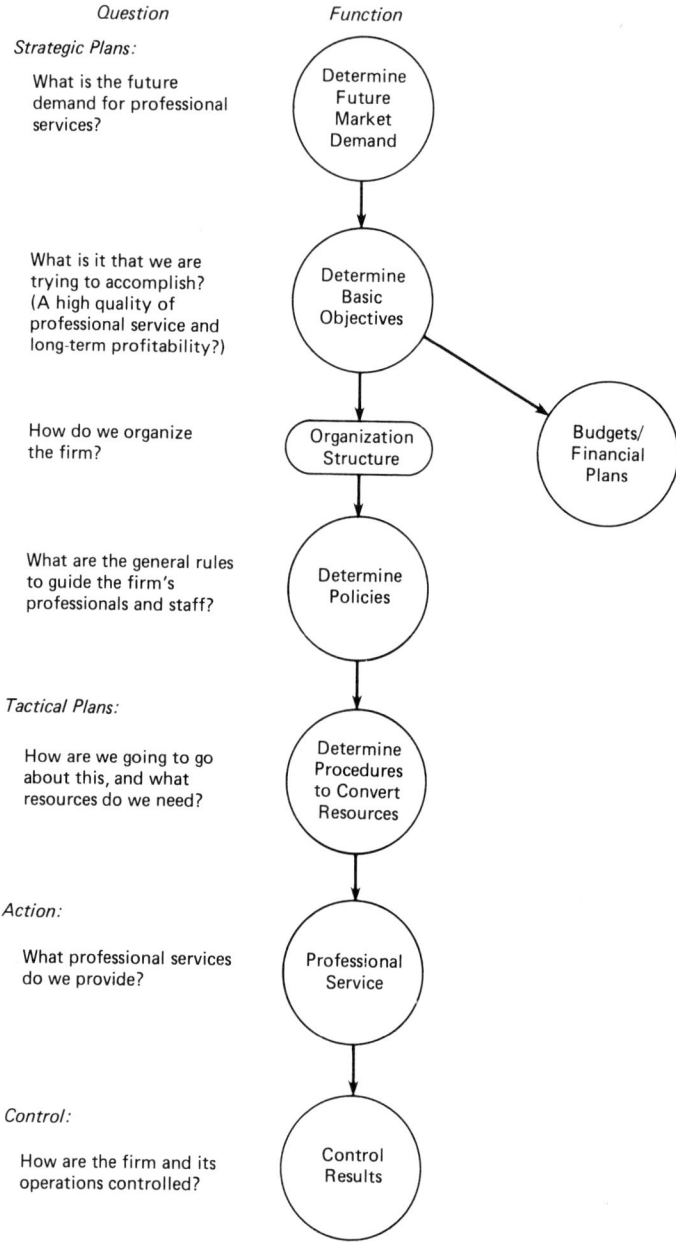

SUMMARY

	Executive Level	
Methodology	*Large Firm*	*Small Firm*

Long-range:
  Economic research
  Client research
  Market research
  Environmental perception
    studies
  Etc.
	Planning partner/
	marketing partner
		Managing partner

Determine:
  Professional service mix
  Level of profit
  For whom
	Managing partner/
	executive committee/
	partners
		Partners

Operating budgets Capital budgets	Administration manager	Managing partner/ accounting staff
Write policy with regard to relationships with creditors, partners, professionals and staff members, government bodies, competitors, etc.	Managing partner/ executive committee	Partners
Define the technology and work methodology. Determine equipment, facilities, staffing, financial, and other needs. Organize the work.	Department heads	Partners and professionals
Operations: management, equipment, facilities, and staff.	Department heads, professionals, and staff	Professionals and staff
Effective referral program. Financial results compared to plan. Studies of professional effectiveness. Management reports. Management information system (MIS)	Managing partner/ executive committee/ administration manager	Managing partner

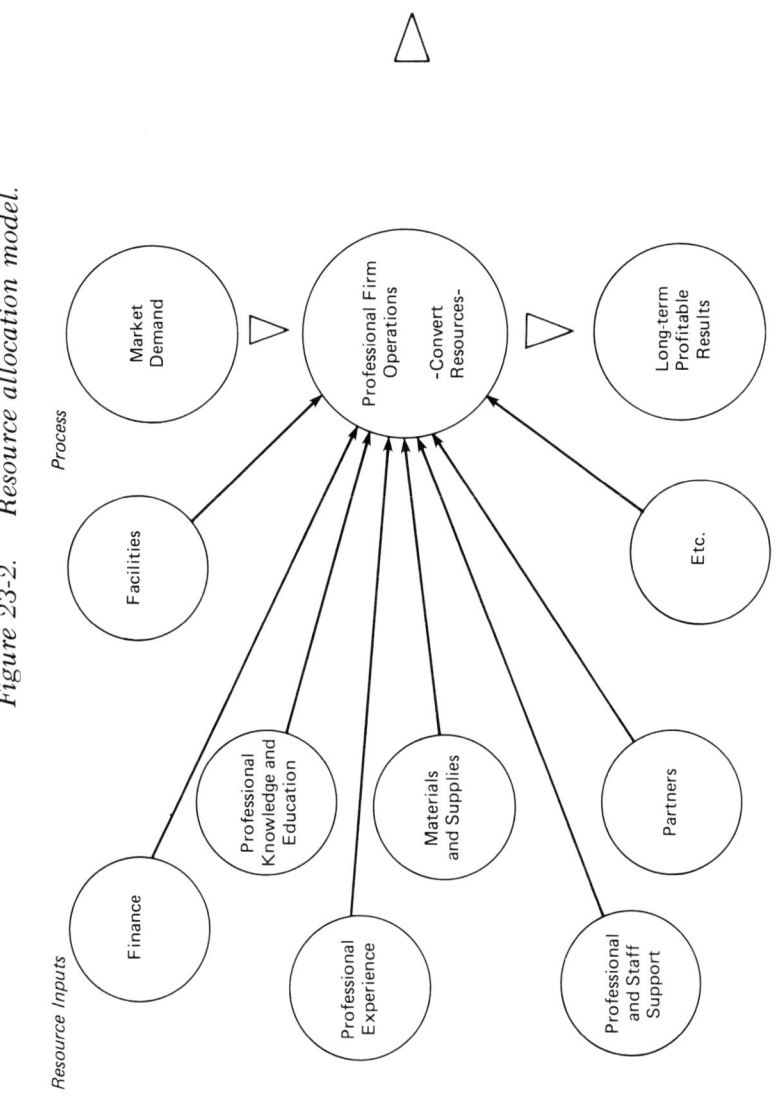

Figure 23-2. Resource allocation model.

age. If there is a predicted shortage, it allows time for planned intervention to generate or acquire additional investment through increased partner equity, borrowings, cost reduction programs, and the like—*before* the money runs out! It also allows planned allocation of surpluses for expansion, modernization, partner drawings, and so on.

Facilities, offices, and equipment must be built or purchased, replaced or abandoned when they are no longer economically viable, and maintained at an optimum level while in use. The size of offices and premises must be considered for optimum efficiency. Expansion of existing facilities or opening of branch offices can be considered. Location of offices is critical—and usually a permanent step. Convenience to professionals, staff members, and employees, and markets for the services offered, are of paramount importance.

Growth policies, major development of the firm, and location all must consider clients' needs, wants, and expectations. The mix of services must be considered. All these, and other items, must be considered in plans of very long range, because we are now planning a firm that will be responsive to client needs long into the future.

Sources of materials and supplies should be conveniently located and available to the firm. There should be methods of checking inventory levels to ensure that materials and supplies will be available in the correct amounts, when needed, at acceptable costs. If heavy reliance is placed on a specific material or supplier, the firm must obtain assurance of future delivery. Even when supplies are available, significant price changes may lead to a search for alternative suppliers or materials.

Human resources must be carefully considered and the firm placed near a source of trained personnel, or provision be made to relocate professionals and staff members. Personnel planning cannot be considered in isolation from total planning of the professional firm. The firm must identify specific skills of each person in the organization. Through a properly designed organization chart, backed by thorough job descriptions, job analysis, and evaluation, the firm must identify the skills it needs at every level.

Potential automation to replace existing human jobs must also be carefully (and discreetly) studied. New professionals and staff must be recruited, trained, and retrained if the firm is to remain viable. Competitive wages and benefits must be negotiated and paid, and increasingly there must be a great deal of job satisfaction to the individual professionals and staff members if the firm is to retain high-caliber, well-motivated personnel.

Senior professionals must have timely and correct information upon which to base decisions. Increasingly, computer-generated management information systems (MIS) are used to provide "on-line" (real-time) information to assist in the complex decision making required of senior professionals.

A professional's central objective must be the optimum use of all resources. Also central to the planning process must be the continual examination and reexamination of those resources to determine methods by which they might be used, modified, or redeployed to attain the firm's objectives most effectively.

The book has been designed to help all professional firms, even the smallest, to find and use appropriate techniques.

Markets must be continually studied and analyzed to determine their needs and receptivity to existing and proposed professional services.

In that sense the application of the tools in this book has no end.

Index

accountants
 client needs for, 66
 core services of, 110
 expansion possibilities for, 112
 feeders for, 152
 follow-up by, example of, 150–151
 incentives from, 158
 marketing departments for, 195
 needs assessment by, 92, 93
 positioning in market by, 144, 145
 publics of, 52
 reduction of services by, 113–114
 survey questionnaire for, sample, 94, 97–101
accounting, responsibility, 248
adaptive planning, 181
advertising, 25–26, 40
 financial constraints on, 168–169
 media for, 169–170
 for promotion, 157–158, 166–170
 quality of service and, 168

advertising *(continued)*
 referrals and, 151
 themes in, 169
agent publics, 51
aggressive marketing, 20
American Marketing Association, 15
analysis
 of clientele, *see* client analysis
 cost-benefit, *see* cost-benefit analysis
 decision-flow, 216–217
 of environment, 3–5
 of macroenvironment, 56–61
 of market structure, 83
 of variance in budgets, 252
appraisal, performance, 253
Argyris, Chris, 47
assets, *see* resources
atmospherics, 156
attitude, of professional services, 187–190
audience, target, *see* target market
audit, market, *see* market audit
augmented services, 110

281

authority, 220
autocratic management style, 47

bad-mouthing, 155
bargaining approaches to compensation, 208
behavior, social hierarchical, 178
benefits, 207, 211–212
   "cafeteria" concept of, 212
billing, *see* fee(s)
blame, acceptance of, 155
branch offices, 123–124
   market-based decision for, 170–173
breakeven charts, 139, 141, 246–247
breakeven fee setting, 139–141
"Breakthrough in Strategic Planning, A" (Marketing Science Institute), 167
Brian, John M., 242
budget(s), 238, 275
   for advertising, 168–169
   in financial planning, 201–203
   flexible, 246–248
   for marketing program, 244, 246
   problems of, 251–252
   profit centers and, 249–251
bulletins, 160
business, *see* firm, professional
"buzz," market, 43, 54, 94, 159
   creation of, by self, 172

"cafeteria" benefits concept, 212
capital, *see* financial resources
cards, holiday, 160
centralization, 123–124
chain of command, 221
change, 240–241
   in environment, 2–3
   in fees, 141–142
   management of, 254
   as objective, 185
   resistance to, 215–216

change *(continued)*
   in technology, 229
   see also growth
charity, 55
charts, breakeven, 139, 141
charts, organization
   functional type of, 73
   marketing function included on, 22
   marketing function lacking from, 19
   matrix type of, 222-223
   for senior-level marketing function, 166
classified advertising, 157
client(s)
   apprehensions of, 27
   awareness of service by, *iv–v*
   convenience for, 120–121, 125
   demographic characteristics of, 83
   discrimination by, in pricing, 136
   ethical considerations for, 28–29
   expectations of, 97, 146–147
   fees and, *see* fee(s)
   first impressions of, 147–149
   geographic factors of, 83
   grouping of, 222
   image of professional and, *see* image, professional
   information needs of, 193
   mix of, 85–86
   needs of, *see* needs of clients
   personal contact with, 157, 191–193
   policy statements on, samples of, 262–264
   psychological characteristics of, 82–83
   as publics, 67
   referrals from, *see* referral of clients

INDEX

client(s) *(continued)*
  responsibility of professional for, 86–87
  satisfaction of, 10, 22–23, 189
  synergy and, 32–33
  target, *see* target market
  welfare of, long-term, 46–47
  see also client analysis
client analysis, 83
  expectations of clients in, 97
  image of professional and, 93–95
  needs assessment in, 91–93
  role modeling for, 96–97
  survey questionnaire for, 97–107
client relations manager, 165–166, 195
client-responsive practice, 44–46, 180
  contact with clients in, 191–193
  viewpoint in, 190–191
client/service mix, 144–145
client services manager, 165–166
client survey questionnaire, 94, 97–107
collective bargaining, 208
comfort phase, in life cycle of firm, 39–41, 179
command, chain of, 221
commercial transaction, 55
communication, 154
  in personal contact, 157
  skills in, 155–156
company, *see* firm, professional
compensation policy, 184, 207–210
  benefits in, 211–212
competition, 63
  fee setting by, 136–137, 139
  market share control and, 243
  MIS and, 230–231
  policy statements on, samples of, 262
  segmentation of, 68

"Competition Comes to Accounting" *(Fortune)*, 195
computers, 170
  see also management information systems (MIS)
confidentiality, when setting up new office, 171–173
constructive synthetic visualization, 96, 274
consuming publics, 51–52
contact, personal, 157, 191–193
contacts list, 160
control, 239
  in life of organization, 179–180
  in MIS, 228
  span of, 220
conversion publics, 67
core service, 109–110
Corporate Market Planning (Brian), 242
cost-benefit analysis, 17, 226
  of marketing program, 244, 245
cost-oriented fee setting, 133–136
credibility, 159–161
cycle, decision, 218–219

decentralization, 123–124
decision-flow analysis, 216–217
decision-making
  cycle in, 218–219
  decision-flow analysis in, 216–217
  modeling and, 217–218
  performance measurement and, 219
delegation, 220–221
demand, 56
  fee setting by, 133, 136
  prestige and, 137–138
  profit and, 130, 131
democratic management style, 47
demographic profile of client, 64–65, 83
depth of service, 110–111

diagram, scatter, *see* scatter diagram
differentiation, *see* segmentation
direct mail, 169–170
direct marketing model, 120
discretionary expense centers, 250
discrimination, in pricing, 136
disincentives, 158
distribution of services
   centralization and, 123–124
   convenience for client and, 120–121, 125
   franchising and, 124–125
   location affecting, 122, 125–128
   planning for, 126–127
   quality control and, 121–122
doctors, *see* medical profession
downtime, 129
Drucker, Peter, 181

economic considerations
   for MIS, 229
   policy statements on, samples of, 258–259
education, iv
   contact developed in, 191–192
   feedback loop in, 36
   on policy, of staff, 255
   training programs as, 191–192, 213–214
   viewpoint renewed by, 191
empathy, 154
employees, *see* personnel
employment transaction, 55
Enger, Norman L., 236
engineers
   client needs for, 66
   core services of, 110
   expansion possibilities for, 112
   feeders for, 152
enlargement, job, 197
enrichment, job, 196–198
environment
   analysis of, 3–5

environment *(continued)*
   internal, *see* microenvironment
   marketplace as, *see* macroenvironment
   motivation through, 213
   policy statements on, samples of, 258–262
equipment, *see* facilities
ethics of marketing, 24–25, 28–29
etiquette, telephone, 147–148
exchange, value, *see* value exchange
expansion of services, 111–113
   market-based decision for, 170–173
   as objective, 185
   see also branch offices

facilities, 279
   atmospherics and, 156
   in growth phase, 39
   in maturity phase, 41
   MIS information on, 233–234
   planning of, 9, 127–128, 203–204
   policy statements on, samples of, 267–268
   in survival phase, 38
fee(s), 25
   in client-responsive practice, 44–45
   complaints from clients about, 16, 53–54
   discrimination and, 136
   in growth phase of firm, 39
   incentives affecting, 158
   increases in, 141–142
   in maturity phase of firm, 41
   minimization of, pressure for, 130
   in objectives statement, 183
   policy statements on, samples of, 265
   prestige and, 137–138
   professional's approach to, 33

fee(s) *(continued)*
  profit affecting, 130
  quality affecting, 121
  in saturation phase of firm, 42
  setting of, *see* fee setting
  in survival phase of firm, 37–38
feedback loop, educational, 36
feeders, 42, 151–152, 159
  ideas of, on expansion, 171–172
fee setting
  breakeven method of, 139–141
  by competition, 136–137, 243
  by cost to firm, 133–136
  by demand, 133, 136
  guidelines for, 139
  objective method of, 132–133
  subjective method of, 132–133
financial information for MIS, 232
financial planning, 201–203, 275, 279
financial resources, 201–203
  policy statements on, samples of, 266–267
firm, professional
  approaches to, 10–11
  control phase of, 179–180
  exchange relationships for, 56
  expansion of, 111–113
  external influences on, 2
  growth phase of, 39–41, 179
  maturity phase of, 41–42
  reduction of, 113–114
  saturation phase of, 42
  self-actualization in, 180
  supersaturation and decline phase of, 42–43
  survival phase of, 37–39, 178–179
first impressions, 147–149
fiscal responsibility centers, 250–251
flexible budgeting, 246–248
flowchart model, 217, 218
follow-up review, 149–151
forecasting, *see* budget(s)

Fortune, 195
franchises, 124–125
fringe benefits, 211–212
functional groups, 221, 222

general publics, 52
geographic groups, 221
geographic location
  of client, 64, 83
  discrimination in pricing and, 136
  planning of, 203–204
  policy statements on, samples of, 265
  of service, 122, 125, 127–128, 279
goal setting, 177
  for advertising, 169
  microenvironment and, 72–74
  for MIS establishment, 226
  rules for, 178
  see also objectives; planning; strategic planning
goodwill, client, 189
goodwill calls, 148
government
  compensation and, 207
  MIS and, 230
  in policy statements, samples of, 260–262
  regulation by, *iii–iv*, 51, 130
Great Britain, 24–25
groups, job, 210
growth, 279
  in life cycle of firm, 39–41, 179
  planning for, 239–242
  see also change

hard-sell approach, 20
holiday cards, 160
holidays, 211
human resources planning, 9, 204, 279–280
  compensation program in, 207–210

human resources planning *(continued)*
  fringe benefits in, 211–212
  management of staff in, 212
  motivation and, *see* motivation
  new staff in, 206–207
  skills in, 205
  staff size in, 205–206

identification, market, 216
image, professional, 16, 17
  atmospherics in, 156
  attraction/retention of client and, 95, 125
  communication affecting, 155–156
  defined, 93–94
  first impressions and, 147–149
  measurement of, 94–95
  in objectives statement, 182–183
  persuasion through, 154
  of senior professionals, 155–156
image enhancement programs, 94
impressions, first, 147–149
incentives, 158
  benefits as, 207
increasing fees, 141–142
individual bargaining approach to compensation, 208
information systems, 217–218
  in management (MIS), *see* management information systems (MIS)
initial impressions, 147–149
innovative planning, 181
input publics, 50–51, 67
institutional advertising, 157
insurance benefits, 211
internal publics, 50
inventories, 232–233
investment centers, 250
investment-to-profit ratios, 133

job enlargement, 197
job enrichment, 196–198
job groups, 210
job rotation, 191, 198
journals, professional, 158

law firms, *see* lawyers
Lawler, Edward E., 200
lawyers
  client needs for, 66
  core services of, 110
  expansion possibilities for, 112
  feeders for, 152
  images of, 95
  market positioning and, 87–90
  publics of, 51
  reduction of services by, 113, 114
  target markets for, 84
layering, 220
lead time, 127
legal firms, *see* lawyers
letters, promotion through, 160
library, professional, 148–149
  for client use, 160
life cycle of firm
  growth phase in, 39–41, 179
  maturity phase in, 41–42
  modification of, 43–45
  saturation phase in, 42
  supersaturation/decline phase in, 42–43
  survival phase in, 37–39, 178–179
lines, service, *see* service lines
listening, 155
location, *see* geographic location
long-term planning, *see* strategic planning
Lovewell, P. J., 239

macroenvironment, 56
  analysis of, questionnaire for, 58–61
magazines, 148
  advertisements in, 169

INDEX

mail, direct, 169-170
management
  of change, 254
  of personnel, 212
  planned, *see* planned management
  policy statements on, samples of, 272
  styles of, comparison of, 47
  top levels of, *see* senior professionals
Management and Organizational Development: The Path from XA to YB (Argyris), 47
management by crisis, 249
management by exception, 248–249
management by objectives (MBO), 198
Management for Results (Drucker), 181
management information systems (MIS), 5, 225–226, 280
  development of, 226–228
  external information for, 228–231
  internal information for, 228, 231–236
  procedures for, 236
Management Standards for Developing Information Systems (Enger), 236
manipulation of client, 29, 153
manners, telephone, 147–148
margins, profit, 40
market(s), 2–3
  audit of, *see* market audit
  definition of, 50, 54, 82
  differentiation among, *see* segmentation
  identification of, 216
  MIS information on, 233
  positioning of, *see* market positioning
  resistance of, 131

market(s) *(continued)*
  target, *see* target market
  see also market share
market approach to compensation, 208
market audit, 56–57
  internal review in, 74–81
  macroenvironment analysis in, 58–61
  market identification in, 69–71
  for MIS, 233
market "buzz," *see* "buzz," market
marketing
  analysis of, *see* market audit
  approaches to, 18–21
  in client-responsive practice, *see* client-responsive practice
  concept of, 28, 187, 189–190
  cost-effectiveness of, analysis of, 244, 245
  defined, 15–17
  department for, separate, 194–195
  ethical considerations of, 24–25, 28–29
  funds allocated for, 242–243
  historical development of, 26–27
  at life-cycle phases of firm, 38, 40, 41–42
  management of, *see* marketing management
  mix in, 16–17, 108–109
  plan for, 242
  research for, *see* research, market
  as senior-level position, 164–165
  as staff position, 165
  synergistic approach to, 32–33
  systems approach to, 31, 33–34
  technique for, *see* technique(s), marketing

marketing *(continued)*
  undifferentiated approach to, 83–84
  see also advertising; promotion; segmentation
marketing management, 18, 31
  balanced approach to, 20–21
  hard-sell approach to, 20
  in maturity phase of firm, 41–42
  traditional approach to, 18–19
Marketing Science Institute (Cambridge, Mass.), 167
marketplace, *see* macroenvironment
market positioning, 87–90
  structured, 69
  synergy and, 143–144
  unstructured, 68–69
market response function, 242–243
market share
  control of, 243
  quality and, 167–168
  return on investment and, 167
market structure analysis, 83
Maslow, Abraham, 178
materials, *see* facilities
matrix grouping, 222
matrix organization chart, 222–223
maturity phase, in life cycle of firm, 41–42
MBO (management by objectives), 195
media, 157–158
  for advertising, 169–170
medical profession
  client needs for, 66
  core services of, 110
  differentiation of practice in, 85
  expansion possibilities for, 112
  feeders for, 152
  images of professionals in, 95
  incentives in, 158

medical profession *(continued)*
  quality level and, 121
  reduction of services in, 113
meetings, 160–161
merchandising, 17
microenvironment
  analysis of, 73–74
  goal-setting for, 72–73
  review of, questionnaire for, 74–81
MIS, *see* management information systems
mix
  of clients, 85–86
  client/service, 144–145
  marketing, 16–17, 108–109
  of services, 86–87
  see also orchestration, market; segmentation
modeling, 217, 218
models, role, 96
Monopolies Commission (Great Britain), 24–25
motivation, 196
  compensation as, 208–209
  employee participation as, 199
  environment and, 213
  factors in, 199–200
  job enrichment as, 196–198
  job rotation as, 198
  management by objectives as, 198
  psychology of, 275
multidisciplinary approach, 192
mutual benefit organizations, *see* professional organizations

needs of clients, 17
  definition of, 91–92
  for information, 192–193
  knowledge of, from clients, 146–147
  projective method for assessing, 93

INDEX

needs of clients *(continued)*
  simulation method for assessing, 92–93
  survey questionnaire for assessing, 97–107
news media, 157, 159
niche, market, *see* target market
nonhuman resources, 201–204

objective fee setting, 132–133
objectives, 239
  characteristics of, 181
  examples of, 182–186
  motivation through, 198–199
  organization and, 220
  policy statements on, sample of, 264
  setting, *see* goal setting
office, *see* facilities
optimizing planning, 181
orchestration, market
  client/service mix and, 144–146
  expansion and, 151–152
  first impressions in, 147–149
  follow-up in, 149–151
  see also mix
organizational groupings, 221–222
organizational structure, *see* structure, organizational
organization charts, *see* charts, organizational
organizations, professional, *see* professional organizations
orientation, of professional services, 187–190

participative approach to planning, 242
peer reviews, 121
P/E (price-earnings) ratios, 133
performance appraisal, 253
performance measures, 219
personal contact, 157, 191–193
personnel, 279–280

personnel *(continued)*
  client-responsiveness of, 190–193
  compensation of, 184, 207–210
  education of, *see* education
  management of, 212
  MIS information on, 234–235
  motivation of, *see* motivation
  planning by, 241–242
  planning of, *see* human resources planning
  policy knowledge of, 255, 257
  policy statements on, samples of, 268–271
  for public relations, 165–166
  recruitment of, 206–207
  size of, 205–206
  skills of, 205
persuasion, 153–154
physicians, *see* medical profession
planned management, 5–8, 239, 273–274
  model for, 274, 276–278
planning, 1, 274
  components of, 177, 226, 227
  of facilities, 9, 127–128, 203–204
  financial, 201–203, 275, 279
  of human resources, *see* human resources planning
  as life-cycle phase for firm, 37–39
  long-term, *see* strategic planning
  organizational, *see* structure, organizational
  philosophies of, 181
  of resources, *see* resource planning
  strategic, *see* strategic planning
  tactical, 8, 275
policy, 254–255
  informal, 255
  statements of, *see* policy statements

policy statements
  advantages of, 257–258
  characteristics of, 256–257
  samples of, 258–272
  writing of, 255–256
political considerations for MIS, 230
positioning, market, *see* market positioning
post-completion review, 149–151
prestige, 137–138
price discrimination, 136
price-earnings (P/E) ratios, 133
prices, *see* fee(s)
privacy of client, 29
process groups, 221–222
production considerations for MIS, 235
production (service) orientation, 187, 188
professional (individual), 274
  image of, *see* image, professional
  management abilities of, 252–253
  psychological profile of, 35–37
  responsibility for client of, 86–87
  self-doubt of, 38
  at senior level, *see* senior professionals
  see also service, professional
professional organizations, v, 26
  anti-marketing stance of, 25
  marketing advice from, 163
profit, 129–130
  budgeting and, 246
  concept of, 28
  fees and maximization of, 130–131
  margins in, 40
  as objective, 185–186, 238
profit centers, 249–251
projective method for needs assessment, 93

promotion
  credibility through, 159–161
  definition of, 153
  persuasion and, 153–154
  policy statements on, samples of, 265–266
  techniques of, *see* technique(s), marketing
  see also advertising; marketing
psychographic profiles of clients, 64, 82–83, 138
psychology
  of educational feedback loop, 36
  of motivation, 275
  prestige and, 137–138
Psychology Today, 200
publicity, 157
public relations, personnel for, 165–166
publics, 31
  functional classifications of, 50–51
  importance classifications of, 52–53
  mutual relationships among, 53–54
  segmentation of, 67
public speaking, 156, 159–160

quality of services
  control of, 121–122
  fees affected by, 121
  market share affected by, 167–168
  policy statements on, samples of, 264–265
questionnaire(s)
  for client survey, 97–107
  for internal review, 74–81
  for macroenvironment analysis, 58–61
  for market identification, 70–71
  for professional-services analysis, 116–119